# BOURBON WHISKEY

## Our Native Spirit

*From Sour Mash to Sweet Adventures
With a Whiskey Professor*

*Third Edition*

Bernie Lubbers

Blue Riv
Indiana

*Bourbon Whiskey, 3rd Edition* © 2015 Bernie Lubbers
ISBN: 9781681570037

Cover designed by Phil Velikan
Packaged by Wish Publishing

Printed in the United States of America
10 9 8 7 6 5 4 3 2 1

Published by Blue River Press
www.brpressbooks.com

Distributed by Cardinal Publishers Group
Tom Doherty Company, Inc.
www.cardinalpub.com

## PRAISE FOR BERNIE LUBBERS AND *BOURBON WHISKEY: OUR NATIVE SPIRIT* 3RD EDITION

*"Bernie has such great enthusiasm when it comes to one of America's greatest spirits. He is continuously learning and teaching others just how special the industry and products are. With Bernie's selflessness along with experience and knowledge working with him is a great pleasure of mine. He has found creative ways through writing, music, and story telling that surely make him a true bourbon historian that enjoys sharing the history and teaching others. I am honored to work alongside Bernie today, tomorrow, and look forward to many years to come."* — Craig Beam, *Master Distiller, Heaven Hill*

*"Bernie Lubbers' passion for Bottled-in-Bond has saved an entire category of bourbon. They may not know it, but every bourbon lover owes Lubbers a dram for making bourbon cool again."* — Fred Minnick, *Whiskey writer/author*

*"...finally a book for the bourbon lover written by someone with the inside line...This is not just something to dip into, this is a book to delve into, soak up and appreciate."* —Rob Allanson, *Editor,* Whisky *magazine*

*"...reading* Bourbon Whiskey *is just like being with Bernie...without the hangover. You know, the book might be better than Bernie!"* —Lew Bryson, *drinks writer,* http://lewbryson.blogspot.com/

*"Just like a fine dram, drinkers will savor Bernie Lubbers'* Bourbon Whiskey. *It's a personal and very enjoyable guide to America's native spirit"* — Noah Rothbaum, *Author of* The Art of American Whiskey *and Columnist,* Daily Beast's

*I dedicate this book to Parker Beam, a man who inspires me with his passionate love of career and of life. He has spent 56 years as a distiller at Heaven Hill and fills his "spare time" as a farmer/rancher. Now he is also a warrior; Parker is bravely battling ALS.*

*He told me once, "Bernie, on the day I die, I hope it's late in the afternoon so I can get a lot done that day!"*

*Me with Parker and Linda Beam.*

STAY BONDED !

Bernie

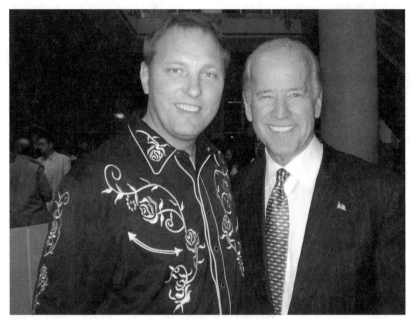

*Whiskey professor Bernie Lubbers and U.S. Vice President Joe Biden.*

# Table of Contents

# Foreword

Bernie asked me to write a foreword for his new book, so I figured I should tell ya'll just who the hell I am. I'm Fred Noe, seventh-generation distiller in the Beam family. My great-grandfather was Jim Beam. He's the one most people know of since his name is on the bottle, and he's the one who started our distillery again after Prohibition in 1934. Pretty amazing for a guy to restart a whole distillery at 70 years old. But it was his great-grandfather, Jacob Beam, who started our family legacy by distilling and selling his first barrel of whiskey back in 1795. To think our family has stuck in this business for over 200 years is really amazing. I'm glad they did, because I don't know what I'd be doing otherwise. It's literally and figuratively in my blood.

*Fred Noe (courtesy of Beam Global Spirits & Wine)*

My dad, Booker Noe (of Booker's Bourbon), taught me all about the business, and I think he was one of the very best. I remember traveling with him on trips where we would promote the small-batch bourbons that Pop created in the early 1990s, actually creating a new category. He taught me not only about distilling, but also how to be a guardian and an ambassador for the brands he created. You see, brands have lives and live on way longer than us human beings. When Dad passed away a few years back, it was just me serving as the ambassador for these brands, and the world was craving more bourbon, more stories, more everything.

I have a son, Freddie, but he needed to get out of college before he can even think about joining the family business. Bourbon had become so popular that we couldn't wait for him to graduate, so we brought in Bernie Lubbers to help promote Knob Creek and our other bourbons from 2005-2012. Now Bernie's not from a distilling family, but he caught on pretty darn quick. I had heard Bernie's name and voice on the "Bob & Tom Show" radio program in the morning, so I knew he'd have a leg up, as a lot of this job is being able to talk to just about any type of person around and to communicate a fairly complicated topic like bourbon.

I guess he had a lot of passion for it since his dad and grandfather worked in a brewery in Louisville, so maybe something rubbed off on him, or poured off on him somewhere along the line. Bourbon is something you don't just learn overnight. It takes years—really it takes a life time—and even though there's a lot more for us all to learn, I'd say Bernie knows his shit pretty damn good.

Being bourbon ambassadors, we have people who come up to us and tell us that they could do our jobs since they love bourbon. But being an ambassador requires quite a few unique skills. Enjoying bourbon and having bourbon knowledge is a good start, but it's just the tip of the iceberg. You've got to enjoy traveling. And when I say traveling, I mean flying more than 100,000 miles a year, sometimes to several cities in a week. A typical ambassador is gone at least two to three weeks a month. We do staff trainings and educational tastings at bars and restaurants with our sales people during the day. Then we might have a bourbon dinner or other type of consumer event that night. Then there are the whiskey shows, where thousands of people attend to taste their favorite whiskies and try new ones. Drink bourbon all night, all day and night sometimes. The next morning you might have to wake up early and catch a plane to somewhere to do it all again, or maybe be on a morning radio/TV show and look and act fresh, and be the life of the party all over again wherever they take you afterward. But if you can, it's a true brotherhood of people, and it's a truly incredible ride.

I think Bernie's book brings some of that to life for you, and I think you'll also learn quite a bit about bourbon, even if you already know a lot about bourbon. Once you finish this book, you may want to come visit us here in Kentucky at our distillery. Come on down and come thirsty and come by and say hey. If you keep drinking it, I'll keep making it.

Here's lookin' at ya.
*Fred Noe*

*John Hansell (*Whisky Advocate Magazine*) at Binny's Beverage Depot during Chicago Whiskey Fest.*

*With Aaron Zacharias and Lew Bryson at Fountainhead during Chicago Whiskey Fest.*

# Prologue: Whiskey Professors Are Born AND Made

The first question that people ask after they find out I'm a whiskey professor is, "How did you get that job?" Well, the truth is that the job came to me. I didn't go after it. I performed stand-up comedy for 20 years, and "whiskey professor" wasn't on my radar screen. Hell, I didn't even know it existed. But it's a career where you use verbal skills and your personality to explain and promote a product, so in many ways, stand-up comedy was a perfect background.

It also may have helped that I grew up in a family in the beer business. My dad worked at a brewery for 45 years, and my grandfather was one of the founders of that brewery. In some ways you could say I grew up "under the influence."

For example, every summer we closed our house in Louisville and moved up to a "camp" my parents owned on the Ohio River in Utica, Indiana. Utica is like that little town in *To Kill a Mockingbird* but without a lawyer and with more Boo Radleys. Our "camp" was (and still is) a two-bedroom concrete block house on a slab that my dad built with his friend Evvers Johnson. Nothing luxurious, but it was awesome to us, and best of all we had our own little beach on the river. We would swim, hike, skip rocks, and fish every day. We had a ball. The Fourth of July was the climax of the summer, with fireworks going off all day, and parties, parties, parties.

We knew all of our neighbors along the river – we referred to ourselves as the "river rats." And river rats are the most friendly and gregarious folk around. Even though Dad went to work every day, it was like a summer vacation for our parents, too.

Beer was a big part of those summers. On weekends, my parents let us take sips of beer when we fetched them one from the house to the beach or patio overlooking the river. Because I had been exposed to beer and adult beverages as a youth, I never went to or threw crazy high school parties like other kids did when their parents went out of town. The idea of playing quarter bounce or anything like that was silly and ridiculous to my siblings and me. The first time we went to a high school party like that, my buddies and I turned around and went home and played pool and poker, and probably drank Mountain Dew or Coke. We never drank beer just to drink beer. It was a nice little treat, but not something you just drank. It just wasn't forbidden fruit at my house, so I really could have taken it or left it.

Do you remember your first official beer? I'll never forget mine. It was July 20, 1969. Something called the lunar module had just landed on the moon with Buzz Aldrin and Neil Armstrong tucked inside. The whole world was glued to their televisions. There are times in your life when you watch history in the making and don't know it. That July night we were watching history, and we knew it. There was no event bigger than this, and I was sharing it with my mom.

My mom's name was "Champie." She got that name by winning the freckle face contest at the Kentucky State Fair in 1939. She had a great sense of humor and everyone who met her, loved her. That July night was a night we would spend bonding along with the entire world.

Walter Cronkite was in great form. He was interviewing a never-ending string of scientists and astronauts. He had the coolest plastic models showing just how the lunar module worked; we were mesmerized. After a couple hours of delay after delay, though, my mom turned to me and said, "How long is this gonna take? Would you be a dear and go get me a beer?" And then she added, "It's not every day a man walks on the moon, so why don't you get one for yourself, too." Two historic occasions in one night! I was so excited.

I was 10 years old at the time.

After another hour of watching for Neil Armstrong's lunar debut she looked at me and said, "If he doesn't come out and climb down that ladder soon, we're going to be drunk!"

Neil and Buzz finally did come out somewhere near the end of my one beer. We watched as they skipped and hopped across the lunar surface. I will not forget that night for the rest of my life.

When I tell people that I travel the world teaching bourbon classes, running consumer events, and hosting bourbon tastings, they just can't believe there's a job like mine. The fact that there is a job called Whiskey Professor is probably why the terrorists hate us so much. I'm sure glad there is because I am having the time of my life. How many people in the world can say "My life is a paid vacation"?

I can. This is a story about living on a paid vacation, the people I've met along the way, and the host of that vacation: bourbon whiskey. So pour yourself a highball and come along for the ride.

*My sister Katie, me (holding a silver mint julep cup), Mom, and my brother Lar.*

I do get to meet some neat people with this job...

*Posing with Celebrity Iron Chef Mike Isabella (photo courtesy of the author)*

*With owner/mixologist Derek Brown of the Gibson in Washington, D.C. (photo courtesy of the author)*

*With singer/songwriters Mayer Hawthorne, Daryl Hall and Booker T. Jones during a taping of "Live from Daryl's House" (www.livefromdarylshouse.com)*

# 1

# How I Became a Whiskey Professor

*"I never drink water; that is the stuff that rusts pipes."*
—W.C. Fields

My name is Bernie Lubbers. I love bourbon, and that's a good thing since I am a whiskey professor. Now that is one sweet job title! And the answer is yes: I do have a business card that says whiskey professor right on it. It's a job your counselor doesn't tell you about when you're in college. And in many ways, it's not really a job, it's a lifestyle. You can't just stop being *The Whiskey Professor*. If you see me in an airport anytime soon, which is pretty likely since I travel 100,000+ miles every year promoting bourbon, odds are I was out late the night before sharing my passion and probably a couple drinks. Just this morning as I was coming through the airport security, a gentleman saw my shirt with bourbon logo and asked me for a sample. I rolled up my sleeve and said, "You want a sample? Here you go, lick my arm."

People ask me just how I got this job and what it takes to be a whiskey professor. Well, besides a strong liver, the first requirement is a deep passion for our country's "native spirit." Second, a person must have an unquenchable thirst for studying the history and heritage of bourbon and the whiskey men and women who forged its legacy. And I guess it doesn't hurt to be born in Kentucky and be part of a distilling family, even though in my case that was brewing beer. But you will soon learn, you've got to make beer before you make bourbon!

My grandfather was one of the 13 saloon keepers in Louisville, Kentucky, who started the Falls City Brewing Company in 1905. They produced Falls City, Drummond Bros., and finally Billy Beer. For those of you under 30, that was named for President Jimmy Carter's famous beer-swilling brother. The brewery couldn't produce beer during Prohibition, so they manufactured soda pop and sold ice to stay viable. My grandfather was also forced to close down his saloon. So he decided to start selling hardware ... and bootleg whiskey. He sold hardware in the front and hard liquor in the back. The back room business was more brisk than the front.

After Prohibition my grandfather moved the bar from the back room to out front and reopened the saloon, and the brewery started brewing Falls City Beer again. When my father graduated from Xavier University in Cincinnati, he went to work at the brewery. He spent his entire career there, starting in the ice house and retiring as Vice President of Purchasing and Labor Relations 45 years later. He would have had 49 years of service at the brewery, but the U.S. Army drafted him in WWII at the age of 32! Because he took a couple law classes at Xavier, he was chosen by the company to be one of the first people in Kentucky and the country, for that matter, to strike deals with the Teamsters and other unions on behalf of the brewery. I'm sure there were some pretty good stories he never shared with us about those times.

### GREASING THE GARBAGEMAN

I guess it was my dad who taught me that if you represent a brand or company, you do it in all aspects of your life. When I was six or seven years old, the garbage was picked up at our house every Saturday. My father gave me the job to go out and count how many guys were working on the truck and then bring them each a frosty cold bottle of Falls City Beer ... two each if it was going to be really hot. Can you imagine doing that today?

I thought this was an awesome responsibility – after all, I was a little boy, and little boys *love* garbage trucks. Here's a giant truck that grown men get to hang off the side of; I mean, how cool is that? And then the men get to take garbage cans and dump them in this big hopper, pull a lever till it smashes the garbage away to the back somewhere and clears the way to dump more in. Fabulous, right? The guys on the truck would ask me every week what I wanted to be when I grew up, and I would smile and shout, "I want to be a garbageman!"

So every Saturday morning about 8:00, I'd look out the living room windows eagerly awaiting the arrival of the magical truck. And every Saturday morning several thirsty garbagemen would look out their windshield eagerly awaiting the sight of this magical little boy who dispensed frosty cold bottles of beer.

Needless to say, our family was very popular with our garbagemen. Our neighbors, who didn't give them beer, never got the same degree of service we did. If they left out old broken swing sets or large appliances, the garbagemen wouldn't pick them up because they were not suppose to fill up their trucks with those kinds of bulky items, so the neighbors would have to borrow a truck and haul it off to the dump themselves. But at the Lubbers household, the garbagemen would take old jungle gyms, dishwashers ... hell, they probably would have hauled dead bodies away without comment! The old man was pretty smart in a couple of ways on that one. Not only did it save him from borrowing a truck and hauling things down to the city incinerator, I bet when those garbagemen bought beer on their own, they'd pick up a 12-pack of Falls City Beer. I didn't know it then, but Dad taught me a valuable lesson in walking the walk, and drinking the talk. Anyone you meet in life–from garbagemen to CEOs—is a potential customer, especially when you're in the beer/liquor business.

My mother was a homemaker and did what most moms did in the '60s. She raised kids, and she was busy with four of us. Back then you didn't have 25 versions of Benadryl or other over-the-counter wonders. When we were teething, she would rub bourbon on our gums. When we were sick, it was whiskey with honey and lemon. We either weren't sick anymore, or we didn't care. Either way, we slept soundly all through the night. Nowadays they'd probably call child services on her for doing that, but that was standard operating procedure for most moms of that generation. My guess is that it got me used to the taste of bourbon, because I never had to acquire a taste for it or beer.

Growing up in Kentucky, at least for my generation, bourbon was sacred. I'm glad to see it's becoming that way again, not only in Kentucky but all over the country and the world. For example, bourbon is extremely popular in Australia and New Zealand. To say they are nuts about it is an understatement. The largest-sized bottles of bourbon we can sell in the United States is a 1.75 liter (about a half gallon). In Australia and New Zealand, they sell 4.5-liter bottles of bourbon! It's so big, it comes on a cradle so you can rock and pour it since it's so big and heavy you can't lift it up easily. I mean, ya don't want to run out of your Jim Beam over the weekend, do ya, mate? Just ask my buds and fellow bourbon ambassadors Jared, Jason and Dylan over there about how popular bourbon (especially Jim Beam) is. They are the best of the best over there (and damn near anywhere in the spirits world), and they love bourbon. As they say in Australia, "Happy Days!"

Other places that bourbon is finding an increase in popularity include Germany and some countries in Asia. Even whiskey drinkers in the U.K. are embracing our native spirit. And in the U.S., bars specializing in bourbon tasting are opening up everywhere from San Francisco to New York. There is a place called Rick House in San Francisco that is decorated like a bourbon rick house, and it's packed. It's the place to see and be seen, and bourbons flow every day there to a young crowd. Char No. 4 in Brooklyn, New York (196 Smith Street), is a very popular place to be, and it features 150 bourbons and American whiskies. Char 4 is the level to which we fire the barrels for the aging of bourbon. PDT (Please Don't Tell) is a speakeasy in the Village that was started by my buddy Jim Meehan who wrote one of the best cocktail books around, *The PDT Cocktail Book*. I suggest you buy the book and then go have a bourbon cocktail at PDT ASAP. Big Star in Chicago (N. Damen Avenue between North Wicker Park and West Pierce Avenues) is a new place started by the same folks who own the famous cocktail bar, The Violet Hour, which is right across

*Here I am with Michael Miller at Delilah's in Chicago during Whiskey Fest.*

the street. While you're in Chicago, you gotta stop by Delilah's, where Fred Noe, Jimmy Russell, and all us ambassadors and distillers hang out after Whiskey Fest there. Michael Miller owns the joint, and you'll find the largest whiskey selection in Illinois! It's a cool, laid-back neighborhood type of place, so go casual, 'cause Michael and his great staff always are. Bar Sable inside the new Kimpton Palomar property in downtown Chicago (505 N. State Street) is another great cocktail bar started by Mike Ryan, who came from the Violet Hour. Ask him what he thinks about Old Grand Dad, Old Fitz and other great bourbons. Are you getting the idea that bourbon is really in vogue? We are smack at the beginning of the Golden Age of Bourbon, so get your ass out there and start enjoying our country's native spirit. OK, off my soap box now, back to my story.

### AGE IS MORE THAN JUST A NUMBER

My mom drank a four-year-old bourbon because she enjoyed highballs. My dad claimed he didn't "trust" a bourbon over six years old. He said that there were too many wood

How I Became a Whiskey Professor • 21

notes from the barrels over six. Pappy Van Winkle of Old Fitzgerald bourbon preferred his whiskey to be around 15 years old. It doesn't make any of them right or wrong, it's just their opinion and preference. That's part of what makes bourbons different. Age and proof. Like any rebellious son, I wanted to find my "own" bourbon to claim.

In college and before, I drank beer, and a little bourbon. Well, we were in the business, so my parents knew I was drinking some, and they kept more than a watchful eye on me. As my dad said, "We don't want the boy to be one of the poor saps to go away to college and never had a sip of liquor in his life, and on his first night on his own, die of alcohol poisoning like those poor Southern Baptist kids do!"

Like most beginning drinkers, I mixed my bourbon. I never had "the talk" from my father that some stricter bourbon parents had with their children about only mixing bourbon with a couple cubes of ice or a little water. I think my parents wanted me to find my own way. So I started out by mixing my bourbon with 7UP and a slice of lemon. Keep in mind, this was before the small-batch and single-barrel bourbon craze of the early '90s. This was late '70s and early '80s. Extra-aged and higher-proof bourbons were rare in the bars, and younger bourbons are fine for highballs.

Soon I was enjoying the flavor of the bourbon, and I was drinking it with either soda water, ginger ale, or a combination of the two. I loved to order the combination because my father told me that drink was called a Presbyterian. I later found out from my friend Chris, who was raised Presbyterian, that it was called that because it looked like a regular ginger ale. If you mix bourbon with ginger ale it becomes dark and looks like you're drinking bourbon. Adding soda water lightens it back to the color of ginger ale. So a Presbyterian could enjoy a drink without appearing to be drinking. Plus it's a deliciously refreshing cocktail.

I think I'll have one right now, since I brought it up. Be right back...

Ahhhhhh, yes indeed, it IS deliciously refreshing. How fun to go to a bar and order a drink named after a religion. Being raised Catholic, I was all over that, and a little jealous to boot! But, back to my story...Eventually, I went from drinking a Presbyterian to just bourbon and soda, and then to just bourbon with ice or water. I had found my way after all. Thanks for trusting me, Dad.

I attended the University of Louisville my freshman year. U. of L. is a commuter school, and it just felt like high school on steroids. So when I visited friends at the University of Kentucky, it seemed more like college life to me. I transferred as a sophomore. It was at UK that I discovered tailgating. "Handles" of Jim Beam and bottles of Old Crow, Ancient Age and Old Forester were everywhere before, during and after football games. Now this was big time college! Because you couldn't major in tailgating, I chose to study marketing because there was little math. I still had statistics and some advanced math to negotiate, but after some summer classes, I graduated on time in four years with a whopping 2.6 cumulative. Actually it was a 2.66, so for résumé purposes, I round it up to a 2.7.

After graduating, I went to work at a local bank as a loan officer (now *that* will make you drink). It was a small family-owned bank that I called Nepotism Fidelity (that's a joke that I earned). I learned that the best thing I could say about working at the bank was that you always knew the time and temperature from staring at the sign out the window, wondering if this was what the next 30 years of your professional life was going to be like.

After three open mic nights at a local comedy club, I quit my job and hit the burgeoning comedy circuit for the next 20 years. I had grown up watching Johnny Carson on TV when I should have been asleep, but I thought his monologues were the most unbelievable things to witness. I wanted to make people laugh and write my own routines, and so I did just that.

When you leave Kentucky, you find that some bourbons that are popular in your home state are not even available in other regions of the country...and vise versa. I took this as an opportunity to try different bourbons and local brews. You tend to drink what your parents drink at first. When those brands were hard to find in other places, I branched out.

I will never forget the day I found *my* favorite bourbon. It wasn't my dad's bourbon or my mom's bourbon, it was *my* bourbon. That bourbon was Old Grand Dad Bonded, and it's still one of the best bourbons out there, in my opinion. I found this bourbon in Drew Carey's stomping grounds in Parma, Ohio, a suburb of Cleveland. When I tasted it on the rocks, it just spoke to me. To this day, I enjoy 100-proof bourbons. It was also the start of what would put me on the bourbon map, teaching people to read whiskey and bourbon labels 20 years later.

This reminds me of a story that happened after I discovered Old Grand Dad bourbon

My longtime friends Paul Halloran and his wife, Amber (which is my favorite color–it's the color of bourbon), entertain frequently at their house. Often Paul's parents would be in attendance, and they were both about 75 years old at the time of this story. Both of Paul's parents, Ryan and Louise, are die-hard bourbon fans and big-time Old Fitzgerald Bonded 100-proof drinkers.

When I got back from working in Cleveland, Ohio, and I enthusiastically shared with Louise the news that I had found "my" bourbon, she calmly and diplomatically informed me that "Old Grand Dad is a fine bourbon, yes, but it's no Old Fitzgerald." Now remember, this is a very proper Southern lady who was well into her 70s. She continued as she sipped her Old Fitz, "Ryan and I prefer the bonded 100-proof, but now that we're older, we drink the 86-proof."

Overhearing her say this, her son, Paul, who had made her drink, informed her, "Hey Mom, that's the 100-proof you're drinking right there." She looked at her bourbon and then up at me and said, "Oh...well, I thought this tasted especially good."

Then as she swirled her bourbon with just two small cubes of ice and looked at it, she continued, "Ryan and I used to only drink our bourbon neat, but now that we've gotten a little older, we cut it with ice." (You just *have* to love her.)

Louise passed away in December of 2009 at the age of 90, and being the "Emily Post of Kentucky" she wore high heels to the end. We all miss Louise, so as you read this, raise an Old Fitzgerald 100-proof to her memory, and if you have to cut it, just two cubes now!

A few years after my Old Grand Dad discovery, the small-batch and single-barrel bourbons hit the market, and I was eager to try them. This was also a time that I learned a very neat trick when it comes to high-end spirits. This is a tip you can use today as it's still true, so pay attention. I found that the Jim Beams, Evan Williams and Wild Turkeys of the world always had a speed pourer on the bottles at the bar so they could be measured out on what bartenders call "a three count." You've seen a bartender pick up a bottle and just start pouring the spirit into a glass. They turn it upside down and count to three, and that's an ounce and a quarter every time, if they count right.

I noticed that the small-batch and single-barrel bourbons had a cork on them, not a speed pourer. So if I ordered an Elijah Craig or similar high-end bourbon, the bartender pulled the cork out and just glug, glug, glugged it into the glass, and as a result I got a double (or more) for the price of a single. I took note, and even though I paid more for that one drink, it was really two really good ones. Buying this book just paid for itself, so use the information to your benefit!

When I traveled the comedy circuit, my big ending was my routine about my father, who was approaching 90 at the time and drank a quart of bourbon a day. That's not my guess, by the way, those were his words to his doctor when he was asked how much he drank. I'd always order a bourbon on stage and salute my dad with a toast.

Oh, all right – I know you want to know what it was

My dad is 90 years old and he's started having trouble with his vision. He's seeing double, and in his mind, it couldn't be the bourbon. Of course it wasn't the bourbon, but then again, he did drink a lot of it. You never know how much they drink, of course. My dad has the magic cup. He drinks from a 24-ounce Styrofoam cup because it doesn't sweat or leave a mark, and it never seems to empty. He has a bottle in the fridge in the garage, so he walks out there with an empty cup, and when he gets back to the dining room—bam!—his cup is full again. My dad is also very quick witted and funny. He told me once, "Son, always date someone that's homeless...that way the next morning, you can just drop them off anywhere."

My dad is an alcoholic. There it is, I said it. I can tell people that my dad is an alcoholic and it doesn't bother me for two reasons. Reason # 1, I like how things turned out. I'd be a different person if my dad was different, and I kind of like myself. So if Dad was a different guy raising us, we'd all be different. Reason # 2 that I am comfortable telling you that my dad is an alcoholic, is that *everybody* has someone in their family, someone they know, who's an alcoholic, and if you don't think you know someone or have someone in your family who's an alcoholic...it's you!!!

Back to my dad's vision problem. So my mom took him to the doctor. Actually it was a new doctor of his ... his fourth doctor, as a matter of fact. You see, he'd outlived the first three. I joked with Dad that we should call this new doctor to make sure he's still alive so we didn't waste a trip!

Now, we all know the questions a new doctor will ask when you get a checkup. How much do you smoke? How much do you drink? And the answers aren't lies you want to rush in to. You try them out on your friends. You'll ask them, "Does three drinks a day sound like a lot?" It doesn't sound like a lot to me, but then again, I'm a whiskey professor.

But for the first time in my dad's life, instead of lying to his doctor, this time he was going to be totally honest. I mean, he's 90, so what's the worse that can happen, he drops over dead? Plus my dad loves to read, so seeing was very important to him. He decided he wasn't going to lie, he was just going to give succinct truthful answers. So the doctor came in and said he was going to ask a few questions and get down to the root of this vision problem. My dad was seated and ready. My mom was there to hear this exchange, and as they say, you can't write stuff like this, it's much funnier when it's the real deal.

*Me and Dad, taken around 2002.*

Doctor: "How old are you, Joe?" Boy, my dad had that one nailed.

Dad: "90," he said loudly and clearly.

Doctor: "Do you smoke?"

Dad: "No."

Doctor: "Do you drink?"

Dad: "Yes."

Doctor: "How much do you drink?"

Dad: "Quart."

Now that made the doctor stop and look up. And that's hard to do.

Doctor: "Did you say quart?"

Dad: "Quart," my dad was on a monosyllabic roll!

Doctor: "A quart of what? Beer?"

Dad: "Bourbon."

Doctor: "In what time frame do you drink a quart of bourbon? A month? A week?"

Dad: "A day."

My dad drank a quart of bourbon each and every day! That sure connected a lot of dots. Kind of explains why I went to a state college!

I don't know what's funnier about that. The fact that my dad drank a quart of bourbon a day or the fact that he still thought we measured bourbon in quarts!

So the doctor left the room and probably went to the nurse's station and said, "Look at this. The man's 90, and he drinks a quart of bourbon a day. And he's breathing … right there in exam room #2."

When he returned, my mom said he looked at my dad and scolded him like a little kid. He said they were going to give him a few tests and get down to the bottom of this vision problem, but as a man of his age, he really should consider *quitting* drinking altogether.

Now I ask you, what the hell kind of doctor could this man be? My dad couldn't, no...no, more like *shouldn't* stop drinking just like that. I mean, how long has he been drinking a quart of bourbon a day? 50? 60? 70 years??? You can't go from a quart to nothing. He'd drop over dead.

You see, my dad's organs are busy! They've been processing and filtering a quart every day for all these years. If my dad did stop drinking, his liver would look at his kidneys and say, "This is the chance we've been waiting for!" and then just shut down.

If my dad dies, and I think it's just an "if," because I don't' think cancer can exist in a bourbon-ridden environment. My dad's probably had cancer seven times and just shook it off.

"Burrrrrrrrr….."

"What's wrong there, Dad? You got a chill?"

Dad: "I think I just had cancer again. Cancer always gives me a headache; I need a drink."

If my dad dies, the second that embalming fluid hits his liver, he's going to sit up straight in the casket and say, "Now this is top-shelf shit right here, boys!"

I also wrote a song about my dad and performed it on the popular syndicated morning radio program, "The Bob & Tom Show." The song is titled "He's My Dad," and it goes a little something like this:

### He's My Dad

He'll eat the fat off your steak, he don't like it too lean

He's outlived three doctors, thanks to ole' Jim Beam

He eats a pork chop sandwich most days for lunch.


Fries everything in butter or bacon grease

Passes constant gas through his BVDs

He swills Citrucel like its gourmet fruit punch.


He's my dad.  He's my dad.

94 years old and still walkin' that ain't half bad.

Claims he's older than Santa Claus and that's a fact.

Graduated with Moses, how 'bout that?

Now that's old school, that's my dad.


He'll do the Sunday crossword without even tryin'

He says, "I can't see" but he's still drivin'

But if he hits you, you won't get hurt, he don't drive that fast.


Tracks the "Storm Team" all through the day

Then checks his rain gauge after every rain

He's going cross-eyed readin' all that crap scribbled on the bottom of CNN.

He's my dad.  He's my dad.

His toe nails look like Fritos corn chips right out of the bag.

He's sittin' home right now with his glass of cheer

I bet he outlives half of us sitting here

He's pickled, he's not going no where, he's my dad.


So here's to my dad

Raise a toast to my dad....

I'm sure glad I got to know ya,

I love ya, Dad.

You can see a version of this sung and performed by me on YouTube.  I recommend watching it with a drink in hand so you can join me in a toast at the end.

My dad passed away just shy of the age of 94.  He lived a long life. He was born in 1911 and passed away in 2005.  Can you imagine what he saw?  When he was a kid, people were still riding horses to get places.  He put us all through college all on his dime. When we graduated we just had to get a job and not worry about loans.  He got to see me perform stand-up comedy and then work in the bourbon industry.  He was really proud of what I was accomplishing, although he didn't really understand how going around drinking bourbon and telling stories was a real corporate job with health benefits.  But then again, he sure thought it was cool.

Truth be told, I didn't get to really know my dad until my mom passed away. We all figured Dad would pass away first, not only because of his age, but in addition to his drinking, he had a horrible diet.  For breakfast he'd take a glazed donut and cut it in half, put a pat of real butter on each half, and put it in the toaster oven.  Then he'd wash that down with half-and-half.  For lunch, he'd eat a fried pork chop sandwich; for dinner, bean soup and a nice marbleized fatty steak. The only thing we could think of was that the fat in his diet clogged his arteries, and the bourbon cleaned them out!

So when my mom passed away at 79 after a brave battle with cancer, we all thought, "Well, what are we gonna do now?" I mean, we really didn't know our dad very well. As odd as that sounds, my mom was the one we all really spent time with. Dad was just kind of "there" through the years. He was cranky most times when he came home, and he was a big intimidating man, so we kinda stayed away from him, and he from us. I mean, he was a great provider, and don't get me wrong, I wouldn't change a thing. But now we were "stuck" with this guy we really didn't know and were a little intimidated by.

He lived alone after Mom passed away and was very self-sufficient. He read five books a week. (On stage I'd joke that with his age, they were the same five every week! He sure loved those mysteries!) He'd read two books at one time and on the side do *The New York Times* crossword puzzles.

He was also still driving, which was scary to think of until you noticed he didn't drive that fast. The impact couldn't have done more than spill your coffee. He would shop, then cook. He cooked food for all of our families and the neighbors. We all took turns having a different "Dad day" and mine was Wednesday. He'd always have a steak he had bought at the store to prepare to my liking. He was always great at finding a good deal at the grocery, too, his favorite pastime. He'd always peruse the sale bin in the meat section, or what I called the "green meat bin."

He'd say, "Hey, look at this, I got this rib eye steak for $1.29."

I'd say, "Dad, there's mold on it."

And he'd retort, "Heat kills everything, son, it'll cook up just fine. Look at all that good fat on there."

He finally did give up driving on his own. I'd drive him to his weekly visit to the grocery store. He'd shop for a good hour and a half, and then when he checked out, I'd pick him up after going to his home to do the cleaning that he couldn't see to do anymore. One time the 18-year-old checkout clerk said to him, "For an old man, you sure do buy a lot of groceries." Without missing a beat Dad fired back, "I have a voracious appetite."

When I drove him to the store for the first time, I pulled up to the second entrance of the store, and he said to me, "You missed the damn exit, boy!"

I said, "Well, I have to drop you off, and so I have to take this entrance to drop you off the right way." He pouted for a couple moments and said back to me, "Well, you're not doin' it the way I'd do it, so you're doing it wrong!"

He was something else.

After a few months of eating lunch with him and spending time actually "talking" to him for the first time in my life, a funny thing happened. I realized my mom gave us all a beautiful gift when she died first: our father. And we all got to fall in love with the man my mom fell in love with. If he would have passed away first, we would have been robbed of that, so cheers to you, Mom. (Sip.)

I found out that I get my wit and humor from him. He was truly hilarious. He'd cut obituaries out of the paper and have me read them. I mean, have you read some of them? They might start out like, "Last night Jane Doe, 42, stepped through the door to Heaven breathing in the wonders and mysteries of being in the presence of God." One of his all-time favorites was, "John Doe, 54, died approximately November 15th, 2003."

Some were *very* long and cost several hundred dollars, especially if a picture accompanied it. He just couldn't believe all that money wasted on someone who was dead. He told me that when he died, we should just say he died and that was that.

When my dad passed away, I wrote the obituary. As he would be the biggest critic of it from "beyond the threshold" (which is where I know he is now reading this book and sipping bourbon), I wanted to have one befitting him. Sorry I wrote more than you wanted, Dad, but here's what it said in the *Courier Journal* that day:

## OBITUARY

LUBBERS, H. Joe, 93, of Louisville, passed away Tuesday

He was born May 5, 1911. At the age of 32, he was drafted in the U.S. Army to serve in WWII. He fell in love with and married Helen, his first wife, and they had a son, whom they named Lawrence "Lar." She unfortunately died too early. He then married Agnes "Champie" Kruse and they had three children: Katie, Bernie, and Gretchen.

He started out working in the icehouse at Falls City Brewing Company and retired as vice president.

He drank good Kentucky bourbon, so let's all raise a glass to Joe. He made it almost 94 years. He was Herman Joseph Theodore Christopher Lubbers–PROST!!!"

(Prost is a shortened version of the old German toast, Ein Prosit.)


So back to how I became the whiskey professor...

Fast forward through 20 years on the road performing comedy in 160 cities from Hawaii to Florida to the day when one of my best friends, Karen ( one of the best liquor distributors in the business), introduced me to a guy named Rob who was just hired by Jim Beam in Kentucky. Rob saw that in my act I talked about bourbon and even ordered and drank his products on stage. He figured that I was a person he'd want to support, since I was on stage for an hour at a time in front of more than 1,000 people a week. So for two years, Rob invited me to tastings and events that Beam put on. One day Rob came to me and asked if I'd be interested in working full-time for Jim Beam hosting events and running promotions. It sounded like fun, and being a personality job, seemed a good fit. So I took the gig, and this is when I started to learn more about bourbon, but with a comedian's approach.

Most bourbon distillers' presentations that I saw focused on how they distilled their specific bourbons. But just about everyone distills bourbon the same way. So I realized it was my job to find a way to talk about bourbons in a new way. We also hired my cousin Bobby and a couple other recent college grads who wanted a career in the spirits industry, and we leveraged their passion and energy with the fact they were out and about a lot by making them ambassadors for Knob Creek. We kicked ass and drove the brand up 129%! The brand manager for Knob Creek took a shine to me and asked if I'd help start the Whiskey Professor Program with them. Too dumb to be afraid, I took on the job, and after two-and-a-half short years, my colleagues David Mays and Steve Cole and I collectively won Whiskey Ambassadors of the Year for 2009 by *Whiskey Magazine's Icons of Whiskey Awards* out of London, England. We won Best Ambassadors of the Year for the United States, and then for the entire world! We were blown away, to say the least. I never thought that stand-up comedy would be a good entrée for a corporate job, but there it is.

We were told by several of the judges that we won that year because we not only had the knowledge and passion for bourbon, but we did things in new and creative ways. I was particularly proud of that because we looked at it from the ground up. We even took a look at how we dressed. I didn't think that wearing slacks, tie and sport coat was ever the way to go. My friends know that if I have a suit on, there's probably a dead body in the room.

With 20 years of experience as a stand-up comic, I knew that we had to look, act, and present in a new and creative way. We decided that we would dress like they do down at the distillery—in blue jeans and a nice shirt. Fred Noe had some really cool cowboy boots made along with the band we sponsor, Montgomery Gentry. So I thought I'd have some custom boots made that had Knob Creek Bourbon on them. The only problem was that custom-made boots are like crazy expensive. So I stopped in to see Nick and Lynn over at Leatherhead down the street from my condo in Louisville. Nick is a true craftsman with leather. He's made custom collars

*Whiskey Professor Bernie Lubbers (photo by Dean Haynes)*

for Oprah's dogs. Nick made the boots for Orlando Bloom in the *Pirates of the Caribbean* movies, and I couldn't think of anyone who could do it better. Plus he and Lynn have a farm next to the Booker Noe Distillery, so serendipity was in full force. Nick and Lynn came up with a solution to have the custom-made look without blowing our budgets. And they are awesome! And I top that off with some really spiffy and blingy belts. Fred Noe calls me "Belt Buckle Bernie."

Along with having a different look than most bourbon ambassadors, I enjoy educating people about how to read a whiskey label. Just like with wine, you can learn how to read a whiskey label and know quite a bit about it before you even taste it. (You will learn how to read a label later on in Chapter 4.) Then we bring to life the fun and riveting stories in the history of bourbon, just like Jimmy Russell, Fred Noe and the guys with the rich family legacies do. And lastly, we have *fun* with it. I don't just give bourbon presentations. We laugh and joke, drink and hang out with other people who love bourbon. Some of the best fun and best presentations I've ever given were just sitting at a bar and getting into a bourbon conversation with a total stranger, and by the time we part company we've shared a few bourbons, talked about history, and bonded. We really have a lot of fun being whiskey professors. When you never feel like you're working, then you really start to take things to another level.

When you visit Kentucky and stay in Louisville, stop by the Blu Café at the Marriott Hotel for Bourbon & Bluegrass Night every Thursday (corner of Second and Jefferson–it's also one of the stops on the Urban Bourbon Trail) and have a Basil Hayden's with Claire at the bar, and listen to some of the best live music with Hickory Vaught, Jeff Faith and Chris Douglas. Be sure to ask them about it. Hickory is my partner in a great whiskey tasting paired with live bluegrass music.

I'm not married and I don't have kids, so I tend to be out listening to live music and meeting friends and family for a cocktail most nights of the week. Being a comedian and a musician, I really enjoy being social and going out, and that really comes in handy as a whiskey professor. Some people ask me why I "gave up" comedy. I use my comedy talents and skills every single day. I travel as much or more now than I did working the comedy circuit. I just integrate it all into my sales and consumer presentation and make it damn entertaining as well as educational. This is not the job for someone that likes to stay home. But it's not for someone who just likes to go out and drink all the time, either. It's a real balancing act. Adding to that is the need to continue educating myself on the category of whiskey and bourbon. Like I said before, my life is a paid vacation, so it doesn't feel like a job to me. Sure I get burned out from time to time, but that usually passes quickly after some time home. Whiskey professor happens to be my job title, but I feel that I'm not just called the whiskey professor, I *am* The Whiskey Professor. For more information, visit www.whiskeyprof.com.

*Shaking hands with Phil Prichard of Prichard's Distillery (Prichard's Whiskies/Rums)*

*At The Chart Room with Phil (Daddy-O NYC), Will and Matt.*

*With Craig and Parker Beam.*

# 2

# What Makes Bourbon, Bourbon?

*"I feel sorry for people who don't drink. When they wake up in the morning, that's as good as they're going to feel all day."*
–Frank Sinatra

Well, now that you know what made me, me, you should ask what makes bourbon, bourbon. People had been making whiskey for hundreds of years. But it took Kentucky to make it bourbon. Make no mistake about it: Because of Kentucky and the Kentuckians who distilled it, their whiskey had a different recipe with the corn, giving it a fuller body and sweetness. They made bourbon in North Carolina, Tennessee, Indiana, Illinois and other states, but Kentucky bourbons were the ones left standing, for the most part.

What makes Kentucky bourbon so special? The big difference is the charred barrels. The interaction of the charred barrels with the aging whiskey enhances the flavor and makes the delicious liquor even more smooth and easy to drink. The specialty barrels also give the whiskey that beautiful amber color it never had before. Kentucky is also responsible for the name–Bourbon–as that was the port city that the liquor came from in the Bluegrass State.

Most–95%–of all bourbon is still produced in Kentucky. There are a few reasons for that. When settlers started moving west, Kentucky was about as far west as you could go. Many of those settlers were displaced after the Whisky Rebellion in western Pennsylvania and were whiskey men. The conditions in Kentucky have always been perfect for whiskey making. Fresh springs, creeks and lakes are abundant, and those aren't

*Limestone-filtered water (Photo courtesy of the Louisville Convention and Visitors Bureau)*

just any water sources; they carry pure, limestone-filtered water. Kentucky has a great limestone shelf, and that limestone filters out all of the iron in the water.

The water in Kentucky also contains a good amount of calcium, which is one of the reasons the horse industry thrives here. When the horses eat the grass and drink the water, they get the calcium they need for strong ankles, which helps them run around the race track on the first Saturday in May and at the Bluegrass Stakes at Keeneland a few weeks before. (Unfortunately, the limestone that filters the water for the bourbon also filters out the extra calcium, so drinking bourbon does not guarantee that *you* will have stronger ankles. So don't go thinking you can outrun Usain Bolt just because you've been enjoying some of our native spirit.)

Then there's the handy location of Kentucky right in the center of the country. We get extreme cold in the winters and extreme heat in the summers. These temperature fluctuations allow the whiskey to work its way in and out of the barrels, imparting that beautiful color and flavor to the bourbon.

Kentucky was also ideally situated right there on the Ohio River, which runs into the Mississippi, so it was easy to get the bourbon to market. That, coupled with the Louisville/Nashville Railroad (L&N), made Kentucky bourbon easily distributed throughout the United States.

Kentucky is also where many of the distilleries were located. If you wanted to start a distillery after Prohibition, you could build a brand new one from the ground up or just buy an empty one. Colonel Beam bought the old Murphy Barber Distillery and started the Beam Distillery in 1934. Heaven Hill built a new distillery on the old William Heavenhill Farm in Bardstown in 1935 — others followed suit.

## FROM UN-CHARRED NEW BARRELS, TO CHARRED USED BARRELS, TO BRAND NEW CHARRED BARRELS

Ben Perley Poore was down in Kentucky representing his employer in 1857 and wrote back to them about his experience: "Everywhere, sir, I am greeted by gentlemen with their hearts in their right hand, and their right hand in mine, and certainly in their left, a bottle of unequalled Old Bourbon Whiskey."

The whiskey of these early settlers in colonial and post-colonial times was a beautiful work in progress. Hard work, along with some lucky mistakes, transformed colorless rye and corn whiskey to the beautiful amber Kentucky Straight Bourbon Whiskey we enjoy today.

When the Scotch and Irish whiskey men landed in the Northeast, they brought with them barley. What grew prevalently in Maryland and Pennsylvania was rye and some corn. So the early whiskey was made with rye and a little corn until their barley plants started to grow. Even George Washington made rye whiskey. We know this from the records kept by his distiller, a Scotsman named James Anderson. The president's whiskey was 60% rye, 35% corn and 5% barley. The whiskey was stored in barrels, and those barrels were made right on site at Mount Vernon. George Washington was of course a very rich man, so he was able to have a cooperage on site. What distinguished a better grade of whiskey back then was how many times it was distilled, not by how long it was aged in the barrels – and no one had even thought of the benefits that charring the barrels would give the liquor within them.

The most expensive whiskey at that time was the highest proof and was distilled four times or more. Multiple distillations not only drove the proof up, but it also distilled out fusel oils and other congeners. Whiskey distilled twice was called "common whiskey" and fetched around 50 cents per gallon, and whiskey distilled up to four times could be as much as a dollar a gallon.

As distillers moved west to Kentucky, barley and rye were not common crops, but corn was plentiful. So corn became the predominant grain used in whiskey making. "Whiskey is made either with rye, barley, or Indian corn. One or all of these grains is used as they are more or less abundant in the county. I do not know how far they are mixed in (all of) Kentucky, but Indian corn is here in general basis of whiskey, and more often employed alone." (Kentucky Bourbon–Henry Crowgey)

Unlike Washington, these whiskey men were not rich and had no cooperage on site. They bought their barrels from dry good stores or from anyone who had barrels to sell. Barrels were handy to use because one person could roll one down the dock and onto the Kentucky boats (simple Tom Sawyer-style rafts, but much larger and able to transport up to 50 tons) or onto steamboats which also sit low in the river.

Frequently, the second-hand barrels had been used to ship pickles, meats, fish and other perishables, and many of the barrels had used salts, vinegars and pickling agents so the contents would not spoil. When the whiskey makers bought these barrels, they didn't just put their liquor in them right away. They would sterilize the barrels by scraping and then setting the inside of them on fire so that their whiskey would not be flavored with what was shipped in the barrels beforehand.

When you snap a branch off a tree, that tree sends sap to that area to heal itself. When the inside of the barrel is fired and charred, the natural sugars in the oak used to make the barrels rush to the damaged area, and a caramelized layer of natural sugars sets where the char ends and the wood begins. This is known as the "red line."

During the day, the sun would beat down on the barrels traveling down the Ohio and Mississippi Rivers. When a barrel heated up, the liquor expanded and went into the wood, passing through the red line to pick up some of that amber color and, more importantly, absorb flavors from the wood. At night when it got cooler, the whiskey would be forced out of the wood and back into the barrel, again passing through the red line, picking up flavor, and rounding out that rough spirit.

In the six months it took the whiskey to travel downstream, it was drastically changed in sight and taste. Remember, it had started differently than traditional whiskey and was sweeter because the predominant grain was corn instead of rye. But the interaction with the charred barrels made it something entirely new. As we like to say in the whiskey business, the barrels rounded off the rough edges and softened up that white dog. When people tasted it, they fell in love with it and asked what it was. The barrel heads were printed with the name of the port the liquor was shipped from, the county in Kentucky named after the French royal family—the Bourbons—just like Bourbon Street: OLD BOURBON KENTUCKY WHISKEY. And so the drink we all know and love came to be. Fans would say, "I sure like that bourbon whiskey from Kentucky."

Did the whiskey makers know what was going to happen to their liquor on that journey? Or was it just an accident that people liked?

Now that's one story of how the barrel became charred on the inside. There are three more. You can decide which one to believe or perhaps believe a combination of two or more.

Here's another: Elijah Craig was a Baptist preacher and a distiller (talk about an oxymoron), and he had some empty barrels stored in his barn. There was a fire in the barn, and being a thrifty God-fearing Christian man who felt that wasting anything was sinful, he went ahead and used those barrels to store his whiskey. When he did this, the barrels did their work and bourbon was discovered because someone was too cheap to replace his materials after a fire. It's a great story and like I said, I really want it to be true, and perhaps it is indeed how *his* barrels became charred.

By the way, Elijah Craig is a damn fine bourbon, and the 12-year Barrel Proof expression is my favorite one to toast Brother Elijah with. There is also a single-barrel 18 and 23 - year-old expression that are quite tasty. And for the price, you can't find a better aged whiskey.

Version three of the barrel charring saga is that the craftsman that make the barrels (coopers) used fires to heat up the wood staves so they would bend more easily when assembling the barrels. Some of the staves caught fire, but the coopers chose to add these charred staves to the barrels anyway.

The last version is that the ultimate consumers in the large market down stream were the folks in New Orleans. They were accustomed to drinking French cognacs that are aged in toasted barrels to impart flavor and color to the brandy. So the bourbon makers began charring their barrels as a response to the demands of the New Orleans market to make the whiskey more similar to the French cognac.

Of course with these stories, you've got to keep in mind that

*Maker's Mark barrels being charred. (Maker's Mark is a registered trademark of Maker's Mark Distillery, Inc. and is used with permission.)*

in France they were storing cognac and brandy in toasted barrels, and barrels were being used to add some color/flavor to other liquor. The French tripped upon extra aging when they were at war with Spain, because Spain was their big export market for cognac. Most of the cognac sat in the toasted barrels for more than 12 years before peace made its export possible again. The VSOP, XO and extra-aged cognacs can trace their origins to this time. So maybe some of the folks in the New World had heard about the benefits of aging liquor in oak barrels. Was it this information that made the folks in Kentucky, North Carolina and other states char their barrels deeper to add more color and flavor? Was it a barn fire? Was it an accident? Perhaps we'll never know, but it sure is fun reading old books and records and seeing the evolution of bourbon aged in charred barrels. I know for sure that George Washington wasn't charring barrels, and David Beam and David M. Beam were charring barrels in Kentucky in the 1800s, so *something* happened somewhere in there.

Regardless of how the barrels came to be charred, until the Bottled in Bond Act of 1897, most bourbons were shipped to a tavern in a barrel right from the distillery. Bourbon makers didn't supply bottles, or ship the liquors in bottles, with the exception of Old Forrester. Old Forrester was bottled in 1870, but that was distributed as a prescription from doctors at the time. So previous to that time, if you owned a tavern, you'd bring your own bottles from home—wine bottles, apothecary bottles—and use them to sell whiskey to your patrons. If you could put liquid in it, you could sell bourbon in it. As an aside, a lot of single-barrel or small-batch bourbon makers, such as Basil Hayden's Woodford Reserve, Knob Creek or Booker's, remember their history by packaging their bourbons in similar bottles today.

Because the bourbon was sent to the tavern in a barrel, some unscrupulous shopkeepers would water down the whiskey to make more money. If you suspected this, you might take a bullet out of your gun belt, take it apart and dump the gun powder on the bar in a little pile. You'd then wet the gun powder with the whiskey. Alcohol will burn at just over 50% alcohol content (57.06 to be exact), so if you lit a match and put it to the gun powder and it burned yellow and fizzled out, the whiskey had been watered down. But if it burned blue and made that gun powder flash, it was *proof* of how good the whiskey was. And that's where we get the term 100 proof or 86 proof. It's also one reason Bottled in Bond bourbon was 100 proof. It was considered the good stuff!

So how did bourbon go from being stored in used charred barrels to being stored in brand new charred-oak barrels each and every time? After Prohibition, the Standards of Identity were written and enforced. The coopers' union lobbied their congressmen and senators, who had a vested interest in the cooper industry in their districts, and to insure the coopers had work forever, these legislators made it a law that bourbon had to be stored in a brand new charred-oak container.

Would bourbon distillers still use a brand new charred barrel if they didn't have to? We'll never know. But when you reuse a barrel, it's like reusing a tea bag. You get less and less out of it with each use. You do get more wood notes and

> *My friend Bill from over at St. Raphael's Men's Club has been retired a little while, and he's known a couple former federal agents who actually lived in the distilleries back in the day. (Agents lived on the distillery up until the 1970s).There were millions of dollars in tax money involved here. They would inspect the "bonded warehouses" and make sure the appropriate taxes were being paid on the right amounts of bourbon. On each warehouse there would be two padlocks on every door. The master distiller would have one key, and the government agent would have the other key. Neither one could get in with out the other.*
>
> *So anyway, a government agent told my friend that several years back, Jim Beam was experimenting with aging bourbon in caves, like wine. Two years later when they came back to taste the barrels that were locked away in the caves, they opened up the doors ... and all the whiskey was gone! So much for national–or alcohol– security.*

characteristics out of a brand new charred barrel than from a used one and in a shorter period of time. But as of now, if you do reuse a barrel even after following all the other laws of bourbon, all you are left with is whiskey, not bourbon whiskey. Examples of this are Michter's American Whiskey and Early Times Kentucky Whiskey. This doesn't mean they are not as good in quality; their wood notes just won't be as pronounced. Some of these can be as enjoyable as bourbon; they are just not bourbon by definition, is all.

### AGING TODAY

As you travel the bourbon trail in Kentucky and visit the different distilleries, you'll notice the rick houses where the bourbon is warehoused dotting the landscape. Most are tin-wrapped wooden structures facing north to south so that they get as much exposure to the sun as possible.

*Heaven Hill rickhouses (Photo courtesy of Heaven Hill Distilleries, Inc.)*

A traditional rick house has from five to nine stories, with three barrels on each floor. It takes a crew of five people to put barrels up in these houses. The newly barreled bourbon is placed in the house from top to bottom, and left to right. The barrels stay in the same place the whole time, and after aging is complete, they are pulled out in the same order. The alternative to this placement is to rotate barrels between storage facilities every two or three years. As you can imagine, rotating the barrels is very labor intensive. However, the distilleries who rotate believe that's the best way to make quality bourbon, and the distilleries that don't feel it's unnecessary. There really is no "better" way, but if you ask them, they will tell you their way is the better way every time! You gotta love distillers! Ha!

Another type of storage facility for bourbon is an escalator house. The escalator house uses a conveyor system to help get the barrels up, so it only takes three people to fill the building. Yet another type of rick house is the palletized warehouse, which is only a couple stories tall, so it only takes one person on a forklift to put the barrels in. They are stacked on top of each other on pallets.

Of course, the fun stories you get told over a drink by a new friend are part of what makes bourbon so special. I wish you all could hear my buddy from Tennessee, Nick Lambert, tell this story. He is an exceptional storyteller. I'll give it my best, though.

One May I was doing a bourbon tasting in Memphis at the famous Bar-B-Q festival. Our team there is the wonderful "Peg Leg Porkers." Pit master Carey Bringle has an artificial leg, a great sense of humor and a great way with BBQ.

I gave my talk to the Peg Leg Porkers and their friends, and it went just great. We laughed, we tasted, we learned about our native spirit, and then we all took the bourbon pledge. One of the guests there was already half in the bag and was heckling me a little during my presentation. It seems my presentation broke into his beer drinking time since he was not a bourbon drinker or fan. So after the tasting, he staggered up to me—I was up close to the beer cooler—and said that he enjoyed my presentation, but he thought I went about 10 minutes too long.

My comedy background turned on like a switch, and I treated him like a heckler. "So just what would you have done in my place?" After toying with him a while and having as much fun as I could at his expense, I thanked him for his honest yet uninvited input. We all moved on to eating BBQ, drinking bourbon, and sharing stories the rest of the night.

When we walked back to the hotel, I noticed the same guy who had been critical of me staggering around with his wife, looking for their car. His wife was totally sober and not at all happy with her intoxicated, boisterous, butting-in husband. After a few minutes, the man started cussing because he realized they had parked in an illegal spot and their car had been towed. He came up to me in our team's car and said, "Can you believe the damn city towed my f@%&ing car?"

I replied, "Well buddy, I guess you parked there about 10 minutes too long."

Anyway, as you can see, all these barrels in these different houses age differently. It takes a distiller experience and know-how to get a consistent flavor profile for their best small-batch or single-barrel bourbons. Should they rotate the barrels over the years? Should they take a cross section from top to bottom, and left to right? There's no single answer for any of these questions. For example, Four Roses is the only distillery in Kentucky exclusively using single floor warehouses so that extreme temperatures never affect the bourbon. Other distilleries want those extreme temperatures and marry barrels from top to bottom. Maker's Mark rotates their barrels. Buffalo Trace has two different types of brick houses and two different types of block houses. A new distiller just has to work with the different methods, taste the results, and then make some choices. That's one of the reasons it is so hard to get into the bourbon business from scratch. There is a *big* learning curve here.

The bottom line is, if you want to get into the bourbon business, you'll find that the most expensive things you'll incur are wood, time and mistakes from lack of experience. A barrel costs around $150 each, and the average rick house holds 20,000 barrels. Experience is priceless. You'll have to cross your fingers and pray over all those years of aging, and hope you distilled and aged it right. What a blow that would be if after eight years in the barrel, the bourbon you made just didn't taste very good.

Even so, there have been hundreds of applications approved for micro distilling in the United States. It will be quite a journey for those new distillers, who will no doubt be calling up the old timers and bourbon experts and bending their ears for advice. Most will be happy to give it. The rising tide raises all ships, so these micro distillers will bring a lot of excitement and pride in regional distilling, just like micro breweries did with craft beers. But whether it's a giant industrial distillery like Jim Beam that makes 1,200 barrels a day, or one that can only turn out a couple of barrels a day, they all have to follow the same strict laws. That's one of the beautiful things about bourbon, there are no short cuts. The word "bourbon" is a quality stamp, like cognac, 100% pure agave or champagne.

# 3
# Distilling and Aging Bourbon

*"I have known several men who drank too much, and they were all extremely interesting."* –Katharine Hepburn

Why the hell did folks distill grains in the first place? Was it just for catching a buzz? Back several hundred years ago, water was the liquid you least wanted to drink in most places. Unless you were located on a spring, the water in ponds or lakes was usually full of bacteria and other nasty things that would make people sick. Our forebearers found that if they fermented the water with fruits, grapes or grains and created mead, cider or beer, the water was then safe to drink and could keep longer.

By the same token, these grapes, fruits and grains could normally only be consumed when they were in season. But fermentation meant that they could be kept around and consumed over a longer period of time. So the earliest distillers were farmers. Whether they were growing fruits or grains, there were certain to be excess crops from time to time. Instead of just throwing that food out, they would preserve it by canning them or (even better) making beer from the grains, or wine from the grapes and fruits.

So how did this lead to distilling? Well, in Spain and France, for example, they had lots of grapes. They would take the excess grapes and make wine, which was great until they started exploring the world. They took wine with them for the voyages since it kept longer than water, but because the wines were made at low alcohol per volume, they would go bad and turn to vinegar. So they began distilling the wine. Those evolved into what we know today as brandies, cognacs and Armagnacs.

Scotland and Ireland grew a lot of barley for their breads and cereals. They often had excess grains after a growing season, so they made beer from it. When they distilled the beer, they got what they called *usquebaugh,* and thus were born Irish and Scotch whiskies. *Usquebaugh* (pronounced Ush-ka-bay-ha) means "water of life" in Gaelic.

Most nations had their own version of the "water of life"—water made drinkable by distillation: Aqua Vitae (Latin), Aquavit (Scandinavia), Eau-De-Vie (French), Zhizennia and Voda (Russian). Some were made from grapes, some from grains, but all were high in alcohol content.

So when the Scottish, Irish, Spanish and French immigrants came to the New World, they brought their knowledge of distilling. If you look at where these various nationalities settled, you get a clear idea of how North American drinking trends were shaped even before 1600.

The Spanish landed in Florida, and the French settled in Louisiana. As the French and Spanish were experienced in making brandy from grapes and fruits, they made brandies and apple jack from the fruit trees that are indigenous in the South. The Irish were more prevalent in the northeastern United States; the Scottish in Canada. Both nationalities were whisk[e]y drinkers, and in those areas of the new continent, rye was the most abundant grain. In Canada, the Scots followed in the tradition of Usher's and Johnny Walker so Canadian Whisky used a neutral grain spirit along with rye, malted rye and malted barley as flavoring grains. Because of their Scottish influence, they also did not spell their whisky with an "e". The Irish and other whiskey men who settled around Maryland and Pennsylvania used mostly rye, and some corn in their whiskey (and beer, for that matter). The Irish influence meant they spelled their whiskey with an "e."

In 1789, George Washington was elected as the first president of the United States. At that time, he had a big debt to repay to France and others for their help in the Revolutionary War. An estimated $54 million in debt was racked up since the 1776 declaration of war. So in 1791, the Secretary of the Treasury Alexander Hamilton suggested an excise tax on domestically distilled spirits. Because of the British embargo on rum and sugar cane, whiskey was the spirit that was being distilled domestically. The people affected most by this tax were the farmers in Western Pennsylvania near Pittsburgh. They had just fought a war based on taxation without representation, and this tax was levied from an Eastern-based national government. Western farmers owned small family stills and did not operate year-round, so they ended up paying a higher tax per gallon, making them less competitive. Farmers in Western Pennsylvania thought that Hamilton was deliberately trying to run them out of business and promote big businesses that could pay more taxes to the new government.

On September 11, 1791 a newly appointed tax collector by the name of Robert Johnson was tarred and feathered in protest in Washington County, Pennsylvania. Shortly after that, a man was sent to Washington County by government officials to serve warrants to those who attacked Robert Johnson, and that government man was whipped, tarred, and feathered as a result. In the frontier Kentucky territory of Virginia, no one would volunteer to take the job of collecting the tax, and all the other states in the Appalachian region followed suit. .

In August 1792 a convention was held in Pittsburgh to discuss resistance to the whiskey tax. A militant group known as the Mingo Creek Association took over the convention and issued radical demands. Washington and Hamilton were embarrassed by this insurrection, since the nation's capitol was located in Pennsylvania at that time. Washington signed a presidential proclamation drafted by Hamilton himself on September 15, 1792, and it was published in every newspaper and plastered in every town. Resistance continued until 1794, when a militia was called up from New Jersey, Maryland, Virginia and eastern Pennsylvania. A force of 12,950 men was gathered, which was larger than the forces involved in the Revolutionary War. The sheer size of the militia helped to squash the insurrection, and there were few casualties. Later Washington pardoned many of the rebels, since he had made his point. He had successfully shown that the new national government had the willingness and ability to suppress violent opposition to its policies. Interestingly, the Washington administration's actions met widespread approval among most citizens. Ironically, George Washington became the nation's largest distiller of rye whiskey in 1797 and 1798 until his death in 1799.

After the Whiskey Rebellion was over, farmers like Jacob Beam and others from Pennsylvania and Maryland moved as far west as they could to get away from the government control. They moved to Kentucky, which had just become a state (actually a commonwealth) in 1792. At the time, new settlers were given a free parcel of land if they built a cabin on it and grew the native crop, corn. This was part of the Corn Patch and Cabin Rights established in 1776 by the Virginia Assembly to encourage western development.

The settlers brought their rye and barley with them to Kentucky and planted that in addition to their corn. As everyone was growing corn to get their free land, there was a lot of surplus lying around in corn cribs at the time. So settlers started distilling it into their whiskey as well. After all, you could more easily transport a bushel of grain in liquid form than in its natural form. The settlers found that they could make more money from a gallon of corn liquor than from an equal amount of grain.

It was soon true that corn became the main grain in whiskey recipes, and they found that it "softened up" the whiskey. Keep in mind, this was clear, like moonshine, and not the "red whiskey" that we associate with whiskies today. But still, it was sweeter than the rye and barley whiskies they were making before in the East and in Europe. This sweeter corn was the foundation that separated what would become bourbon from the barley-based Scottish and Irish whiskies and from the rye whiskies from the northeastern United States. The corn-based whiskey was so popular that some farms used all of their crop to make whiskey – you've probably heard the songs about how people drank their corn from a jar.

### DISTILLATION

Let's take a look at just what distillation is. I'm not going to cover every holding tank, pipe and temperature...I'm

*Pot stills at Laphroaig Distillery "The Magnificent 7" (Laphroaig is a registered trademark of Beam Global UK Limited and is used with permission.)*

basically going to distill down the distillation process. I am not going to mention how many gallons a cooker or fermenter holds, or what temperatures are set, etc. This can get a little confusing, plus it's slightly different from distillery to distillery. I'm just going to talk about distilling overall. I don't want to get too technical, and trust me, folks, I can't, since I was publically educated in Kentucky!

The word *distill* literally means "to strip away." So the higher proof you bring the whiskey off the still, the more congeners, flavors and character you strip away. The more times you distill something, the more you strip away. The highest you can bring anything off the still is around 190 proof.

With single-malt scotch, distillers must use copper pot stills by law. A copper pot still is kind of like an old-fashioned tea kettle. Each time a distiller makes a new batch of whiskey, he puts the fermented beer in, gets the temperatures up, and the whole time the proofs are going up and down erratically. That's where they split off the heads and tails and just keep the heart.

*A column still (photo courtesy of Heaven Hill Distilleries, Inc.)*

They make their distillates in batches. Then when they finish distilling that batch, they clean out the still and start a new batch.

Most bourbon distilleries, however, use a column still. All but one of the 10 distillers in Kentucky use column stills. With a column still, once the steam under the column still gets to the correct temperature, you can pump in the fermented distiller's beer 24 hours a day at a constant level proof. Temperatures and proofs are more constant in a column still, so it's very efficient and does extremely well. It doesn't mean scotch or pot stilling is inferior, it just means there are different ways to do it.

So here's how the process works: Let's say you're making vodka (God forbid). With vodka, your goal is an odorless, colorless, and tasteless spirit. (Damn, I can't wait to taste that vodka.) You might not just double distill, but triple distill, quintuple, or continuously distill. Each distillation strips away most of the character, and you end up with a very clean, crisp, tasteless spirit. (I know I'm selling vodka pretty aggressively here, but that really is the definition of vodka.) Distilling to that high proof over and over again has stripped away most of all the characteristics of whatever you fermented.

The lower proof we bring a distillate off the still, the more characteristics we leave in the distillate. With bourbon, we want the flavors from the grains we have fermented. So we only use two distillations to achieve more flavors from these grains. The laws of bourbon state that it must be distilled under 160 proof. In practice, most bourbons are brought off the still at under 140 proof.

The whole process begins with the grains. The grains are sent to a grinding mill. Mill grinds are set to get maximum breakdown of the starches so they convert better. Each grain is milled separately, weighed according to the percentage of the recipe of that mash bill, and added to a cooker. In that cooker the grain is mixed with pure limestone-filtered water and a thin slop, known as the *sour mash process.* All are cooked until proper pH

*Grains before milling (photo courtesy of the Louisville Convention and Visitors Bureau)*

conversion and flavor consistency are achieved. *Sour mash* is the liquid that is left over from the previous distillation minus the alcohol. When the mash is first put into the fermenter it is sweet since all the starches and sugars are present. After fermentation, the yeast eats all the sugars, and at the end it actually tastes sour. The corn and the rye are where we will be getting body and flavor, and the enzymes in the malt turn the starches into sugars. Are you with me so far? To summarize, we've just added the ground-up grains to water and thin slop.

So now that we have grains and liquid in a large vessel, we heat it up and cook it. This helps to release the grain starches into fermentable sugars. After cooking, we take all this liquid and grain and put it into a fermenting tank where

*Cooker at Jim Beam (Jim Beam is a registered trademark of Jim Beam Brands Co., and is used with permission.)*

Distilling and Aging Bourbon • 57

*Jug yeast and fermenter at Maker's Mark (Maker's Mark is a registered trademark of Maker's Mark Distillery, Inc. and is used with permission)*

the liquid jug yeast is added along with more thin slop for the sour mash process for consistency of flavor. Each distillery has its own proprietary yeast strain. Yeast is very important congener-wise. You can take the same grain bill, but if you add two different yeast strains in two different fermenters,

*Greg Davis (black shirt) explains to Gary Crunkleton (The Crunkleton, Chapel Hill, NC) and his staff about fermentation. (photo courtesy of the author.)*

you would end up with two totally different-tasting bourbons at the end of it all. Yeast is a living enzyme that feeds on the sugars. As the yeast feeds, they produce three things:

(1) carbon dioxide

(2) alcohol

(3) heat/temperature

We're not so interested in the carbon dioxide and heat, but we are interested in that low-proof alcohol. The fermenters produce a 17.5-proof beer or 8.75% alcohol (this differs from distillery to distillery) which actually does taste like a stale beer. Well, that's probably because—minus the hops—it *is* beer! We call it distiller's beer.

Now we take this distiller's beer, and we pump it continuously into our column still. This will be the first distillation. We pump the beer and grains into the still about 2/3 of the way up. Imagine a tall cylindrical column with steam heat underneath it. In this column are a series of plates/trays with tiny holes and weirs (troughs) in the bottom of each plate, kind of like a thick pizza tray with smaller holes.

As the liquids and solids fall down from plate to plate from top to bottom, the heat from the steam works its way from bottom to top. Water turns to vapor at 212 degrees. Alcohol turns to vapor at a lower temperature. So the alcohol vapors rise through the perforated trays to the top of the still, and the beer stair-steps down from tray to tray to the bottom of the still.

---

*Fred Noe asked his dad, Booker, the legendary distiller and grandson of Jim Beam, why the new bourbon whiskey was called white dog. Booker said, "Well, Dumbass..."*

*Fred claims he thought that his real name was Dumbass until he was 20.*

*"Well, dumbass, it's called white dog because it's clear (white), and if you drink enough of it, it'll bite you in the ass like a dog!"*

---

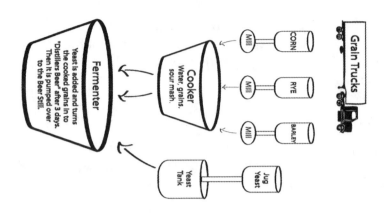

## Beer Still / First Distillation

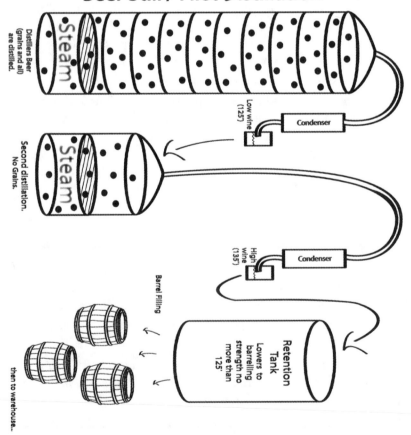

The leftover solids (grains) are taken and spun in a centrifuge and further dried by heat and steam and sold as high- quality feed grain for livestock. The liquid is used for the sour mash process; that is the thin slop that is added to the next cook and fermenters so the flavor of the next batch is consistent with the previous batch (kind of like a starter loaf in a friendship bread).

The vapors that escape from the top are then surrounded by tubes of cold water, and this condenses that vapor back into a liquid. This is called *low wine,* and the proof of the alcohol has been raised from 17.5% to 125 proof. This differs from distillery to distillery. I'm using the example of Jim Beam. This low wine is clear like water or vodka. We've taken out most of the congeners and fusel oils (the stuff that gives you a headache) in this first distillation. But we need to distill it one more time to get the proof up slightly and to eliminate the rest of the undesired fusel oils and congeners.

We send this low wine down to what we call the *doubler.* The doubler is not a column still; it is a hybrid between a column still and a pot still. We don't have any grains in this liquid, so we just pump the low wine in over steam coils underneath, and that alcohol is turned to a vapor and escapes out the top. Once again the pipe for the vapor is surrounded with tubes of cool water, and it condenses it back in to a liquid. Viola! We have *high wine,* or what is called *new bourbon whiskey.* It is at 135 proof now. It tastes cleaner and not as oily as the first distillation, because we have taken out more of those fusel oils. Out of around 44,000 gallons of fermented distiller's beer, we only yield around 6,000 gallons of new bourbon whiskey. New bourbon whiskey is also called *white dog.*

Now we need to put that new bourbon whiskey into a brand new charred-oak barrel and put it up in the rick houses to let it age. But according to law, we cannot store that distillate at more than 125 proof. So we add enough de-mineralized water to get that new bourbon whiskey down to just under 125 proof, and then we put it into the barrel for aging.

The laws of making bourbon are very strict. So if we put that white dog directly into the barrel at 135 proof, even if we

# Hot and Dry / Proof Raises

Higher Floors It Is · The In the barrels.

27
Barrels
Tall

Proof → 145°  **9**

140°  **8**

**7**

130°  **6**   C E N T E R

**5**  120°

**4**

**3**  115°

**2**

**1**  110°   three high / two high / one high

Proof →

1 million
gallons
in each
rackhouse.

Lower floor It Is

# Moist and Cool / Proof Lowers

In the barrels.

*How barrels age inside a traditional rackhouse.*

put it in a new charred-oak barrel, the resulting product could not be labeled bourbon. It could only be labeled as whiskey. So we have to add more of the limestone-filtered water to get that down to 125 proof before it enters the barrel. Also, if you distill to 150 or 160 proof, you'll have to add even more water to get it down to the 125 in the barrel, resulting in a lighter end product.

*Buffalo Trace Barrels in rackhouse (photo courtesy of Buffalo Trace Distillery)*

The reason for barreling at 125 proof or less is because, as the whiskey ages, we lose approximately 4% a year to evaporation, also known as the angels' share. It's what the angels drink. The old boys say that if the angels don't take their share, it's not worth drinkin'. The barrels that age on the higher floors where it is very hot and dry will rise from 125 proof to 145 proof after evaporation. If we put the 160-proof whiskey in the barrel, it could rise all the way up to 180 proof or so. And if you add water after aging to get that bourbon

---

**BOURBON AND MOONSHINE**

*You'll find that some bourbons now have flavorings added to them as a shout-out to the tradition of adding a flavor to moonshine. Wild Turkey and Evan Williams make a honey and cherry flavor, and Jim Beam's Red Stag is black cherry flavored. There are some folks that scoff at this or say distillers shouldn't add flavors, but I'd argue moonshiners have been doing it longer than we've been aging in barrels.*

---

*The Jim Beam Rackhouse*

down to 80 or 100 proof in the bottle, you've just watered down everything you worked so hard for, and you don't get the flavors you need at the end. So bourbon can't enter the barrel at anything more than 125 proof.

For small-batch bourbons or single-barrel bourbons, the proofs of the low wine and high wine are typically lower, leaving in more flavors and characteristics from the grains. The process of making all bourbon is the same, so if you do want to make a more flavorful, or "premium" product, you can really only change the grain bill, yeast strains, or bring it off the still at different/lower proofs or bottle it at higher proofs. Are you getting the hang of just how regulated bourbon is?

After distilling, we go into the aging process. Aging is just as important to the final flavor of the bourbon as the distillation. You can take the same recipe, put it in two barrels at the same proof, and then bottle one after four years and the other after six years, and you will get two very different bourbons. This is where it really starts to become interesting.

*Barrels charring at Independent Stave Cooperage (Jim Beam is a registered trademark of Jim Beam Brands Co., and is used with permission.)*

## HOW THE AGING PROCESS WORKS

If you've ever had moonshine (and you should once in your life), you'll remember it being served in a mason jar with something else in it. There's often fruit in it, like strawberries, cherries or a peach. The fruit softens up the taste of the harsh moonshine and adds some sugar and flavor to it. The barrel serves a similar purpose. It just takes a lot longer to do it.

Aging sounds pretty simple. You take your whiskey off the still, put it in a "brand new charred-oak container" as the law specifies, and then store it until you decide to bottle it, right? Sounds simple. But there is way more to it than that. How long do you store it? Where do you store it? Do you move the barrels around or just let them rest? From where do you pull the barrels after aging?

First of all, let's put to rest the myth that bourbon has to be aged for two years in the barrel. This is not true. The Standards of Identity only say that bourbon should be "stored" in a brand new charred-oak container. As Jimmy Russell from Wild Turkey says, with bourbon you can use the "Fifteen/Fifteen" rule: As long as you put the new under-125-proof bourbon whiskey in the new charred-oak bucket for 15 seconds or carry if for 15 feet, you've got bourbon. It wouldn't be very tasty, but by law it would be bourbon. The designation of "straight"

*Buffalo Trace Warehouse C (photo courtesy of the Louisville Convention and Visitors Bureau)*

bourbon means that you have followed all the laws of bourbon and have stored (aged) the whiskey for a minimum of two years.

Let's talk about the barrels. We all use white oak, since that variety allows the bourbon to penetrate the wood but also can hold the liquid for the years needed without losing integrity. Before being made into barrels, the wood is cut and set outside in the open air for several seasons to allow it to age in the elements. This helps get all the green out of the wood and tempers the wood against some tannins and other elements that are undesirable during the aging process.

As I explained in the last chapter, charring makes the natural sugars come to the surface of the interior of the barrel so that the bourbon can imbibe the qualities, flavor and character of the wood, which is what gives bourbon its beautiful color and seductive taste. Most distilleries use the deepest, or level four, char. In contrast, wine is typically aged in lightly toasted barrels with no char. Bourbon distillers are allowed to select their char level, but barrels must be charred, not just toasted or seared. The way the coopers char the barrels is to assemble the barrel staves, and before they put the heads on the ends, they introduce a flame through the inside of the barrels. If you've ever seen a hot air balloon and its burners, it's similar to that.

Storage while aging has developed differently at each distillery, and each master distiller or warehouse manager has his/her own opinion about it. Some use brick rick houses and others use wood-and-tin construction. Some use four-story rick houses that are 12 barrels tall and others prefer nine-story rick houses standing 27 barrels tall. Maker's Mark rotates its barrels the old-fashioned way. Four Roses only uses one-story warehousing. Buffalo Trace and Woodford Reserve use brick rick houses. There are as many ways to age the liquor as there are ways to make it, and one way is not necessarily more correct or better than the other; they are all just different. Although if you ask one of the distillers, he might say his way is better ... I just love the pride in this industry.

*Barrels resting at Heaven Hill Distillery (photo courtesy of Heaven Hill Distilleries, Inc.)*

*Bernie the bourbon thief?*

The atmospheric pressure in the rick house and location of the barrels make barrels age differently from top, to middle, to the bottom of the rick house. It's very hot and dry at the top of the rick house—think of it as being just like your attic. So the barrels on the top floor start out at 125 proof and will rise all the way up to 145 proof (or more) due to evaporation during the aging process. Barrels on the bottom floor, however, where it is moist and cool, will have the alcohol and water molecules interact. Those barrels start out at 125 proof and will go down in proof to 115 or so. The middle of the rick house is where the temperature is the most consistent, so the barrels will stay around the 124 to 128 range. Confusing? Well keep in mind that the bourbons on the outer parts of the rick houses will get more heat than those on the inside.

Where do you pull the barrels from after aging? From one floor in the rick house? From all floors? How much from each floor? Do you rotate the barrels? Do you just use a single-story rick house? Are you discovering that generations of experience passed down from distiller to distiller really comes in handy here? That's why distilleries talk about their family lineage and experience all the time.

Distilleries used to rotate barrels as standard operating procedure. Maker's Mark still rotates its barrels, but as the number of barrels has increased for everyone, the practice of rotating has been replaced by letting the barrels rest, and then taking a cross section of barrels from the top to the bottom, and left to right diagonals.

Distillers also found out that by rotating the barrels, the barrel bung would dry out at the top of the barrel after a couple years, and by rotating it and rewetting the bung, they lost another 1% or 2% angels' share. That translates into thousands of gallons of bourbon we could all be sipping here instead of passing it on to the angels through evaporation.

Each distiller has a different opinion on the optimal age for their bourbons. Baker Beam (Baker's Bourbon) says that after seven years you've gotten everything out of the barrel you can, and it's the perfect time to dump the bourbon. Fred Noe says that number is nine years for his Knob Creek, and you've really hit the wall at 12 years. Bill Samuels says between five and six years. He ages by taste, not years. Julian and Preston Van Winkle age their bourbons from 15 to 23 years. Parker and Craig Beam age the Elijah Craig bourbon 12 to 18 years. Remember, my dad thought that six years was the perfect time. Jimmy and Eddie Russell

*Great Whisk(e)y Debate with Dan Tullio (Canadian Club) and Simon Brooking (Laphroaig/Ardmore)*

like between four and five years, but they like to distill and barrel at very low proofs, the old-fashioned way. If all bourbon tasted the same, it would be a boring category of whiskey indeed. But thank God they all *do* have a different opinion.

Another way to age whiskey that's a lot quicker is the Lincoln County Process that Tennessee whiskies employ. Many people think that Jack Daniels is not a bourbon because it's made in Tennessee. This is not true. Bourbon can be made anywhere in the United States. But Jack Daniel never wanted to make bourbon. Back in the 1860s was a dangerous time to live, and people didn't want to wait six years for a bourbon to age when they didn't know whether they'd be alive in six days. So they found a way to speed up the aging process.

They burned the maple trees that grew around their distillery and then took the charcoal that was left after burning and piled the ashes and char in a 10-foot column. Then they took the white dog and put it in this column and let it slowly drip, drip, drip through all that charcoal. After a good six or seven days of dripping through all this charcoal, they'd put it into a new charred barrel. This process is called charcoal mellowing, not filtering. This adds flavor to the whiskey. That's why Jack Daniels has the smoky quality that Tennessee whiskey drinkers like. If you spent a week in a vat of charcoal, you'd taste a little smoky, too.

Small-batch and single-barrel bourbons are typically aged longer than main line Wild Turkey, Jim Beam and Evan Williams. Some people think that scotch is higher quality than bourbon because it is aged 10 years or more, but that's not true. Keep in mind that every year a barrel of whiskey is aged in Kentucky is equivalent to about four years in Scotland. The average temperature in Scotland is 55 degrees, so they aren't getting the variety of temperatures we're getting, and they are not using a brand new, charred-oak barrel on top of that. They are using one of our once-used bourbon barrels, so they have to age it longer. I'm not saying our bourbon is better than scotch or vise versa; I'm just explaining the differences. Each distiller in Scotland or Kentucky uses their experience and geography for what's best for their whisk[e]y. That's also why scotch tastes so good. Every drop of scotch has some of our bourbon in it!

They did a test a few years ago. Makers Mark sent a barrel of bourbon to Scotland to age, and the Laphroaig Distillery sent a barrel of scotch to Kentucky to age. It turned out that the switch just didn't work. Both tasted below par, proving that bourbon and scotch need to be aged in the environment and landscape of where they are distilled.

I had the great opportunity to visit Scotland, and it was a magical experience. I visited the Dalmore Distillery in Inverness, Laphroaig on the Island of Islay, and then the Ardmore Distillery, home of Teacher's Blended and Ardmore Single Barrel, in Aberdeenshire. The highlands of Scotland really resemble Kentucky. Both places are basically the same size geographically and population-wise (around 4.5 million). Both are known for excellent water and whisk[e]y making, and both are full of excellent whisk[e]y men and women who are extremely passionate about their craft.

Although I don't get to see them as often as I'd like to, I'm lucky to call John Campbell at Laphroaig and Alistair Longwell at Teacher's my colleagues and friends. But I do get to work with, debate, and drink good whisky with Simon Brooking and John Cashman, their global ambassadors. If you ever get the chance to see any of these whisky men, by all means do!

## A Word About Recipes or Grain Bills

By far the most frequently asked question that I get is "What is the recipe for your bourbon?" Some people seem to want to know the exact percentage of barley, rye and corn that we use. It's a question that every distiller and ambassador has been asked. A couple distillers will just tell ya straight out. Maker's Mark is 70% corn, 16% red winter wheat and 14% barley malt. It's right

*Bourbon flowing from the barrel in the dump floor (Jim Beam is a registered trademark of Jim Beam Brands Co. and is used with permission.)*

up on the wall at the distillery on a chalkboard. That's pretty damn cool. Maker's Mark just makes one recipe. Other distilleries have two or more different recipes for their bourbons. Jim Beam and Buffalo Trace don't reveal their different grain recipes. It's a family secret, if you will, and that's pretty damn cool, too. I mean, do you think you could discern that one bourbon could possibly be "better" than another simply because it had 1.5% more rye or corn than another? And would that make a big difference over four to 12 years of aging in a barrel?

No one ever asks what the grain bill is for a single malt scotch, do they? That's because there is only one recipe, and that's 100% barley. And there are over 90 distilleries in Scotland producing the same recipe in the same whisky. It depends on where that distillery is and how that location affects the whisky in production and during aging. The size and shape of the still has an effect on the final product as well. But everyone wants to know the exact percentage of grains in bourbon and then pretend that this combination defines what is, in their own head, a "good bourbon." I think that's ludicrous. I personally think that some people just don't know what to ask, so that seems to be a good question, especially in front of a group of people.

Now that being said (and I'm glad I got that off my chest), a considerable change in the percentage of grains can have an effect on a bourbon. In studying bourbon and being around all the distillers, I have concluded (and I'm not the first one to conclude this, but it's an "aha" moment when you get to this point) that there are only three (that's right, three) recipes in *all* of bourbon. From this I've put together the following "chart." This chart is based on information from articles and books I've read and distillers I've talked to. It shows what you can learn when you read *Whisky Magazine*, *Malt Advocate*, *The Bourbon Review*, Liquor.com, straightbourbon.com and books on the subject.

**Corn** is what gives bourbon its signature flavor and is considered the "engine" that provides the highest yield of alcohol per bushel of all the grains. The flavor of corn is very prevalent fresh off the still in the white dog. But over years of aging, corn becomes neutral and lends mostly in the overall sweetness to the finished product.

**Barley** is prized mainly for its enzymes that convert starches to sugar for the fermentation process so the yeast can feed on the sugars. Where corn is the "engine," malted barley is considered the "work horse" that delivers these enzymes. Barley provides some of the underlying malty and chocolate notes, along with some dryness. Usually around only 5-12% of any grain bill, barley is mainly used for those enzymes, and not so much for flavor, but it does gives the bourbon that biscuity texture.

**Rye and Wheat** contribute most significantly to the flavor of mature bourbon. They are referred to as the "flavoring grains." Any grains can be used, like oats or rice, but these two are the only ones used, with rye being the dominant flavoring grain with distillers.

**Rye** brings a range of spice notes including pepper, nutmeg, clove and cinnamon, which are all intensified during the aging process. Think of eating a piece of rye bread. Rye gives bourbon that wonderful flavorful "bite" that it is known for.

## WHAT ARE SOUR MASH AND SWEET MASH?

*Back in the 1830s, distillery owner Oscar Pepper made the smartest decision of his career by hiring Dr. James Crow as his Master Distiller. Crow was from Scotland, so he was familiar with whiskey making, but he was also a doctor and a chemist. He was determined to use modern methods in making his whiskey. One of the first things he did was to move the livestock away from the distillery for a cleaner environment in which to distill. Most distilleries had farms attached to them to dispose of the spent grains (known as "thick slop") to feed the hogs and cattle.*

*Another way, Crow modernized his distillery was in testing the levels of sugar in his mash. He didn't just taste it; he used a litmus paper test called a "saccharimeter." To measure the strength of the spirit coming off the still, he used a hydrometer. He also found that saving the "thin slop" (the water that was left from distillation that did not become alcohol) and putting that back in the next mash tub really helped with the ph levels in the mash. It also helped in making a more consistent product. This is called the "Sour Mash" process, and it's akin to using a "starter" in baking. If a distiller does not use thin slop or, as it is sometimes called "set back," but uses new water to cook the grains in the mash each time, then this is called "Sweet Mash."*

*Dr. Crow is often credited with inventing the sour mash process, but there are several written accounts of distillers using thin slop or set back way before Crow's time. But he was the first to consistently employ the sour mash process as a daily standard operating procedure. I'd say 99% of whiskey made today uses the sour mash process.*

**Wheat** results in a sweeter-tasting bourbon, but not because the grain is sweeter. Wheat is not as rich as rye, so it allows more of the sweetness of the corn and vanilla to show through, compared to rye, which can overshadow some of those sweet flavors.

THE THREE RECIPES OR MASH BILLS IN BOURBON

- Traditional Bourbon Recipe—70-80% corn, balanced with rye and some barley. Think of a sweet-and-spicy, back- of-the-tongue experience. *This is my term for this, not the industry's, but I think it describes it well since the next two are accepted terms in the industry.

- High Rye Bourbon Recipe—20-35% rye–dials back on the corn and keeps the same amount of barley as a traditional bourbon.

- Wheat Bourbon Recipe (or simply referred to as "Wheated")—70-80% corn--similar to traditional, but re-places the rye with wheat. Wheat allows the sweetness of the corn and the sugars from the barrel to be more pro-nounced. Think "soft and sweet," with a front-of-the-tongue experience.

## BARRELS AND AGING

The recipe is the soul of the bourbon, and the barrel and aging provide varying flavors depending on how long it is aged, the type of warehouse and the location of the barrels inside the rick house. Barrel aging is responsible for 50% to 75% of the final flavor of a bourbon. Smaller barrels (five gallon, for example) have the advantage of getting a lot of color and flavor quickly. The disadvantage of a small barrel is that oxygen never really gets into the barrel to work with the spirit well, and shorter aging means not many confection notes like vanilla, caramel or toffee.

There are at least six different types of vanilla flavors you can get from a barrel. And it takes six years to get those vanillas. Bourbons aged six years or more will have more pronounced vanillas, and other barrel notes like maple, butterscotch, brown sugar, caramel, ginger, clove, toffee, cinnamon, nutmeg, orange, graham cracker, walnut, almond, butter, anise, bacon, toasted nuts and many, many more.

## BARRELS: BIG VS. SMALL

There are a lot of craft distillers getting in the arena, and making some whiskey and bourbon. This will be great for the category, and like craft brewing, will bring a lot of excitement to bourbon and eventually some great products I can't wait to try. There's a lot of buzz going on about small barrels, and their advantages and disadvantages. Some are using smaller size barrels (five to 10 gallons) as opposed to our industry standard size of 53 gallon (200 liter), I have discussed this with several experts and here are some of their comments:

*"A small barrel with give you color and extract quickly"*

*"There is more surface area of oak to volume of spirit ratio in a small barrel, so the amount of extractives from oak will be larger than a regular size barrel."*

*"I don't think small barrels are the answer to quick aging. However, I think you will still get the confection notes (vanilla, brown sugar, caramel, toffee, etc) just not a mature whiskey flavor."*

*"It will not age properly." (in a small barrel)*

*"The 30 gallon barrel Koval uses seems to yield positive results."*

*"Also I would think that a small barrel would be very cost prohibitive for a number of reasons, cost per gallon for oak, labor, storage etc. I also suspect that you will have a greater 'angels share'."*

*"Buffalo Trace Distillery did some extensive experimentation with 5 to 15 gallon barrels and found that their Buffalo Trace bourbon did not mature well in them, and the smaller the barrel used (the 5 gallon barrel) the worse the bourbon tasted. Buffalo Trace has also tried experiments with different parts of the tree used for barrels with positive results, but that was in 53 gallon barrels."*

Distilling and Aging Bourbon • 75

*"The oxygen uptake will be more too, for the same reason of larger surface area. The slow oxygenation in a regular size barrel will never happen in a small barrel even if the intensity of aromatics is diminished by a different char or toast, so a small barrel will never have the balance of oxidation products achieved in a spirit aged in regular sized barrels."*

The 53 gallon (200 liter) barrels have been used for generations. Rick houses built in the late1800s are still around and designed for this size. So 200 liter (53 gallon) barrels have been and looks like will be the industry standard...and well, they just work beautifully.

The most expensive items in making bourbon are time, wood and mistakes. It would be a shame to make great whiskey, and then ruin it by trying to save some money by putting it in inferior wood. Choose your barrels carefully, and give that bourbon all the chances it can to develop in to the special whiskey that it is!

*Picture from Independent Stave on how they cut the staves from a white oak tree for a barrel (courtesy of the author)*

# Three General Bourbon Recipes

*(Visit WWW.WHISKEYPROF.COM for more cool in-depth info!)*

## Grains and What They Contribute

**Corn** is what gives bourbon its signature sweetness and is considered the "engine" that provides the highest yield of alcohol per bushel of all the grains. The flavor of corn is prevalent fresh off the still in the White Dog, but over years of aging, the corn becomes neutral, and lends mostly to the overall sweetness of the finished product.

**Barley** is prized mainly for its enzymes for converting starches to sugar during the fermentation process so the yeast can feed on the sugars. Where corn is the "engine," malted barley is considered the "horse power" that delivers these enzymes. Barley provides some flavor with the underlying malty and chocolate notes, along with some dryness. Usually only around 5% - 14% of any grain bill, the use of barley is mainly for those enzymes, and gives bourbon that slight biscuity texture.

**Rye and Wheat** contribute most significantly to the flavor of mature bourbon. They are referred to as the "flavoring grains." Any grains can be used, like oats or even brown rice, but these two are primarily used, with rye being the dominant flavoring grain with distillers by 90%.

*Rye* brings a range of spice notes including pepper, nutmeg, clove, caraway and cinnamon, which are all intensified during the aging process. Think of eating a piece of rye bread. Rye gives bourbon that wonderful flavorful "bite" that it is known for.

*Wheat* results in a sweeter-tasting bourbon, but not because the grain is sweeter. Wheat is not as rich as rye, so it allows more of the sweetness of the corn and vanilla to show through.

## BOURBON RECIPES OR MASH BILLS

**Traditional Bourbon Recipe (my term, not the industry's):** 70-80% corn, with the balance rye and some barley. Think of sweet-and-spicy, back-of-the-tongue experience. Bourbon can be up to 100% corn, but corn becomes neutral during aging and only contributes to the sweetness, so a flavoring grain of rye is used, and of course barley is used for converting those starches into sugar and for giving the bourbon that biscuity quality and hint of chocolate.

**High Rye Bourbon Recipe:** 18% + rye – dials back on the corn, keeping basically the same amount of barley as a traditional bourbon, but doubles up on the rye. Rye is a back-of- the-tongue experience, and it gives the bourbon that nice white pepper spice like a slice of rye bread. These bourbons will be less sweet and more spicy.

**Wheat Bourbon Recipe:** 70-80% corn — similar to the traditional, but the rye is replaced with wheat. Wheat allows the sweetness of the corn, and the sugars from the barrel to be more pronounced. Think "soft and sweet," with a front-of-the-tongue experience.

**Straight Rye Whiskey Recipe:** 51-100% rye — includes a corn/barley mix like a traditional bourbon, but the majority grain is rye instead of corn. Rye whiskey can be up to 100% rye, (just as bourbon can be 100% corn), but some distillers argue that you should have at least 6% of barley malt to ensure the conversion of starches to sugars, so the yeast can then convert those sugars to alcohol. Otherwise, additional enzymes need to be added to the recipe to help with that conversion, so 100% to 94% rye whiskies will need that help. Canadian rye is typically 100% — Monongahela Pennsylvania style is high in rye with some barley and maybe some corn. George Washington made rye whiskey with 60% rye, 35% corn, and 5% barley. They didn't plan any particular recipe, they just used the grains that grew around them and then tailored it to the best-tasting whiskies from those ingredients. So find the style you like, know what/where it came from, and most of all, enjoy.

## YOU ARE THE MASTER DISTILLER...

What recipe would you make?

\_\_\_\_% Corn \_\_\_\_% Barley \_\_\_\_% Rye

## BARRELS AND AGING

The recipe is the soul of the bourbon, and the barrel and aging provide varying flavors depending on how long it is aged, what type of warehouse, and the location of those barrels inside a rick house. Barrel aging is responsible for anywhere between 50% to up to 75% of the final flavor of a bourbon.

There are six different types of vanillas you get from a barrel, and it takes a good six years to get bold vanillas out of a it. So younger bourbons will not have pronounced vanillas. Bourbons six years or more will have more pronounced vanillas.

Resulting barrel notes are: *vanilla, maple, caramel, ginger, clove, toffee, cinnamon, nutmeg, fruits and toasted nuts.*

I got this great piece of information from Greg Davis the master distiller over at Makers Mark. It's what he calls the Distiller's Rule Of Thumb. To determine a Bourbon's end flavor breakdown: 25% come from the small grains, 15% from distillation, 10% yeast strain , and 50% maturation

## YOU ARE THE MASTER DISTILLER...

Where would you put your barrels in Rackhouse? ____ Floors For How Long?____

## HIGH RYE BOURBON RECIPES

| | |
|---|---|
| Old Grand Dad | Basil Hayden's |
| Four Roses | Bulleit |
| Very Old Barton | Kentucky Tavern |
| 1792 | Old Forester |
| Woodford Reserve | |

## WHEAT BOURBON RECIPES

| | |
|---|---|
| W.L. Weller | Maker's Mark |
| Old Fitzgerald | Van Winkle |
| Rebel Yell | David Nicholson 1843 |

## TRADITIONAL BOURBON RECIPES

| | | |
|---|---|---|
| Jim Beam | Evan Williams | Booker's |
| Wild Turkey | Knob Creek | Eagle Rare |
| Elijah Craig | Buffalo Trace | Old Crow |
| Heaven Hill | | |

## WHAT'S YOUR BOURBON COMMON DENOMINATOR?

- If you like Bulliet bourbon, which is a nice high rye bourbon, try Old Grand Dad, especially the 114 proof.

- If you like Four Roses, maybe try Basil Hayden's since both are high rye bourbons, and lighter but flavorful.

- If you like Van Winkle, it's hard to find, so try Maker's 46 since it's wheat with big wood-influenced notes.

- If you like Jack Daniel's whiskey, try Devil's Cut bourbon with big wood influence and cinnamon spice.

- If you like reposado or anjeo tequila, perhaps you'd like Jim Beam Black or (oak/vanilla influence).

- If you like Highland single malt scotch, try Eagle Rare, Basil Hayden or Maker's Mark, which have a delicate, quick finish.

- If you like Bacardi Rum, perhaps you'd like Maker's Mark, W. L. Weller or Old Fitz, since they're soft and sweet.

- If you like Cpt. Morgan/Sailor Jerry, then Devil's Cut with all the spice, and/or Maker's 46 with French Oak would appeal.

- If you like Crown Royal, try Four Roses or Basil Hayden's for their light body and high rye content.

- If you like cognac, try Baker's Small Batch Bourbon for its sweetness and long finish.

*Four Roses single-story rackhouse at Cox's Creek*

*Rackhouses at the original T.W. Samuels distillery location, now aging Heaven Hill bourbon.*

Distilling and Aging Bourbon • 81

*Bonded tattoos of Joshua Gonzales, Devon Boyll an me after a Bourbon
Thru Bluegrass show at Thunderbird in Indianapolis.*

# 4
# How to Read a Label

*"Always carry a small flagon of whiskey in case of snakebite and furthermore always carry a small snake." –W.C. Fields*

Growing up in Kentucky I would hear from many people that "All bourbon is whiskey, but not all whiskey is bourbon." But when I got into the bourbon business I also learned that "All scotch is whiskey, but not all whiskey is scotch," and "All Irish whiskey is whiskey, but not all whiskey is Irish." So after my head started hurting, I asked, "What makes bourbon different from all whiskey?" It had to do with aging it in barrels, but then I found out that all whiskies are aged in barrels. I threw my hands up in disgust and decided not to even think about it anymore.

It wasn't until working with distillers Fred Noe, Jerry Dalton and Tommy Crume at the Clermont Distillery that it all became clear to me. What really did it was when Jerry Dalton gave me a copy of the Standards of Identity from the Bureau of Alcohol, Tobacco, and Firearms (now called the TTB), which defined whiskey and bourbon.

The Standards of Identity came out shortly after bourbon was named the native spirit of the United States in 1964. But it wasn't the first paperwork on bourbon; the Standards of Identity were preceded by a couple other acts. The Bottled in Bond Act of 1897 was a bill championed by one of my heroes in the bourbon world, Colonel Edmund Taylor along with Ezra Banks and others. Bottled in Bond is still in effect today. If a whiskey is labeled "bonded," then it was aged in new, charred oak for a minimum of four years and is exactly 100 proof. It comes from one distillery and from whiskies distilled from one season (January to December). So if you see "bonded" or "bottled in bond" on your bourbon label, you are guaranteed that it is an honest 100 proof, at least four years old, and distilled in one place in a specified period of time. In short, the good stuff. Up until the 1970s federal marshals used to actually live at the distilleries and inspect the bonded warehouses on a daily basis. It doesn't take long to inspect a warehouse with added barrels, or barrels being removed, so I've heard that those federal agents were really good golfers.

However, the second law that affected the bourbon business was 1906's Pure Food and Drug Act. The act defined three different types of whiskey:

1. Straight Whiskey–aged for two years

2. Bonded Whiskey–aged for four years, 100 proof, and from one distillery and one season

3. Imitation Whiskey–product of rectifiers and compounders

Imitation whiskey? Let me explain a little: Rectifiers do not distill. They buy whiskey stocks from one or more distilleries and then process and bottle them under another name. They can buy barrels from one or several distilleries and marry them. They can age them longer and come up with their own flavor profile, or bottle it at varying proofs.

Some use a variety of aged whiskies to create a different flavor profile. If you know the meaning of the words on a label, and you know whether some words are missing, you can tell a great deal about the liquor. You can find some bourbons that are diamonds in the rough, that are really great whiskies at low retail prices. Others you can see are still a great quality, but perhaps a little overpriced for what the label is telling you. When I see these, I'll just wait for someone to buy me one instead of me putting my own money down for them.

Compound whiskies are those that contain grain neutral spirits for filler. These are better known as "blended whiskies." Brands like Seagrams 7 and Eight Star come to mind. These are still quality products, but they have a very different flavor profile than straight bourbon whiskey and are produced much more cheaply.

The 1906 Pure Food and Drug Act was further refined in December of 1909 by the Taft Decision. This created the formal definition of whiskey that is still present today. Taft said that for a whiskey to be called "straight," water was the only thing that could be added. If anything other than water was added to the whiskey, it had to be called "blended" whiskey.

But of course, you can't really know what bourbon is until you know just what whiskey is. So let's look at the definition of what I call the four foundation words: Kentucky - Straight - Bourbon -Whiskey. We'll look at them one at a time and learn how each word is defined by the Standards of Identity for Distilled Spirits. (Please note that the Standards spell whisky and bourbon whisky without an "e" in all definitions.)

### WHISKY

Whisky is "an alcoholic distillate from a fermented mash of grain produced at less than 190 proof in such a manner that the distillate possesses the taste, aroma, and characteristics generally attributed to whisky, stored in oak containers and bottled at not less than 80 proof, and also includes mixtures of such distillates for which no specific standards of identity are prescribed."

So the general category of whiskey requires that whiskey should be made from grains (similar to vodka) distilled under 190 proof (similar to vodka) and aged in oak (a distinction from vodka).

You can add neutral grain spirits (pure grain alcohol which is basically vodka). And you can add colors and flavors to get it to meet the requirement that it looks, smells, and tastes like whiskey (not vodka).

### BOURBON WHISKY

*(Rye Whisky, Wheat Whisky, Malt Whisky and Rye Malt Whisky)*

"Bourbon whisky, rye whisky, wheat whisky, malt whisky, or rye malt whisky is whisky produced at not exceeding 160 proof from a fermented mash of not less than 51 percent corn (rye, wheat, malted barley, or malted rye grain respectively), and stored at not more than 125 proof in charred new oak containers, and also includes mixtures of such whiskies of the same type."

How to Read a Label • 85

So unlike just plain whiskey, bourbon can't be made from just any grains. The majority has to be corn. Whiskey can be distilled up to 190 proof, but bourbon must be distilled at under 160 proof. Whiskey can be stored in any type of barrel at any proof, but bourbon must be stored in a brand new, charred-oak container, and at less than 125 proof. (Remember: The reason they put an upper limit of 125 proof on bourbon in the barrel is that barrels at the top of the rack house will rise in proof.) Whiskey can have colors and flavors added, but bourbon can only have water added to achieve barreling and bottling strengths. Ah, now I get it! All bourbon is whiskey, but not all whiskey is bourbon.

As they all share a definition, this means that rye whiskey has to be at least 51% rye and follow the same standards. As do wheat, malt and rye malt whiskies.

### STRAIGHT

"Whiskies conforming to the standards prescribed in the definitions of Bourbon whisky, rye whisky, wheat whisky, malt whisky, rye malt whisky [and corn whisky] which have been stored in the type of oak containers prescribed [charred new oak] for a period of two years or more shall be further designated as 'straight.'"

So basically "straight" means that all grains were distilled at lower proofs and contain no grain neutral spirits. Only water has been added, and the whiskey has been stored for a minimum of two years in new charred oak.

I was told that when the railroad was being laid across the country, two railroad ties were called a "straight." I don't know if the term comes from aging whiskey two years, but until you can prove me wrong, I'm running with this one here.

### KENTUCKY

"State of distillation of domestic types of whisky and straight whisky, except for light whisky and blends…"

Bourbon can be distilled anywhere in the United States, but if you list a state on the label, it must be the state of distillation. Kentucky makes 93% of all bourbon because of the reasons we've already discussed: It has iron-free water and a suitable climate, and, perhaps most significantly, it was where many of the distilleries were already located when Prohibition ended. It is much easier–and cheaper–to retool an old distillery than to build one from the ground up.

There is a bourbon called Virginia Gentleman (General McArthur's favorite bourbon), and it says "Virginia Bourbon" on the label. There are over 200 applications for the development of microdistilleries to make bourbon, whiskey and other distillates. So you'll see many regional whiskies popping up all over the United States, from New York to Montana. This will be great for the industry. It is hoped that people will embrace them, just as they did microbreweries, and I think it will increase awareness and sales in bourbon and rye in general.

Kentucky state law requires that in order to put the word "Kentucky" on a bourbon label, the bourbon should be aged at least a year and a day in Kentucky. This is for Kentucky state tax purposes, since $2 per barrel property taxes are levied per year. Doesn't sound like a lot, but when you figure distillers have anywhere from 100,000 to 1.5 million barrels on hand, that starts to add up. More than half the price you pay for a bottle of bourbon is taxes!

### WHAT TO LOOK FOR IN A LABEL

So if you see the words "Kentucky Straight Bourbon Whiskey," that's a quality stamp. I call these words the four foundation words. If you see these words, you know where/how it's made. Just like if I see a bottle of brandy, that's one thing, but if I see the words Courvoisier Cognac XO, that's another story altogether. That word "cognac" is a quality stamp, and the designation XO is a statement of age.

Look for the words "distilled and bottled by" when you are selecting a bourbon. If it says "distilled and bottled by" then you know by law that bourbon was distilled at that distillery. If it just says "distilled in Kentucky, bottled by..." then all you know is that bourbon was made in Kentucky, but not by any specific distillery. Pappy Van Winkle of Old Fitzgerald Bourbon used to say you should look for "distilled and bottled by" because "any fool with a funnel can bottle whiskey."

## LABELING LAWS

There are labeling laws for bourbon whiskey. These laws require:

Information about the aging process

- If the bourbon is under four years old, an age statement is required.

- If the bourbon is over four years, an age statement is optional.

- If an age is stated, it has to reflect the age of the youngest whiskey in the bottle.

Proof/alcohol by volume must be printed on the label. The higher the proof, typically the less water has been added after aging to get it to the bottling proof.

Are you starting to clearly see the differences between whiskey and bourbon? If so, that's a huge step in the right direction. So pour yourself a nice 100 proof bourbon, grab some bourbon/whiskey bottles, and let's sip and read some labels together.

# WHISKEY PROFESSOR

BERNIE LUBBERS · www.whiskeyprof.com

## HOW TO READ A LABEL

**Distilled BY** – If it says "distilled and Bottled by" then that bourbon was produced by that distiller. So "Distilled by the Old Grand Dad Distillery" means it was made at that distillery.

**Distilled IN Kentucky, Bottled BY** usually means it is the product of a rectifier, and purchased bourbon on the open market and then bottled under their name.

Pappy Van Winkle of Old Fitzgerald famously said to always look for the words distilled an bottled **by** because "any fool with a funnel can bottle whiskey!"

**Kentucky** – A damn fine state, and if the label says it's from KY, that means it was the "state of distillation of domestic types of whiskey.

Kentucky State law further states that if it spends a year and a day in Kentucky, a $2 a barrel property tax is then due to the Commonwealth.

**Straight** – "Straight bourbon Whiskies conforming to the standards" prescribed in the definitions of whiskey and bourbon "which have been stored in the type of containers prescribed for a period of two years or more shall be further designated as 'straight.'" Straight is where is was originally designated only water could be added to bourbon in The Taft Decision of 1909.

**BONDED, or Bottled In Bond**

The whisky must be bottled at exactly 100 proof, aged for a minimum of four years, be a product of one distillery, and distilled during a single season; (today that season is January through December).

the result of this law makes Bonded the most restricted of all the bourbons

**WHISKY** – "an alcoholic distillate from A fermented mash of grain produced At less than 190 proof in such a manner that the distillate possesses the taste, aroma, and characteristics generally attributed to whisky, stored in oak containers, and bottled at not less than 80 proof, and also includes mixtures of such distillates for which no specific standards of identity are prescribed."

**"Bourbon whisky", "rye whisky," "wheat whisky", "malt, whisky", or "rye malt whisky"** Is whisky produced at not exceeding 160 proof from a  fermented mash of not less than 51%corn, rye, wheat, malted barley, or malted rye grain, respectively, and stored at no more than 125 proof in charred new oak containers, and also includes mixtures of such whiskies of the same type.

Tennessee Whiskey – has no definition in the Standards of Identity, so if falls under the class of Whisky. Tennessee Whiskies also differs from bourbon when it passes through the column of maple Charcoal adding some of the sweetness and characteristics of those embers.

Scotch Whisky – is a distinctive product of Scotland, and the main difference is that it must be made from malted barley, and produced in pot stills, and aged in oak for at least 3 years. Blended, Single Malt, and Blended Malt Whisky.

Irish Whiskey – Is a distinctive product of Ireland, distilled in pot or column stills but most often triple distilled and aged for at least 3 years in oak. Both blended, and single Malt - so it is barley based.

Canadian Whisky – A distinctive product of Canada, from a variety of grains, aged in oak for a minimum of 3 years, and no less than 50% neutral grain spirit. or more than 50% straight grain spirit. Canadian whisky may include up to 9.09% of any other type of distilled spirit. (e.g. Sherry, port)

*Blended Scotch, Irish, and Canadian whiskey has a high percentage of neutral grain spirits, which also must be aged for 3 years in oak.

Neutral Spirits – are distilled spirits produced from any material at or above 190 proof..."

American Blends – Blended Bourbon/Whiskey "a mixture which contains straight whiskies or a blend of straight whiskies at not less than 20% on A proof gallon basis, excluding alcohol derived from added harmless coloring, flavoring, or blending materials, and, separately, or in combination whisky or neutral spirits". % of neutral spirits is declared.

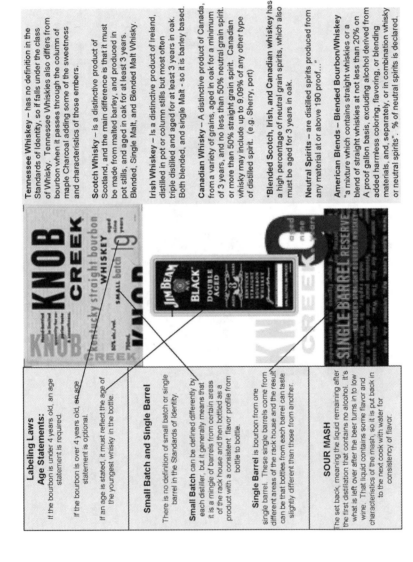

## Labeling Laws
### Age Statements:
If the bourbon is under 4 years old, an age statement is required.

If the bourbon is over 4 years old, an age statement is optional.

If an age is stated, it must reflect the age of the youngest whisky in the bottle.

## Small Batch and Single Barrel

There is no definition of small batch or single barrel in the Standards of Identity

**Small Batch** can be defined differently by each distiller, but it generally means that it is a mingle of barrels from certain areas of the rack house and then bottled as a product with a consistent flavor profile from bottle to bottle.

**Single Barrel** is bourbon from one single barrel. These single barrels come from different areas of the rack house and the result can be that bottles from each barrel can taste slightly different than those from another.

## SOUR MASH
The set back, meaning the liquid remaining after the first distillation that contains no alcohol. It's what is left over after the beer turns in to low wine. That liquid contains some flavor and characteristics of the mash, so it is put back in to the next cook with water for consistency of flavor.

## BOTTLED IN BOND

*Have you ever wondered what the words "Bottled In Bond" mean on a whiskey label? The seven most important words on a label are **KENTUCKY STRAIGHT BOURBON WHISKEY BOTTLED IN BOND**. That phrase means that the whiskey is of highest possible quality. The Bottled In Bond Act of 1897 was the first consumer protection legislation in the history of the United States. It was passed nine years before our government passed laws regulating our food in the Pure Food and Drug Act of 1906. Our forefathers cared more about our whiskey than our food. You gotta love America!*

*After the Civil War the US Government imposed a big tax on whiskey to rebuild the country. Some companies were buying neutral grain spirits and doctoring it up to look and taste like whiskey. They would buy bulk whiskey or grain alcohol and then add colors and flavors like iodine, tobacco, prune juice, etc. and market the product as whiskey. Distillers Col. Edmund H. Taylor, Jr. at the O.F.C. (Old Fashioned Copper) Distillery and Ezra Brooks, who were diligently making bourbon the right way, decided to put a stop to the imposter bourbons. Taylor also happened to be the mayor of Frankfort, Kentucky (and the great nephew of Zachary Taylor). Working closely with the U.S. Secretary of the Treasury, John G. Carlisle (also from Kentucky), Taylor drafted and then helped pass the Bottled In Bond Act of 1897. Some folks credit this act with saving bourbon and other straight whiskies from the rectifiers and blenders. So if the words "Bottled In Bond" appear on the label, that whiskey must meet these criteria (as cited by the Alcohol and Tobacco Tax and Trade Bureau):*

- *Composed of the same kind of spirits composed from the same class of materials*
- *Produced in the same distilling season by the same distiller and the same distillery*
- *Stored for at least four years in wooden containers*

- Reduced in proof by the addition of pure water only to 100 degrees proof, and bottled at 100 proof
- The label shall bear the real name of the distillery and the plants registered DSP, ex D.S.P. KY-1

To further illustrate the point, I'll compare the BIBs to all other whiskies of the world, from least restricted to most restricted:

**Whiskey:** Whiskey can be made from any grain, anywhere in the world and is distilled up to 190 proof. I've also just described vodka, so what makes whiskey different is that it must be stored in wooden containers and must posses the taste, aroma and characteristics generally attributed to whiskey. The makers can add colors, flavors and sugars to achieve this. Must be bottled at no less than 80 proof (40% ABV).

**Canadian Whisky:** Canadian Whisky is made from cereal grains and mashed, distilled up to 190 proof. It must be aged for a minimum of three years in "small wood" (defined as containers less than 700 liters {185 US gallons}) in Canada and posses the aroma, taste and character generally attributed to Canadian Whisky. The makers can add caramel coloring and also contains up to 9.09% of another spirit (typically sherry).

**Blended Scotch Whisky:** Blended Scotch is a mingle of whiskies from any number of distilleries in Scotland. It is made with a neutral grain spirit and matured in excise warehouses in Scotland in oak casks not exceeding 700 liters (185 US gallons) for a minimum of three years. The makers may add water and/ or caramel coloring.

**Single Malt Scotch:** This scotch is made from one grain (malted barley) from one distillery and in pot stills only. The scotch is then aged in oak casks for minimum of three years in containers of under 700 liters. Water and caramel coloring may be added.

**American Corn Whiskey:** Distilled from a mash of no less than 80% corn, Corn whiskey is distilled not to exceed 160 proof. If it is aged, it must be stored in used oak or uncharred new oak at no more than 125 proof and aged for a minimum of two years (hear all these restrictions?). If it says "STRAIGHT" on the label, nothing but pure water has been added (no caramel coloring or flavors).

**Bourbon, Rye and Wheat Whiskies:** – These drinks must be made with a minimum of 51% of the respective grains, distilled not to exceed 160 proof, stored at no more than 125 proof in charred new oak containers and aged for a minimum of two years. If it says "STRAIGHT" on the label, nothing but pure water has been added (no caramel coloring or flavors).

**Bottled in Bond Bourbon:** The BIB must be aged a minimum of four years in the appropriate type of barrel, composed of the same kind of spirits that were produced from the same class of materials and produced during the same distilling season by the same distiller at the same distillery. It must also be reduced in proof to 100 proof, and the DSP of the plant registry must be listed on the label!

Clearly BIBs are the most restricted of the most restricted whiskies in the world.

# BOURBON LABELS

## OLD CROW

Kentucky Straight Bourbon Whiskey

"Distilled and bottled by"

Aged for 3 years

80 proof

I know where it was distilled (Kentucky), I know it was distilled by the company that bottled it, so they had control from grain to glass. I know that it was more than 51% corn, stored in new charred oak at no more than 125 proof, and that nothing was added to it other than water to get it to barreling or bottling strength. We also know that it was aged for a full three years in new charred oak and bottled at 80 proof.

Since it is under four years old, an age must be stated. It follows all the laws and is a true bourbon. As you can see, the word "bourbon" is the largest word on the label of the four foundation words. It will be a lighter bourbon since it aged for only three years, but it is a bourbon nonetheless. Bourbon = quality.

Let's compare and contrast:

## EARLY TIMES

Kentucky Whiskey

"Distilled and bottled by"

Aged for 36 months in reused cooperage

80 proof

## MICHTER'S, SMALL BATCH, UNBLENDED AMERICAN WHISKEY

"Decanted and bottled by"

no age statement

91.4 proof

On the Early Times, two of the four foundation words are missing: "straight" and "bourbon." It is 36 months old, so you can figure out why it cannot be called "straight." If you look at the back label, it states that it is aged a full 36 months in "reused cooperage," which means that they are storing the whiskey in used barrels. So this is a whiskey instead of a bourbon.

But it's over two years old, so why isn't it "straight" whiskey? Remember, straight whiskey has to be aged in *new* charred barrels. I can tell by this piece of information that this will also be a lighter whiskey, even lighter than Old Crow because they are reusing the barrels. This is still a purer product than a blended whiskey, but it is not a true bourbon. Early Times is a well-made, perfectly fine whiskey, but it just won't be as full-bodied and flavorful as a bourbon.

With Michter's, "unblended" means they are trying to alert you to the fact that there are no grain neutral spirits, and by the statement "unblended," and "American Whiskey" means that is it is not a bourbon. This probably means that it, too, has been aged in used barrels. There is no age statement, so it must have aged for at least four years. This is a $30 bottle of whiskey, so I have a few questions about this product. "Decanted and bottled by" means the producers are rectifiers that purchase whiskey on the open market and then age and process it to their standards, but they have no distillery. The proof is a nice high proof that would be worth a few more dollars, but I would like some more information on the age for it being a whiskey and not a bourbon.

### Seagram's 7, Kessler

"American whiskey–a blend of distinctive character"

"Bottled by"

80, 80 proof

75% and 72.5% grain spirits

A "blended whiskey" or "whiskey–a blend" is a mixture which contains straight whiskies or a blend of straight whiskies that are not less than 20% on a proof-gallon basis, excluding alcohol derived from added harmless coloring, flavoring, or blending materials, and separately, or in combination, whiskey or neutral spirits. Also, the percentage of neutral grain spirits must be printed on the label for U.S. whiskies.

Sure enough, if you look on the back label of Seagram's 7 it states "75% grain spirits." A neutral grain spirit comes from a grain (usually corn, as there is a bigger alcohol yield from corn than from small grains like rye, wheat or barley) that is distilled up to 190 proof. What's an example of a grain spirit? I'll bring back a high school or college memory–Ever Clear Pure Grain Alcohol. Ever Clear is made from corn and distilled to 190 proof. As a side note, I also get a kick out of the other words on the Ever Clear label:

DO NOT APPLY TO OPEN FLAME

CONTENTS MAY IGNITE OR EXPLODE

CAUTION!! EXTREMELY FLAMMABLE

HANDLE WITH CARE

NOT INTENDED FOR CONSUMPTION UNLESS MIXED
WITH NON-ALCOHOLIC BEVERAGES

Have you ever been to a party where grain alcohol is being served by your classy host? How do they usually serve it? With a mixture of fruit juices. That hootch is equivalent to putting colors and flavors and sugars into it–much like the peach or strawberries in our moonshine example earlier. You have to soften it up and make it palatable, so you make a blend of juices to do so.

Back to Seagram's 7. So 75% of this is pure grain alcohol, and 25% is whiskey (which can also be produced up to 190 proof), so you've basically got Ever Clear that has been watered down to 80 proof. It must "look, smell, and taste" like whiskey to be a whiskey, so they add caramel coloring, sugars and flavors to get it to look, smell, and taste like whiskey. This is done instantly. And there you have "whiskey–a blend."

To show you what sugar and coloring can do, in my youth I would make Kool Aid in the summertime. My mom always bought the concentrated pouches that had no sugar added. I always liked the sour sensation the Kool Aid would give me without the sugar, but I could only drink a spoonful. But as soon as I added a cup and a half of sugar to it, I could drink the whole pitcher! Same thing with blended whiskey. It starts out kind of harsh because it's basically pure grain alcohol watered down to 80 proof. But as soon as you add caramel color and sugar to it, it becomes really smooth. And how do people drink Seagram's 7? In a seven-and-seven: They mix it with 7UP, which has more sugar and flavor. No wonder it's so smooth, and no wonder you wake up with a giant headache the next morning from all that sugar!

There is absolutely nothing wrong with drinking blended whiskey. Some people prefer it over other whiskey. But know what it is. Blended whiskey is cheap whiskey by definition. They do not cost much, and they shouldn't, but there are still some bourbons like Old Crow which cost several dollars less than blended whiskey. I'll buy Old Crow or Old Charter over blended whiskies when the occasion calls for it. Knowing how to read a label could be saving you money, too!

## JIM BEAM, EVAN WILLIAMS, OLD FORESTER, OLD FITZGERALD, WILD TURKEY

Kentucky Straight Bourbon Whiskey

"Distilled by"

4 years old stated

Some state no age

80 proof

I don't have to wonder how these bourbons are made. I know this is a quality stamp since the words Kentucky Straight Bourbon Whiskey appear on it.

Jim Beam states four years of age, the others state no age. I look at the back to see whether they are four years old. If the bourbon is four years old, the age statement is optional. Jim Beam makes four-, five-, seven-, and eight-year-old bourbons. They put age statements on their white labels to distinguish the differences between the bourbons.

Evan Williams, Old Forester, Old Fitzgerald and Wild Turkey do not state an age on their labels. What I assume here is that these are four years old. That's what the label is telling me, anyway. Some have varying proofs, but the ages are the same according to the labels.

Remember, it takes at least six years to get pronounced vanilla notes. So if you like big vanilla, caramel, maple and ginger flavors, look for something that is at least six years old.

## JACK DANIELS, GEORGE DICKEL, PRICHARD'S

Tennessee Whiskey

Old No. 7, Old No. 8

"Distilled and bottled by"

80 proof

Tennessee Whiskey is not a designation in the Standards of Identity, so Jack must follow all the rules of whiskey but not of bourbon. Jack uses the same basic rules of bourbon regarding grain bills and distillation. They distill to 140 proof, so that's well under 160. They use new charred-oak barrels. The big difference is what is called the "Lincoln County Process" of aging and leaching the whiskey off the still through a 10-foot column of maple charcoal. Gravity propels the whiskey to drip down through the charcoal into the barrel. It takes a whole week to get this done.

Jack Daniels uses new barrels to get as much flavor out of the wood as possible in the time that they age. If they used a previously used barrel, they would have to age the whiskey longer than the four to five years they do. The "No. 7" on the label is not an age statement. Even folks at their distillery aren't sure what it really means. I know this because I was watching the History Channel one night and on came a show about whiskey. They were at the Jack Daniel's Distillery, which was fascinating, but the representative for the distillery said that no one at the distillery had any idea what Old No. 7 stood for. The first thing that came to my mind was, "Dude, you're on the History Channel! Make some shit up at least!"

Old No. 8 for Dickel Tennessee Whiskey is a fine tradition, and they produce good whiskey. But it is not bourbon by their design and tradition in Tennessee. I don't see anything on the website about what Old No. 8 stands for, but my guess is that it is a play on Old No. 7 from Jack, which would be really hilarious since Old No. 7 means nothing.

Apart from Jack Daniels, George Dickel and Prichard's are the only other Tennessee Whiskies. They do it slightly differently, but still in that same style. Mr. Prichard is also using white corn to mirror the style of the Tennessee whiskies made in the 1800s in the Volunteer State.

## OLD GRAND DAD, HEAVEN HILL, OLD FITZGERALD, OLD BOURBON HOLLOW—BOTTLED IN BOND

Kentucky Straight Bourbon Whiskey

"Bonded – Bottled in Bond"

"Distilled by"

All are 100 proof

No age statement

We know by definition that these are at least four years old and exactly 100 proof, from one distillery and from one season.

## KNOB CREEK 9-YEAR, ELIJAH CRAIG 12-YEAR, PAPPY VAN WINKLE 23-YEAR, RUSSELL'S RESERVE 10-YEAR

Kentucky Straight Bourbon Whiskey

"Distilled and bottled by"

Small Batch

Aged 9 to 23 years

100, 94, 95.6 and 90 proof

These all have the four foundation words, so there's the quality stamp. Every drop in that bottle is at least as old as the age that is stated on the label.

"Distilled and bottled by" shows that they are each controlled by their own standards. Some state "small batch," which has no definition, but was coined to differentiate it from a single barrel bourbon. It's a mingle of barrels.

I'm left with few questions, if any, about these bourbons. I know how they are made, where they are made, and how long they have been aged. But there is a risk in putting an age statement on a bourbon label. If the demand for that bourbon outpaces the supply of barrels that are in a warehouse, you might see a shortage or outage of a product until the next lot of barrels reaches maturity.

*The 1,000,000th barrel produced after prohibition by the Sunny Brook Distillery in front of one of the bonded warehouses. (Photo courtesy of the Louisville Convention and Visitors Bureau)*

## A NOTE ON SMALL BATCH

*There is no definition of small batch or single barrel in the TTB's Standards of Identity. "Small batch" is a term that was first coined by legendary distiller Booker Noe in 1987 with the introduction of Booker's Bourbon a few years after Elmer T. Lee came out with Blanton's Single Barrel in 1984. Booker's "small batch" became a designation that was supposed to mean it was not a single-barrel bourbon. I like to say, it's a "mingle" not a single.*

*A single-barrel bourbon is agreed upon that it's bourbon bottled up from only one barrel. That barrel and its location in the rack house are sometimes noted on each bottle. Small-batch bourbons are taking more than one barrel (no agreed upon amount) from certain places in the rack house and then mingling those barrels for a consistent flavor profile. Conversely a single-barrel bourbon can taste different from barrel to barrel, and that's the magic of single-barrel bourbon. We don't make batches of bourbon since we use continuous column stills, so the small batch is at the end where you take selected barrels from the distiller's "sweet spots" of the rack house.*

*The definition of small batch can differ from distiller to distiller. Now Parker Beam at Heaven Hill introduced Elijah Craig around the same time as Booker's, and he defined his Small Batch Bourbon as a batch of 100 barrels or less. Because Booker and Parker are cousins, and both buddies with Elmer T. Lee, it's probably a logical assumption that they were picking each other's brains without really telling each other completely what they were working on. So even though Small Batch Bourbons are not distilled in small batches, it still defines the category. So small batch is kind of like an oxymoron, like peace keeper missile. Oxymorons that I came up with on my own include vodka tasting, vacation Bible school, mild heart attack, and Fox News.*

### Woodford Reserve, Bulliet, Maker's Mark, Buffalo Trace, Four Roses — Larceny

Kentucky Straight Bourbon Whiskey

"Distilled by"

Small batch

No age statement

90.4, 90, 90, 90, 90 proof

You don't have to worry about quality with the four foundation words. We know the bourbon in the bottle is at least four years old since there is no age statement. But with many small batch or other handmade bourbons, their stocks are limited so they often mingle ages. If you mingle bourbons from four to eight+ years old, you get a unique flavor profile. Some call this "bottled to taste." They are not trying to mislead you about the age of the bourbon, but they are most likely trying to keep themselves from running out of older whiskey and not being able to supply the demand. If there is an age on the bottle, that number must reflect the age of the youngest bourbon in the mix. If you don't state an age, the youngest bourbon has to be at least four years old. So the distiller can use younger bourbons with the same flavor profile to continue the run if they run out of the older stock, as long as the youngest is at least four years old.

Bourbon with ages on the bottle aren't "better" than those without ages, but remember, if you like big vanilla or other barrel notes in your bourbon, age statements might be more important for you.

### Corner Creek, Rowan's Creek, Jefferson's Reserve, Pogue Master's Select

Kentucky Straight Bourbon Whiskey

Small batch

"Distilled in Kentucky, bottled by"

No age statement

88, 100.1, 82.3, 91 proof

These are quality products with the four foundation words. But the language "distilled in Kentucky" means that it was not distilled *by* them. This means that they are buying the bourbon from one of the distillers that sells on the open market. What are they doing to make it "their" bourbon? Look for age and proof.

There is no age statement, so we can assume that the bourbon in the bottle is at least four years old. It could also be a mingle of ages, but we are going by the label here. Then note the proof. For additional information, you can check the "necker labels" that often dangle from the bottles or check the companies' websites. In many cases this can give more information than the label. But remember, there are not the same strict laws on neckers or the web that there are for the label itself.

Make no mistake, I would *love* to be a rectifier and have my own bourbon. It's a way for passionate people (some who are descendants of famous whiskey distillers) to continue or start a bourbon legacy. Distilleries cost millions of dollars to build and maintain, so rectifying is a great way to get into the business. I just like as much information on the label as I can get.

BLANTON'S, FOUR ROSES, HANCOCK'S, SINGLE BARREL BOURBONS, NO AGE STATEMENT

Kentucky Straight Bourbon Whiskey

"Distilled and bottle by"

Single barrel

No age statement

93, 100, 88.9 proof

Elijah Craig **18,** Eagle Rare **10,** single barrel with age
statements

Kentucky Straight Bourbon Whiskey

"Distilled and bottled by"

Single barrel

Proof

18 years old, 10 years old

Single barrel means that all the bourbon from one barrel is bottled at one time. Because every barrel in a rack house can have a slightly different taste, distillers usually list on the label or necker the location of each barrel from which they pulled the bourbon. If you find that you consistently like high-storage or low-storage barrels, you can go for that single barrel over another. Or you might enjoy the varying flavor from barrel to barrel. That's the magic of single barrel bourbon. And that explains the difference between "small batch" and "single barrel."

If no age is listed, all you can assume is that it has been aged for at least four years. With small batch and single barrel bourbons that have no age listed, I look for "distilled and bottled by." I'd like to know that I'm dealing with a distiller and then I can assume they are bottling to a flavor profile. An example of this is Buffalo Trace with their Blanton's and Hancock's brands—it is important to know which warehouse the bourbon was pulled from since they age different labels in different warehouses to get a certain flavor profile. You also want to check the proof and see how much water has been added after the aging process. When the age is stated, I get a very clear idea of what to expect from the taste.

Now let's check out some straight rye whiskey labels. Rye whiskey has to be at least 51% rye, and all the other rules are exactly the same. Check out wheat whiskey. There's only one, Bernheim Wheat Whiskey. It has to be 51% wheat and follow all the same laws.

## STRAIGHT RYE WHISKEY

Rye brings a range of spice notes, including pepper, nutmeg, clove and cinnamon, which are all intensified during the aging process. Think of eating a piece of rye bread.

### RITTENHOUSE RYE, PIKESVILLE RYE, JIM BEAM RYE, OLD OVERHOLT RYE, SAZERAC RYE, (RI)1 RYE

Look for state of distillation, if any

Straight Rye Whiskey

"Distilled and bottled by"

Age

80, 80, 90, 92 proof


### RITTENHOUSE RYE BOTTLED IN BOND

Straight Rye Whiskey

Bottled in Bond means at least 4 years old, from one distillery, exactly 100 proof, and all from barrels from one season (January-December of one year)

"Bottled by"

100 proof

Rye whiskey has to follow the same laws as bourbon. Rye indicates that the whiskey must be made from a fermented mash of at least 51% rye instead of corn. That's the difference between it and bourbon. Less corn and more rye means that the spirit will be less sweet and have more spice to it. Some of the companies (and this is just my opinion) leave off "Kentucky," even if they are distilled there, to tie their product to the history of the classic Pennsylvania or "Monongahela" rye whiskies.

It's also a distinctively American spirit, and the category is on fire right now. Rye is enjoying its second "Golden Age."

## STRAIGHT WHEAT WHISKEY

### Bernheim Original

Kentucky Straight Wheat Whiskey

Small Batch

90 proof

What is this telling you? Well, we know it's 51% wheat. Wheat results in a sweeter-tasting whiskey, but not because the grain is sweeter. Wheat is not as rich as rye so it allows more of the sweetness of the corn and vanilla to show through, compared to rye, which can overshadow some of those sweet flavors.

Hey, you're catching on. I wonder how long it will take for someone to produce a straight malted rye whiskey?

So now you know how to read a label. Head out to the liquor store and spend some time looking at the labels. You will find that instead of just looking at the price of a bourbon and assuming it's really good, you'll be able to read the label and know something about it before you even taste it. When you do that, you'll find some real diamonds in the rough. Old Grand Dad, Ancient Age, Elijah Craig and Old Forester are just a few.

Some do cost more and are more than worth it. I'm always surprised when someone asks me why a bourbon can cost anywhere from $25 to $50+. Remember, distillers have to use a brand new barrel every time and then age the liquor for at least four years. I'm surprised we sell it as cheaply as we do. These are the same people that go to dinner and think nothing of spending $50 on a bottle of wine, and it's gone when dinner's over. That $50 bottle of bourbon will be around a little longer than that, and you get more than four glasses out of it! So quit bitching and buy the bourbon...jeez!

## JUST WHO ARE THE PEOPLE BEHIND THE NAMES ON LABELS?

To be a true expert in bourbon, it's good to also have a working knowledge of the guys who have contributed their names to the beverage. Here's a list of the who's who in the history of bourbon making:

*A.H. Hirsch:* The bourbon was commissioned by Adolph Hirsch, a former Schenley executive. Four hundred barrels of bourbon were made in the spring of 1974 at the Pennco Distillery in Schaefferstown, PA. Schenley was formed after Prohibition and was one of the largest operations. It later became United Distillers when it joined with Glenmore, and then UD became Diageo.

*Baker's:* Baker Beam is Carl Beam's son and Park Beam's Grandson, two legendary master distillers at Jim Beam and Heaven Hill. Baker worked at both these distilleries himself, and has his own small batch bourbon in the famous Jim Beam Small Batch Bourbon Collection. Baker is retired and does a few appearances at the Beam distillery throughout the year, but is an avid motorcycle enthusiast. He is also a fan of high storage for his Baker's Bourbon. He feels that seven years is the maximum when you use high storage.

*Bernheim Original Wheat Whiskey (and I.W. Harper):* Bernheim is the gentleman who is linked to these two brands. I.W. Stands for Isaac Wolfe, and Bernheim is his last name. He's the same gentleman who donated the 40,000 acres that is now Bernheim Forest right off Hwy 245 on the way to Bardstown. Bernheim had his distillery in downtown Louisville at 17th and Breckenridge, and there's one there still today: DSP KY 1 is the Heaven Hill Bernheim facility. Back in the day because of the prejudice against people of Jewish heritage, Bernheim didn't want to put his last name on his label, so instead he used his friend's: Harper. Thus I.W. Harper was born. Today, Heaven Hill is proud to put Bernheim's name on its Original Wheat Whiskey.

*Blanton's (Col. Albert Blanton):* Born on an adjacent farm, Blanton joined what was then George T. Stagg's Distillery as an office boy at the age of 16. Over the next several years, Blanton was promoted and given experience in every department at the distillery. In 1921, Col. Blanton was promoted to president of the George T. Stagg Bourbon distillery. Col. Blanton kept the Distillery alive through Prohibition, obtaining a special government license to produce "medicinal whiskey." It was one of only four distilleries in the country to obtain this special permission. After a disastrous flood in 1937, Col. Blanton had the distillery back to normal operation in just 24 hours. He was also responsible for much of the aesthetic growth of the distillery throughout his tenure, building a clubhouse and several gardens as well as his own personal property, the Stony Point mansion that overlooks the distilling grounds.

**Booker's (Booker Noe):** Frederick Booker Noe was born December 5th, 1929 and passed away in 2004. He introduced Booker's Bourbon in 1987 and coined the phrase "small batch" to describe his uncut, unfiltered bourbon. Master Distiller for over 40 years, Booker was a a larger than life character. He played football for Bear Bryant at the University of Kentucky. Standing 6'4" with fingers like sausages, crowds in New York and San Fransisco fell in love with him as he would taste his bourbon and smack his lips aloud. Journalists called that "The Kentucky Chew." Along with his friends, Elmer T. Lee, Jimmy Russell and his cousin Parker Beam, Booker was one of a handful of legends that propelled the industry in its second golden age today. His son Fred and grandson Freddie are also Frederick Booker Noe, the III and IV respectively.

**Bulleit:** Augustus Bulleit was a tavern keeper in 1830s in Louisville, Kentucky. He liked a lot of rye in his bourbon so his contained a "high rye" recipe. One fateful day, while transporting his barrels of bourbon from Kentucky to New Orleans, Augustus Bulleit vanished. What happened is still unknown, but his great-great grandson Tom and Tom's daughter Hollis both continue with representing the family legacy.

**Col. Edmund H. Taylor:** As a descendant of two U.S. presidents, James Madison and Zachary Taylor, you might say that E.H. Taylor, Jr. had leadership and ambition in his blood.

While Madison went down in history as the "Father of the Constitution," E.H. Taylor, Jr. sealed his own prestigious legacy as the "Father of the Modern Bourbon Industry." Taylor is celebrated for the countless innovations he contributed to the bourbon industry in his time. His first involvement in the industry came as a banker, aiding in the organization and financing of several distilleries. Through his experience as a banker, Taylor became personally acquainted with several prominent whiskey makers. Taylor's 1869 purchase of a small Leestown distillery that he christened O.F.C. (Old Fashioned Copper) was his foray into distilling, making an immediate mark on the industry by modernizing, expanding and upgrading the plant. Among his innovations were copper fermentation tanks, state-of-the-art grain equipment, columnar stills, modernized buildings, a more efficient sour mash technique and a first-of-its-kind steam heating system still used in the warehouses today. Also a skilled politician, Taylor was instrumental in fighting for higher standards in the bourbon industry, pushing for the passage of the Bottled in Bond Act of 1897 along with the Secretary of Treasury (and another whiskey man) Ezra Brooks. As if his involvement in the bourbon industry weren't enough, Taylor served as mayor of Frankfort, KY for sixteen years.

*Elijah Craig:* Born in Orange County, VA, Craig was ordained a Baptist minister in 1771. Arrested for preaching without a license or for disturbing the peace by his preaching, so you could say the good reverand was out of the ordinary to say the least. In 1781, his brother (also a preacher) led an exodus of 600 members of what they called the "Traveling Church" to the Kentucky Territory of Virginia, and Elijah followed him there through the Cumberland Gap a couple years after and bought 1,000 acres of land in Fayette County Virginia. He preached at the Great Crossing Church which is still active today in Georgetown, KY (a community Craig himself helped design). He founded the first classical school in Kentucky in 1787 and then later donated the land for Georgetown College, which still exists and operates today.

The story goes that Elijah Craig opened a distillery in 1789, and a barn that held some empty whiskey barrels almost burned down. As the heads were not on them, the barrels were burned only on the inside, so Craig decided to use them anyway. The charred barrels imparted color and flavor to the whiskey, and his customers raved about the taste. The distillery has been doing it ever since.

Craig continued to prosper, coming to own more than 4,000 acres (16 km²) and operating a retail store in Frankfort, KY. He died in Georgetown in 1808. John Taylor wrote of him in *A History of Ten Baptist Churches*: "His preaching was of the most solemn style; his appearance as of a man who had just come from the dead; of a delicate habit, a thin visage, large eyes and mouth; the sweet melody of his voice, both in preaching and singing, bore all down before it."

*The Kentucky Encyclopedia* refers to the *Kentucky Gazette* for his eulogy, "He possessed a mind extremely active and, as his whole property was expended in attempts to carry his plans to execution, he consequently died poor. If virtue consists in being useful to our fellow citizens, perhaps there were few more virtuous men than Mr. Craig."

*Elmer T. Lee:* Kentucky born and bred, Elmer joined the distillery as a maintenance engineer in 1949 after serving as a Radar Bombardier in World War II and returning to earn an engineering degree at the University of Kentucky. Quickly rising to Plant Engineer, then Plant Superintendent and eventually the shared title of Plant Manager and Master Distiller, Elmer oversaw much of the distillery's modernization and growth up until his retirement in 1985.

In 1984, Elmer honored the man who hired him by introducing the world's first single barrel bourbon, Blanton's Single Barrel. Not long thereafter, Elmer himself was honored with his own single barrel namesake. Both bourbons have received the highest worldwide acclaim and honors since. Elmer T. Lee passed away July 2013 at the age of 93. What a long and great life, and he's no doubt one of the main reasons for the modern Golden Age of bourbon!

***Evan Williams:*** Kentucky's first licensed distiller. Williams' distillery was located in downtown Louisville, and he was also a city councilman. There were many complaints about the smell and slop of the stillage that were brought to the council meetings, but when Williams brought whiskey with him, he rarely got fined or even slapped on the wrist about it. Like a lot of people in Kentucky, Evan Williams came from Virginia. Kentucky was actually part of Virginia until 1792 when we became the 15th state. When he moved to Kentucky he became Louisville's first harbor master.

***Ezra Brooks:*** I can't find a lot of information about Ezra Brooks, but Ezra Brooks was a pioneer in the early shaping of Kentucky. He was also a passionate whiskey man who helped push through the Bottled In Bond Act of 1897 along with Col. Edmund H. Taylor.

***George Dickel:*** Born in Darmstadt Germany in 1818, George immigrated to the U.S. in 1844 and ended up settling in Nashville, TN where he went into business as a cobbler. Ten years later he entered the rectifying and bottling business where he bought whiskey from several distilleries, mingled them together, bottled them under another name and sold them at his own store (kind of like private labels today). He tended to like the whiskey from the nearby Cascade Distillery and ended up buying their whiskey exclusively.

In 1881 George's brother-in-law, a partner in George A. Dickel & Co., gained controlling interest in the Cascade Distillery, and the distillery gave them sole bottling and distribution rights . They bottled "Cascade Whisky — Mellow As Moonlight." George was forced into retirement after a fall from a horse in 1888 and died in 1894. Cascade Tennessee Whiskey actually moved to Louisville after Tennessee voted for statewide Prohibition in 1910, ten years before the nation! It wasn't until 1964 when whiskey giant Schenley finally put George Dickel's name on a bottle of whiskey.

***George T. Stagg:*** Stagg was born December 19, 1835, in Garrard County, Kentucky. While little is known of his early years, the impact his adult life had on the bourbon industry was quite impressive. Working as a whiskey salesman in St. Louis, he had the good fortune to team up with bourbon icon E.H. Taylor, Jr. Together they built the most dominant American distillery of the 19th century. A leading industry expert at the time declared the distillery "one plus ultra of its class," the best of the best.

Stagg's salesmanship and financial acumen helped build the distillery into one of the world's leading bourbon producers. In 1904, the distillery was rechristened to bear Stagg's name, a title that was maintained for nearly a century.

*Hancock's Reserve:* Named after Hancock Taylor who was a surveyor who laid out and surveyed the Leestown, KY area in 1774. He was tragically killed by Native Americans in that area shortly after. (I'm not sure if he was related to Edmund H. Taylor, but probably not)

*Henry McKenna:* Henry McKenna was born in the Irish county Derry in 1819 and came to Kentucky in Nelson County in 1838. Several years later he opened a flour mill, and in 1855 he used the excess grains to make wheat whiskey with his friend and master distiller from Country Derry, Patrick Sweeny. A few years after later, the duo made corn whiskey (bourbon). In 1880 McKenna opened an office in Louisville Kentucky, and in 1883 he built a new distillery with a three barrel per day capacity! Henry passed away in 1893, and the business was taken over by his sons: Daniel, James and Stafford.

*Jack Daniel:* Jack Daniel was born in Tennessee in 1846, and his mother died a year after he was born. His father remarried, but young Jack didn't get along with his parents so he moved out and stayed with neighbors and friends until he was 20 years old. At that point he opened the Jack Daniel Distillery in Lynchburg, TN. Because of the confusion and disarray after the Civil War, most distilleries in the South didn't register their stills with the government, but young Jack did. He became known as a "stand-up" distiller and the still became known as the Jack Daniel's Number 1 Distillery. Jack was called 'Little Jack' because he was 5'2" tall and weighed 120 pounds. Quite the Tennessee Squire, he always went around in a colorful vest, string tie, frock coat and planters hat. By 1884 his nephew, Lem Motlow became the Jack Daniels plant manager. Jack Daniels Whiskey won a gold medal at the Louisiana Purchase Exhibition in 1904, and shortly after that Jack and Lem began shipping it overseas where it won four more gold medals and two more awards.

*James E. Pepper:* James Pepper is the son of Oscar Pepper, who made one of the smartest moves in distilling history by hiring Scotsman Dr. James Crow to be his distiller in 1838. That bourbon became the most popular bourbon during the civil war, enjoyed by folks such as Daniel Webster, Andrew Jackson, U.S. Grant and Henry Clay. James only ran the Old Oscar Pepper Distillery until 1878 when he sold it to James Labrot and James Graham (site of where Woodford Reserve is made today at the Labrot and Graham Distillery). James was one of the people (if not THE person) responsible for the Old Fashioned Cocktail. In 1889 he walked into his club in downtown Louisville, The Pendennis Club, and ordered a bourbon drink the "Old Fashioned" way. (muddling fruit and using sugar and bitters). The story goes on that when he visited New York he asked for the same drink the way they made if for him in Louisville, and the rest if history.

*Jefferson's Reserve:* Thomas Jefferson – Do I really need to go in detail here? Here's a few hints: founding father, wrote the Declaration of Independence, hired Lewis and Clark, Louisiana Purchase, founder of the University of Virginia, inventor, architect, slave owner and after all that…he died broke.

*Jim Beam:* Col. James Beauregard Beam was born near the end of the Civil War in 1864. He took over the Old Tub Distillery (later to become the Jim Beam Distillery) before Prohibition. He decided not to apply for a license to sell bourbon medicinally, and so during Prohibition he went into the citrus farming business in Florida and rock quarrying in Kentucky. He was not successful in those ventures and folks in town said Col. Beam was only good at making and selling whiskey. They joked that if Jim Beam decided to open a funeral home in town, everyone in Bardstown would suddenly stop dying!

When Prohibition ended in 1934, Col. Beam at the age of 70 went into business with a couple of businessmen from Chicago. He bought the old Murphy Barber distillery and insisted on the same DSP (Distilled Spirits Producer) number as he had before, and they started making whiskey again under the Old Tub and Pebble Ford labels. After he passed away in 1947, his son, T. Jeremiah Beam, launched the brand Jim Beam to honor his father, and that brand has become the #1 selling bourbon in the world today.

*JTS Brown:* John Thompson Street Brown opened his distillery in 1870, along with his two sons and his half brother George Garvin Brown. It was George Garvin Brown who also started Old Forester. If you're a fan of classic movies you'll recall this is the brand that Fast Eddie Felson (Paul Newman) drank when he played Minnesota Fats in *The Hustler.*

*J.W. Dant:* Joseph Washington Dant was a blacksmith and only 16 when he opened his distillery in 1836. This hard-working boy had a taste for bourbon, which wasn't odd back in the tough world of the 1800s. Instead of the more common copper stills of the time, Dant used the "running on a log" still method, using a hollowed out section of a tree trunk and running a copper pipe through it which was considered old fashioned even then. He fathered 10 children, and his son John led the distillery into the 1900s.

*Mattingly and Moore (also Tom Moore):* It all started late in the 1800s when two gentlemen — Tom Moore and Ben Mattingly — fell in love with the Willett sisters. For those of you unfamiliar with the Willetts, they have been one of the premier families in Kentucky bourbon distilling from the early days to the present. Both Tom and Ben married their sweethearts, and years later, their father-in-law signed over ownership of the Willett & Frenke distillery to them. I'm not really sure what happened to Frenke, but Tom and Ben rechristened their operation Mattingly & Moore. One of the first products out of the Mattingly & Moore distillery was Belle Of Nelson Bourbon Whiskey.

*Old Crow:* Dr. James Crow was a Scottish chemist and physician that arrived in the U.S. in 1820 and worked for a couple different distilleries until Oscar Pepper made the best move of his career, and probably the best in the bourbon world, by hiring Dr. Crow in 1838 to be his master distiller. Dr. Crow didn't "run on a log" like J.W. Dant was doing or use copper pot stills like everyone else. He used the newly invented Coffey Still (a column still that brought the white dog off the still at a consistent strength). Crow checked that strength with a hydrometer while most still shook the jars to see the beads and guessed the proof or used gunpowder and a match. Crow also used litmus paper and a saccharimeter to check acid and sugar levels. He didn't invent the "sour mash" process but employed it on a daily basis to give the whiskey consistency and help in the mash tubs with pH levels. His Old Crow bourbon was the most popular of the era and was known as red whiskey (AKA red liquor or red eye) since he aged all of it in charred barrels. Because of its popularity, you can be sure his competitors also started using those same techniques, so you can see Dr. Crow's influence on the entire bourbon industry.

*Old Fitzgerald (John E. Fitzgerald):* Old Fitzgerald Distillery started up in 1870. John E. Fitzgerald was not a distiller, but a treasury agent at the old W.L. Weller distillery who was known to have good taste. He also had the keys to the rack house and would help himself to the best tasting of the wheated W.L. Weller barrels. Those special barrels became known simply as "Fitzgerald Barrels." Fitzgerald's good taste was so legendary that he started his own distillery in 1870 and sold his brand on steamships, trains and in fine gentleman's clubs the world over. Except that's not true. This was the myth that Pappy Van Winkle came up with to market the brand when he acquired Stizel-Weller Distillery. His unique brand of myth creating seems to have worked. He made it one of the most popular bourbons in the 1950s and 60s. The brand is still wheated today by Heaven Hill's Craig and Parker Beam, and The Fitzgerald name appears on the Larceny Bourbon Label since it's out of the same distillery and mash bill.

*Old Forester (Dr. William Forrester):* "Old Fo" is the flagship brand of Brown-Forman, named after the Civil War surgeon Dr. William Forrester (spelled with two "r"s) and was the first bourbon to be labeled and bottled as a medicinal bourbon since Geo. Garvin Brown was a pharmaceutical salesman. It's been sold at a 100 proof for a while now, but they've just applied to make a B.I.B., and that's exciting! Brown's good friend, Dr. Forrester, told him that doctors couldn't trust bulk whiskey. So Brown was inspired to buy the best bourbon he could and sell it to doctors, and to further increase the brand's credibility, Brown put his good friend's name on the label. Old Forrester was introduced in 1870. After the good doctor passed away, they struck one of the "r"s off and it's been Old Forester ever since. The only bourbon to be produced before, during and after Prohibition by the same company.

*Old Grand Dad and Basil Hayden (Basil Hayden, Sr.):* Hayden was a Maryland Catholic that led a group of 25 Catholic families from Maryland to what is now Nelson County, Kentucky (near Bardstown) in 1785. This area is home to many of the famous bourbon brands, including Jim Beam. Hayden donated land for the first Catholic church west of the Alleghenies, and the first Catholic church in what is now the Commonwealth of Kentucky.

Around 1885, Hayden's grandson Raymond B. Hayden founded a distillery in Nelson County and named his label "Old Grand-Dad" in honor of his grandfather. Raymond's mother, Polly, was a member of the Dant family by the way. The picture on the bottle was copied from a rendering of Basil Sr.'s likeness. When Beam Industries introduced their "small batch" collection, among the four was "Basil Hayden's", which the company says uses a mash similar to that originally utilized by Hayden in 1788.

*Old Overholt:* Abraham Overholt was a farmer and distiller in the Pennsylvania region known as Monongahela, named for the river. Overholt starting making a rye whiskey around 1810, which became known as Monongahela Rye. His son Jacob and his cousin Henry continued to grow the business from that point in time.

*Old Pogue:* In 1876, Henry Edgar Pogue (H.E. Pogue I) purchased the Old Time Distillery from O.H.P Thomas. Pogue was the head distiller for O.H.P Thomas at the time of the acquisition, producing "Old Time" Sour Mash and "Old Maysville Club" Rye. The distillery became Kentucky Registered Distillery No. 3. According to some records, the H.E. Pogue Distillery's original brand was "Old Pogue" Kentucky Straight Bourbon Whisky.

*Pappy Van Winkle:* Julian P. "Pappy" Van Winkle Sr.'s mantra was "We make fine bourbon at a profit if we can, at a loss if we must, but always fine bourbon." His name has now become synonymous with quality in the bourbon industry. Pappy's involvement with bourbon began in 1893 as a traveling salesman for W.L. Weller and Sons. He and a friend, Alex Farnsley, eventually purchased the A. Ph. Stitzel Distillery, which produced bourbon for Weller. The two companies merged to form the Stitzel-Weller Distillery. Opened on Derby Day of 1935, Stitzel-Weller quickly became known for its wheated bourbon recipe, using wheat instead of rye in the mash for a softer, smoother taste. Pappy remained highly involved with the Distillery up until his death in 1965 at the age of 91.

*Parker's Heritage Collection:* This bourbon is named after the legendary 6th generation Beam distiller, Parker Beam. He's named after his grandfather, Park Beam, who was the brother of James Beauregard Beam, otherwise known as Jim Beam. Parker learned the business from his grandfather and his father Earl. Earl turned the reigns of Heaven Hill distillery over to Parker in 1975. Parker's other passions (after bourbon) are farming, driving trucks and tractors. Parker's son Craig Beam is overseeing the distilling at Heaven Hill now along with Denny Potter and Charlie Downs. However, all are under the watchful eye of Parker who's motto is, "quality, quality, quality!"

*Rittenhouse Rye:* David Rittenhouse was a surveyor for Great Britain. He helped draw the famous line that was the Mason-Dixon Line. He was also named as first Director of the U.S. Mint in April of 1792 and hand struck the first U.S. coins made from silver donated by George Washington himself.

*Rowan's Creek:* John Rowan was a statesman in Kentucky during the late 1700s and early 1800s. His mansion is said to have inspired the Stephen Foster song "My Old Kentucky Home."

*T.W. Samuels:* This rye bourbon dates back to 1844 when T.W. Samuels opened his distillery in Deatsville, KY. The company was known for its unique stair-step-designed rackhouses, which give a greater chimney effect to force more heat to the top floors. T.W. Samuels' grandson went on to start a little bourbon called Maker's Mark.

*Wathen's:* Henry Hudson Wathen was known to have operated a distillery in Lebanon, KY in 1788. The Wathens later acquired the Old Grand Dad label and produced that bourbon for some time. The Wathens were vitally important in the western part of the Bourbon area. At one point, they owned and operated three distilleries all in a row along the western side of Owensboro.

*Willett Reserve:* Shortly after the Civil War, John David Willett began the Willett distilling tradition in Kentucky. He was Master Distiller and one-third owner of the Moore, Willett and Frenke Distillery in Bardstown. In her book, *Historic Nelson County*, Sarah B. Smith states that, "failing eyesight caused John David Willett to sell his interest in the distillery to his brothers-in-law, Ben F. Mattingly and Tom Moore, yet his knowledge and skill was such that he shrugged off the handicap and went on to serve as Master Distiller for five plants; three in the Bardstown area and two in Louisville." John David developed mash bills that were later used by the Willett Distilling Company in some of their whiskies, and now in the recipes at Kentucky Bourbon Distillers. (See also the entry about Mattingly and Moore.)

**W. L. Weller (William Larue Weller):** A true distilling pioneer, W.L. Weller is credited with being the first distiller to produce Kentucky Straight Bourbon Whiskey using wheat instead of rye in the mash bill. Weller's original "wheated bourbons" became so popular, in fact, it's been said that Weller was forced to put a green thumbprint on his invoices and barrels to ensure that customers were receiving the real deal.

Weller's namesake company eventually went on to merge with Pappy Van Winkle's A. Ph. Stitzel Distillery to form the Stitzel-Weller Distillery, becoming renowned for such brands as W.L. Weller, Old Fitzgerald, Rebel Yell and Cabin Still.

**Woodford Reserve:** Woodford County, Kentucky is named for William Woodford, an American Revolutionary War general from Virginia who died while a prisoner of war in 1780. The county was formed from a part of Fayette County, Virginia in 1788. It was the last of the original nine counties established that formed the Commonwealth of Kentucky in 1792.

## WORDS ON WHISKEY LABELS
## ARE LIKE BOY SCOUTS EARNING BADGES

*When you look at words on a whiskey label, think of the whiskey as a boy scout earning badges. Just like the scouts, not all whiskies earn all the badges. The words DISTILLED BY or DISTILLED AND BOTTLED BY is a badge. This means that the company named actually made the whiskey. If it says PRODUCED BY, BOTTLED BY, DISTILLED IN INDIANA BOTTLED BY or DISTILLED IN KENTUCKY BOTTLED BY this usually means that the company sourced and bought the whiskey from someone else but did not distill it. It's not necessarily a bad thing. It's like if you bought Ethan Allen furniture from someone other than Ethan Allen. It's still Ethan Allen furniture, you're just paying more for it than if you had bought it directly from the company.*

*The word WHISKEY or WHISKY on the label is another badge. It's telling you that the drink is not just vodka or neutral grain spirits: it is Whiskey. Whiskies may be made from any grain, anywhere in the world, produced up to 190 proof and aged in oak. They must also look, smell and taste like whiskey, and the producers can add colors and flavors to make that happen. Whiskey has to be bottled at no less than 80 proof. If you meet these criteria, you earn the WHISKEY BADGE.*

*BOURBON is another badge. It's not just whiskey, it's Bourbon. The majority grain has to be corn. It must be distilled in the United States, distilled at under 160 proof and aged in a charred new oak container at no more than 125 proof. RYE, WHEAT, RYE MALT, and MALT are also badges. Just the majority grains change accordingly.*

*STRAIGHT means that it is aged in wooden containers for a minimum of two years with nothing added except pure water.*

*KENTUCKY is also a badge. You might not think so, but would you prefer to drink Kentucky Straight Bourbon Whiskey or Florida Straight Bourbon Whiskey? We have the limestone filtered water here in Kentucky, as well as the extreme heat and cold. In Florida it would be mostly hot and*

*little cold. So just like there's a difference between a Brandy and a Cognac, Kentucky also sets a certain standard.*

*An AGE STATEMENT is also a badge since every drop must be no younger than the stated age on the label.*

*SMALL BATCH and SINGLE BARREL are badges, and — although not legally defined — they are still important designations. With no age statement on the label, this can mean the bourbon is composed of a mingling of ages with SMALL BATCH or that it has been pulled from certain areas of the rickhouses with SINGLE BARREL or SMALL BATCH.*

*These are great badges to look for in a whiskey, but if you want the EAGLE SCOUT of whiskey (or spirits in general) then BOTTLED IN BOND has all the badges. If the words BONDED, BOTTLED IN BOND or AGED IN BOND are on the label, then they must meet all the badge requirements above, but also be composed of the same kind of spirits produced from the same class of materials, produced in the same distilling season by the same distiller at the same distillery and stored for at least four years in wooden containers. The bourbon can also be reduced in proof by the addition of pure water only to exactly 100 degrees of proof. The label shall bear the real name of the distillery and the registered plant number in which It was bottled (DSP# or Distilled Spirits Premisis #).*

*This might not guarantee that you will like the flavor of each and every Bottled in Bond Whiskey out there, but it does insure that it is the most regulated. So I ask you, why wouldn't you want every single one on your bar!? I do on mine!*

*STAY BONDED my friends!*

For more information about all things bourbon, check out my website: www.whiskeyprof.com.

# 5
# The Evolution from Unaged Corn Whiskey to Bourbon Whiskey

May 27, 1778 – Two years after America declares its independence, the highest ranking officer in the Northwestern Territory, Lieutenant Colonel George Rogers Clark takes his Kentucky Militia and 60 civilians and settles on a 43-acre island at the Falls of the Ohio River in the Virginia Territory. Because it grows so well there, they name the island, "Corn Island." After the militia leave, civilians move to the mainland and a town charter is granted from the Virginia General Assembly. The city is named for the King of France, Louis XVI, since he loaned the colonies money, troops and firepower to fight the red coats: *Louisville*. Coincidentally, the French royal family's surname was "Bourbon."

Louisville was a portage city at the falls of the Ohio River. Boats couldn't pass through the falls, so they had to be unloaded and all the inventory had to be taken by land to other boats below the falls. As a result, Louisville was a natural stopping place for travelers so the town started to grow. Many men wore many hats. A Welshman by the name of Evan Williams served on the town council, presided as the Warf Master and also worked as a builder, but what he is most remembered for is the whiskey that he distilled.

Evan Williams was Kentucky's first *legal* distiller, but there were many farmers distilling out in the territory who had small pot still operations. Distilling was used to preserve fruits and grains by making them into beer, cider and wine. Those products were then distilled into whiskey and brandy. Most farmers didn't obtain a license to do so, but there were other distillers in Kentucky that followed Williams' lead: Basil Hayden, Elijah Craig, Jacob (Jake) Beam and Elijah Pepper, just to name a few.

To make whiskey or brandy you've got to make beer or cider/wine first. Unlike the beer, cider and wine of today, the beverages of the past were typically very low proof (around 2%) and were served in place of water at meals as the water of the time was often unclean and carried a lot of bacteria and disease.

To make whiskey, beer was distilled up to four times in small pot stills. For each time the beer was distilled in the process, the distillers would put an "X" on the jug that held the end result. For example, if the whiskey was distilled three times, the jug would be labeled "XXX." At the time whiskey was not aged, clear and more potent each time it was distilled (130 to 150 proof or more after the third or fourth distillation). No wonder it was called white lightning!

Of course, in the years immediately following the revolution, whiskey was not something to be sipped and savored next to a fire (although you could have started a fire with it). People just slugged a shot or took a couple pulls from a jug after a long day of working on the farms. It was high proof alcohol, so it was used as medicine to heal a body from the inside out or to pour on wounds to heal from the outside in. Many farms had a pot still or could borrow/lease time from a neighbor. Most were probably making enough for only their family and friends, with a few extra for bartering in the months ahead.

Farmers could plant seeds or buy trees from a nursery and within the span of seven years be harvesting the fruits from those trees to make cider, wine and eventually brandy. The Port of Louisville custom house records show that the export of whiskey and brandy from January to May of 1801 was

42,562 gallons of whiskey and 6,157 gallons of peach brandy. (For a more detailed account, see Henry Crowgey's *Kentucky Bourbon - The Early Years of Whiskey Making.*)

## GEORGE WASHINGTON – EX PRESIDENT/DISTILLER

A man couldn't give more for his country than George did, by George! Not only was he a founding father, the Commander In Chief of the Continental Army that defeated the British and our first President serving from 1789-1797, he was also a distiller of whiskey.

After leaving the office of President in 1797, George Washington went back to Mount Vernon in Virginia and hired a Scotsman by the name of James Anderson to start up a whiskey distillery. Whiskey wasn't a passion for George. It was merely another way to keep cash flow robust. Mount Vernon wasn't cheap to keep running, and George saw whiskey as a viable source of income. George also knew he had a guaranteed market for his whiskey with the U.S. Calvary. As an ex-President and general, George knew that each soldier was given a daily/weekly ration of whiskey as part of their pay. And also as the ex-President and general, George had first dibs on being a big provider of that whiskey and getting paid for it by the U.S. government.

James Anderson made the Mount Vernon whiskey with a recipe that consisted of approximately 60% rye, 35% corn, and 5% malted barley. It was sold to the Calvary in two variations: whiskey that was distilled twice at $.50 a gallon and whiskey that was distilled four times at $1.00 a gallon. Did the officers get the XXXX distilled whiskey and the enlisted men the XX distilled?

I don't know, but I do know that George needed to get the whiskey to his customer, so he used barrels to transport it. He built a cooperage at Mount Vernon, and as he had plenty of money and a lot of cheap labor in the form of slaves, it didn't really add a lot of cost to his process. The whiskey was always shipped in brand new barrels, without any charring or aging to change the taste of the alcohol.

Mount Vernon started distilling in 1797, became the top distiller in the United States with 11,000 gallons of whiskey by the end of 1798, and then in 1799, a life changing thing happened to George Washington. He died. I don't care who you are, that's a life changer. George and Martha had no children together, Martha didn't want to mess with it, and it wasn't James Anderson's still, so the operation closed at the end of the 18th century.

Around this time, the Kentucky whiskey producers began charring their barrels — remember the four different origin stories in chapter two? — and that proved to be a game changer. Regardless of who discovered it, did it first or how it came about, the charred barrel is what separates bourbon from all other whiskies, even today.

Charring a barrel is much different than toasting one for wine. Imagine we are at a bonfire roasting marshmallows. There are two distinct roasting marshmallow techniques. Some gently put the marshmallow near the fire, carefully turning it often to toast it evenly. Others just jam the marshmallow right in the flames and watch it catch fire. When they pull it out and blow out the flame, it has turned black from the sugars caramelizing which causes an explosion of great flavor (and possibly a burnt tongue).

That illustrates the different between toasting a barrel for wine and charring a barrel for whiskey. Toasting is a passive fire inside the barrel that lightly brings some of the sugars in the wood forward. But charring actually means catching the wood inside the barrel on fire, and all of those sugars in the wood rush forward to form caramelized layer called the "red line." Each time the whiskey passes through the red line while it is aging (during the hot summers and cold winters), it picks up amber color and barrel notes like vanilla, maple, caramel and ginger.

So when the distillers in Kentucky started to char their barrels, it was a game changer. It started happening consistently in the 1820s when both the makers and their customers realized how much the whiskey's flavor was enhanced and improved simply by using a charred barrel to store it. As the barrels traveled down river to customers, the barrels also gave the whiskey an amber hue or straw color, so the resulting product was very different from the clear "White Lightning" they received from other distillers.

The other thing that made the Kentucky whiskey different from others was that the water that was used to produce it was very pure, so it did not change the taste of the whiskey. The limestone shelf that sits under a good bit of Kentucky filters out iron from the water and adds other minerals that help in the PH levels and other chemistry used in distilling whiskey. The limestone-filtered water is what attracted and kept many distillers in this region. That same limestone shelf also dips down in to Tennessee and up in Indiana.

In 1836 a 16 year old blacksmith named Joseph Washington Dant set up a still. He has little money, so he uses an old fashioned log still, made by putting a copper pipe through a section of a log like the early pioneers did. He was also probably determining the proof of the whiskey by the old fashioned method: shaking it and gauging the bubbles and beads or mixing it with gunpowder and lighting it. (If it burned yellow and fizzled out, it was a low proof; but if it burned blue, it was "true blue" and was a high proof of over 50% and good whiskey.)

Dant's passion for making whiskey was evident in the delicious final product which he named J.W. Dant, and he eventually grew his business to include a proper modern still and his own cooperage. His two sons, Joseph Bernard and George Washington Dant both followed him in the business and saw it through Prohibition. The brand still lives on today through Heaven Hill Distilleries.

Around the time Dant starts making his whiskey, Oscar Pepper, the largest land owner in Woodford County Kentucky, started a distilling operation with his dad Elijah. Unlike Dant, he had money so wanted to make whiskey the modern way. To do that, he hired a Scotsman named James Crow who is a doctor and a chemist to run his distillery in Millville (now home to Woodford Reserve). It was to be one of the best decisions of his life.

Dr. Crow employed scientific methods to the business of distilling whiskey. First, he moved the livestock father away from the distilling operation for cleanliness. Then he applied scientific tools to the entire process of distillation. He'd measure the sugar content of his mash with a saccharimeter, which is a litmus paper test to determine the mash acidity. He didn't use gunpowder and matches to determine proof, but a hydrometer. The resulting consistent quality of the whiskey, "Old Crow" made it the favorite bourbon of Mark Twain, Daniel Webster, U.S. Grant and Henry Clay. The Old Crow brand still remains a solid seller for Jim Beam today.

### Old Bourbon Whiskey From Kentucky

In 1857 a man by the name of Ben Perley Poore was in Kentucky securing business for his employer. He enjoyed meeting the people of the state very much and is reported to have written to his employer back home the following: "Everywhere, sir, have I been greeted by gentleman with their hearts in their right hand, their right hand in mine, and, certainly must I say it, with bottles of unequalled Old Bourbon in their left hands."

So it looks like Kentucky has a reputation for making good whiskey by the mid 1850s. And the good whiskey wasn't just called just *whiskey*, it was called *bourbon whiskey*. Just how that happened we don't really know. But according to whiskey lore, it may also come from those charred barrels that are so much a part of the bourbon story. The main port in Kentucky for shipping downstream to Southern markets was in Maysville, KY: the Port of Old Bourbon County. (Remember Louis XVI? That county was created in 1786 and given his family name.) On the ends of the barrels, the shippers would list the port it was shipped from and the contents inside. So each barrel would have been marked with both OLD BOURBON KENTUCKY (the port) and WHISKEY (the contents). Customers would know when they saw the markings that the distillers in that area were using the charred barrels, and that the barrels contained a far different product

*A HAND WRITTEN RECIPE FOR SPONTANEOUS YEAST from JW DANT from the 1890s. Used with permission by John Dant, Louisville, KY.*

from the other whiskeys coming from other parts of the country. And all of the Kentucky bourbon was being served from those barrels, because bourbon wasn't bottled yet. Bottling would have added expense and inconvenience to an already labor-intensive product. To take a bottle of whiskey home, a customer went to a Public House (a Pub) where it was drawn directly from the barrel it had been shipped in and put into a bottle that the owner of the pub supplied or the customer brought with him. The bottles weren't new bottles. They were recycled from all different uses. You could have been drinking bourbon from a perfume bottle!

## A SETBACK FOR BOURBON

But right when things were going along just fine, the Civil War breaks out in 1861. The South made bourbon distilling illegal so it could use the corn to feed the soldiers and their horses. Kentucky did not side with the South, so they continued to distill. However, most of their customers were in the South, and the war made it difficult to get their product to market. A lot of small distilleries found that they could not sustain their businesses.

After the war ended, things began looking up again with the new railroads spreading out across the country. It became much easier to get bourbon to market. The Louisville/Nashville Railroad (L&NRR a.k.a. "Old Reliable") was also a big help in transporting whiskey, grains and other equipment. But you still had to be creative to survive post-Civil War.

George Garvin Brown and his half-brother J.T.S. Brown (John Thompson Street – one of the best names on the planet!) went into business in 1870. George was a pharmaceutical salesman, and his good friend was the most respected doctor in Louisville, Dr. William Forrester. Dr. Forrester told George and J.T.S. that doctors could not rely on bulk whiskey when prescribing medicinal whiskey. This prompted the Browns to acquire the best bourbon they could, bottle it to insure that quality and then sell it to physicians/druggists. To give the "medicine' credibility, they put their friend's name on the label: Old Forrester was born. After the doctor's death, the Brown boys removed one "r" from the name, and Old Forester is still around under the watchful eyes of the same family in Louisville (Brown-Foreman).

## Rye Whiskey

At the same time bourbon was evolving down South, Rye whiskey was flowing up North. Rye was prevalent in Maryland and Pennsylvania and New York. Maryland Ryes (Pikesville Ryes) were known for having more of a grassy quality, and Pennsylvania Rye's being more spicy. Old Overholt Rye (1810), Bininger's 'Old Time' Rye (1848) and John Gibsonton Mills Old Monongahela Whiskey (1856) had discovered the same affect that barrel charring was having on bourbon down South.

It was during the Presidential election of 1876 that the next evolution of whiskey cocktails occurred. Jennie Jerome, age 20, from Brooklyn was quite the world traveler when she met Lord Randolph Churchill from Great Britain and they married. To say Lady Randolph was politically well-connected was an understatement. Her first son Winston (the future British Prime Minister) was only two years old when Lady Randolph and her husband hosted a fundraising party for their friend Samuel L. Tilden. Tilden was the Governor of New York and running for President against Rutherford B. Hayes. A welcoming cocktail was provided for all guests made with American Whiskey (which in New York in 1876 would have been a rye whiskey), Italian Vermouth (sweet vermouth), and a dash of bitters. Since the party was held at the Manhattan Club, they simply called the drink the Manhattan.

By the 1870s the business and shipping offices of 150 different bourbon/whiskey companies were located along Main Street in downtown Louisville, Kentucky. Distillers from all over the state had offices there to be close to the financial center, buy and sell bulk whiskey and to keep a finger on the whiskey pulse. You can still see the office facades for J.T.S. Brown, Stitzel-Weller, and many more on Main Street today, which is still referred to as "Whiskey Row." There is also a recreation of "Whiskey Row" at the Evan Williams Bourbon Experience at 6th and Main Street.

In 1879 a man by the name of Frederick Stitzel applied for and received a patent on an improvement in Racks for Tiering Barrels. Here is a copy of a portion of that patent:

Specification forming part of Letters Patent No. 22 L945, dated November 25, 1879; application filed August 22,1879.

To all whom it may concern:

Be it known that I, FREDERICK STITZEL of the city of Louisville, in the county of Jefferson and State of Kentucky, have invented a certain new and useful Improvement in Racks for Tiering Barrels containing whisky and other similar liquids; and I do hereby declare that the following is a full, clear, and exact description of the construction and operation of the same, reference being had to the accompanying drawings, forming part of this specification, and to the letters of reference marked thereon.

Figure 1 is a side view of the racks, showing the manner of arranging them in the house. Fig. 2 is a cross-sectional view of the rack, showing the barrels and projecting ledges of the rack on which they rest. Fig. 3 is a perspective view of the racks, showing their general construction.

This my invention relates to a certain new and useful improvement in racks for tiering barrels containing whisky or other spirituous liquors, the object of which is to provide a portable rack or frame made in sections that will be sufficiently strong to bear the weight of as many barrels as may be tiered between the floors of the house without resting upon each other, thereby avoiding the danger of crushing the staves by the weight, as each tier is made to rest on separate rails projecting on the inside of the frame independent of the others, thereby causing a free circulation of air between the barrels, and at the same time making it easy to remove any of the barrels in the lower

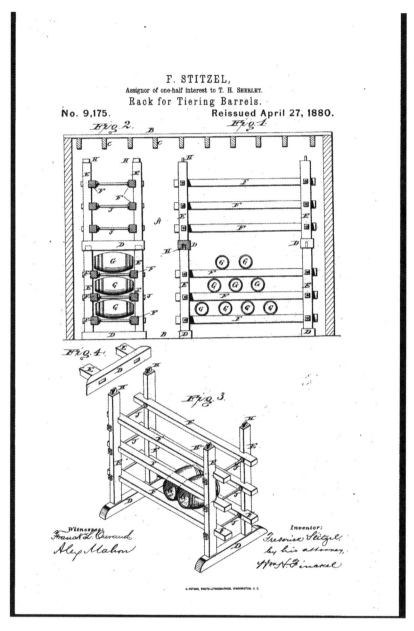

tiers without interfering with those above or below. These racks are made of square pieces of timber of suitable size, consisting, first, of four posts tenoned into two cross-pieces as a base, sufficiently wide apart to admit a barrel endwise loosely, to the illside of which three horizontal rails are secured, leaving sufficient space to permit a barrel to pass between them without touching the one above it. These rails are let into the inside of the posts about one -third of their breadth, leaving the remainder to project, so as to answer as a ledge for the barrels to rest upon. In order to secure them firmly to the posts, bolts are provided long enough to pass through the entire frame at each connection.

Before the Stitzel system, barrels were stored as they were in Dunnage warehouses in Scotland: stacked on top of each other. This meant a lot of weight was heaped on lower barrels, which caused leakage or sometimes the destruction of the barrels on the bottom. The rick system meant many more barrels could be stored in a warehouse and without damage.

Between 1880 and 1920, 20 million immigrants poured into the United States. A thousand people arrived every day at Ellis Island from Southern and Eastern Europe as well as Russia. Angel Island in San Francisco welcomed hundreds of thousands from China and Japan. This influx of people brought a lot of new workers and many of them were thirsty for more than just success. They needed a drink, and it didn't necessarily have to be something of high quality.

The population explosion also meant that saloons became more numerous. Because a lot of immigrants (and others) lived in just one room of a house or in very small apartments, the neighborhood saloon was an important part of life. The saloon is where a person could cash a paycheck, read a paper and find out about a job. Unions, veterans groups, fraternal organizations and immigrant associations met in saloons. Christenings took place in saloons, and after someone died, they'd hold the wake there. The saloon in the last quarter of the 19th century was the average Joe's gentleman's club. It seemed everyone just wanted something (anything!) alcoholic to drink, and companies were happy to provide it.

To meet the new demand, the whiskey business began to turn more to rectifiers and blenders. According to Mike Veach's book *Kentucky Bourbon Whiskey: An American Heritage,* rectifiers and blenders of whiskey would take any whiskey they could buy, add a high proof neutral grain spirit (like a vodka) and then add some iodine for color and cherry or prune juice for a little sweetness and flavor. The resulting product was cheaper to produce and could be bought by the consumer for less money. This didn't sit well with some distillers in Kentucky that were making "straight whiskey," whiskey that was distilled and aged in barrels with nothing added to it. Their products were of higher quality, and they didn't want people to think their product was the same as those that were produced by other companies.

At the end of the 19th century a very passionate distiller by the name of Colonel Edmund H. Taylor of Frankfort, KY got together with another distiller, Ezra Brooks, and the Secretary of Treasury, John Carlisle (also from Kentucky), and they drafted the first consumer protection legislation in the history of the United States called The Bottled In Bond Act of 1897.

The Bottled in Bond Act of 1897 stated that if the words "Bottled In Bond" appeared on the label, then that whiskey must be aged for a minimum of four years in charred oak and bottled at exactly 100 proof. The whiskeys must be made from barrels that were filled in one distilling season (back then there were two seasons, Spring {Jan-June} and Fall {July-Dec}). Lastly, the whiskey must be a product of one single distillery, and that distillery must be named on the label. For example if you look at a bottle today of Evan Williams White Label Bottled in Bond, it states that is was produced at DSP KY 1. DSP means Distilled Spirits Producer. KY designates KENTUCKY, and the number one is the number assigned to the Bernheim distilling plant owned and operated by Heaven Hill in Louisville, KY.

The Bottled in Bond Act guaranteed the customer that the whiskey was a good age and a good strength, and he or she knows exactly who made it and when. To me, this is a BIG deal. If it wasn't for the Bottled In Bond Act of 1897, we'd all be sitting around drinking Seagrams 7 today! Nothing against Seagram's 7, it's a popular blended American Whiskey, but I think you know what I'm saying.

The Bottled in Bond Act was also a great job creator. Fred Minnick's book, *Whiskey Women, The Untold Story Of How Women Saved Bourbon Scotch And Irish Whiskey*, reveals that the act gave distillers a reason to bottle bourbon instead of just delivering barrels to a bar. Bottling lines were expensive to run, and it took a lot of man or woman power and would have raised the final cost to the consumer. But Bottled In Bond made it advantageous to put their products in bottles to ensure nothing was tampered with or watered down after it was delivered to the tavern – the quality was expected to be higher so customers were willing to pay more. Those jobs on the bottling lines were good paying jobs, and women proved to be as good if not better at the job than the men.

The Bottled in Bond Act was followed by the Pure Food & Drug Act of 1906 which also set guidelines for whiskey making, but these two laws did not end the controversy between the rectifiers/blenders and the straight whiskey manufacturers. Legal battles slogged through the courts regarding who could call their product what from 1897 until President William Howard Taft stepped in and made a decision in 1909.

I only knew one thing about William Howard Taft when I was a boy, and that's the story of how he got stuck in a bathtub at the White House. But in reading more about him, I've learned that he was the first president to ride in a car and throw out the first pitch of the baseball season. After he was president, he was named by his successor to be the Chief Justice of the Supreme Court. I'm sure that last fact will not occur again in my lifetime.

Taft decided that there should be two categories of whiskey: *blended whiskies* and *straight whiskies*. Blended whiskies were just that — a rectifier could blend many whiskies together and add colors and flavors. The rectifier must list the percentage of grain spirits in the product.  If you look at a label of Seagram 7 for example, it states that 75% of the contents are Grain Spirits (vodka if you will).

Straight whiskies are those that only add water and nothing else, and must be aged for at least two years.  Straight whiskies can use whiskies that have been produced at more than one distillery and can be bottled at any proof.

## Prohibition

So everyone is in agreement about what constitutes what kind of whiskey, the standards for quality have never been higher and the drinks are flowing throughout the United States. What could stop whiskey now?  Well none other than the 18th Amendment which enacted Prohibition. Organizers like Wayne Wheeler of the Anti-Saloon League and activists like Carrie Nation and their followers got the votes to prohibit the

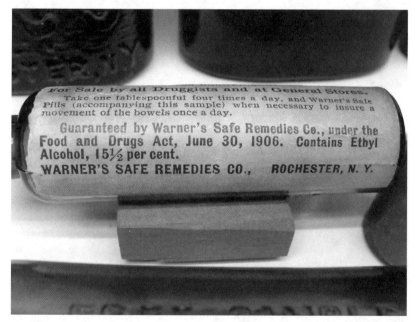

*Products would reference the Pure Food & Drug Act of 1906 on their labels.*

The Evolution from Unaged Corn Whiskey • 137

*Tax stamps told the date made and bottled: Made Spring 1936, Bottled Fall 1942. (Yes, it was delicious still.)*

manufacture, sale, transportation and import/export of alcohol. This drove a wedge through the country. You were either a "wet" or a "dry." No one rode the fence on this one. If you were for Prohibition, you were for total abstinence with a capital "T," called a "T-Total'er" or "Teetotal-er"

The 18th Amendment was passed on January 16, 1919. One year later the law was enforced. So January 15, 1920 was the last day you could buy a legal drink or bottle, and it was known as "Thirsty Thursday." From January 16, 1920 to December 5, 1933 Prohibition was the law of the land. Almost 80 years later the United States is still affected by Prohibition. First of all, nearly 13 million Americans today still live in Prohibition through "dry" counties. In Kentucky alone, there are 75 dry counties out of 120.

The only way you could get a drink legally was through a doctor's prescription. And according to the Ken Burns documentary on Prohibition, six million prescriptions were written in those 14 years. There were ten distilleries in Kentucky that were granted a license to sell "medicinal whiskey." Medicinal whiskey was Bottled in Bond, and prescribed by pint size. It came in a box which listed the medical benefits of the whiskey. Patients was permitted one pint every ten days. If they wanted more, family members often came down with the same affliction.

Here's what a box of Old Grand Dad claimed to have cured:

*"Old Grand Dad is an unexcelled distillation and has proven itself meritorious on treating pulmonary conditions, LaGrippa, Influenza, colds, bronchitis, fever, stomach and other digestive organs and malaria.*

*Especially indicated for exhaustion due to mental or bodily overwork, run down conditions, nerves, sleeplessness, etc.*

*Also in weakness of convalescence and debility of old age.*

*Whiskey is used as an antiseptic dressing for wounds, ulcers, etc. "*

When traveling around the U.S. today, you will still witness the effects of Prohibition. People in the south still drink a lot of rum-based drinks (Pina Coladas, Hurricanes and Rum punches) because the Caribbean was so close and rum was easily sneaked in by boat to Florida or New Orleans. In Texas and other states along the Mexican border, tequila flowed into the country so certain salt and lime beverages still enjoy popularity there. In Michigan and the other states along our northern border, Canadian blended whisky was quietly slipped in to quench the thirst of their American neighbors.

But in the states not enjoying a close neighbor with legal booze manufacturing, Kentucky, North Carolina, Tennessee, West Virginia and others, what do you think they were drinking? That's right, moonshine! They were forced to make their own and send it off in souped up Chevys, Fords and Dodges that could outrun the feds. After the madness was all over, these drivers went legit on the new NASCAR circuit because of their unique expertise.

Prohibition did have a couple positive effects on our culture though. Before Prohibition women were not allowed in most bars, and it was actually against the law for a woman to bartend. Most bars and nightclubs were also segregated. African Americans and whites did not mix for the most part. But in the speakeasy culture during prohibition, everyone who wanted a drink was already doing something illegal. Whether you were a woman or a man, black or white, didn't matter, and no one cared who bartended. You've always suspected that a shared drink could save the world, right?

After Prohibition, Canadian whiskey makers like Hiram Walker (Canadian Club) and Sam Bronfman (Seagrams) had a big leg up on most of the U.S. companies. In Kentucky, the handful of distillers that had been granted the right to produce medicinal whiskey during those 13 years were also ahead of the game. Brown-Foreman's Old Forester is the only bourbon that was produced before, during and after Prohibition that is still owned by the same company.

## TIME TO GET BACK TO WORK

After Prohibition the scenario for the most part was that there were 1) people who knew how to make whiskey but didn't have the money to start back up and 2) folks who had money, but didn't know how to make whiskey. Colonel Jim Beam purchased the old Murphy Barber Distillery in Clermont, Kentucky backed by Chicago businessmen Harry Homel and H. Blum. Colonel Beam had lost quite a bit of money during Prohibition due to his involvement in citrus farming in Florida and the rock quarry business in Kentucky. The scuttlebutt around town was that if Colonel Beam decided to open a funeral home in town, people in Bardstown would stop dying!

There were five Shapira brothers and each owned a department store in small towns in Kentucky. Even during the depression and Prohibition people still needed hats, jackets and underwear, which meant they were doing just fine. So when the opportunity was presented to them to invest in a distillery and make whiskey, they had the funds and decided to take the leap. The start-up eventually ended up costing them $30,000, which is a lot of money even today! Can you imagine investing that kind of money in to a venture that had no distillery, no brands, no inventory and no product for several years? Because the Shapira boys didn't know a barrel from a box, they hired folks who knew how to make whiskey: Joe and Harry Beam. If you've read Paul Pacult's book, *American Still Life,* it maps out the Beam family tree and shows which Beams were distilling whiskey at which Kentucky distillery.

Jim Beam's company is still distilling today at the same location in Clermont, Kentucky, with Beam's great grandson Fred Noe and his son Freddie still involved in the business. Heaven Hill is still operating on the 150 acres of land that Mr. Joe Beam bought, and the company is still owned and operated by the Shapria family with Parker and Craig Beam serving as Master Distillers along with Denny Potter and Charlie Downs. Heaven Hill filled their first barrel on December 13, 1935 and put Serial #1 on it. Today they are stamping the barrels with Serial #7,000,000 and counting.

To differentiate themselves from the Canadian and American blended whiskies that Hiram Walker and Seagrams and others were making, the Kentucky distillers like the Beams made straight whiskies (whiskies aged for 2 years in charred oak with nothing but water added). In December of 1937

Heaven Hill introduced Bourbon Falls Straight Whiskey, a two year old whiskey that wasn't full bodied or deep and complex, to get some much needed cash flow coming in. In December 1939, after they'd aged the whiskey for four years so that it could be labeled Bottled in Bond, Old Heaven Hill Kentucky Straight Bourbon Whiskey Bottled In Bond was released. It immediately became the best selling bourbon in Kentucky. That put the little distillery on the map. Other distilleries like Old Tub, Old Crow, Old Grand Dad, Early Times were all brands that went back to the Pre-Prohibition standard of Bottled In Bond. When you hear the term today "Pre-Prohibition style whiskey" thrown around, they're referring to Bottled In Bond.

Larger operations were capitalizing on the repeal of prohibition too. Well financed and headquartered in New York, Schenley Distilleries opened up with a powerful bourbon brand line up including I.W. Harper, Ancient Age and Old Charter. The also created a blended whiskey: Black Velvet Blended Canadian Whisky.

But wouldn't you know it, just as bourbon stocks were mature enough to begin replenishing the shelves, World War II started. Kentucky distilleries were drafted to make high proof alcohol synthetic rubber to defeat the Axis powers. Their involvement in the war effort kept bourbon from making a real comeback until the late 1940s. By that time, blended whiskies really were soaring, as were rum and gin. The Martini, Aviation, and Negroni are all gin cocktails that became very popular post war, and then the Tiki Bar craze hit with the Mai Tai, Cuba Libre and Hurricane.

The whiskey category was booming at the time, but it was being driven by the blended whiskies: Seagrams 5 Blend, Seagrams 7 Blend, Kessler, Philadelphia, Canadian Club, VO, Black Velvet, Windsor Canadian and other American and Canadian whiskies were all flowing to the public. American Ryes like Ritthenhouse and Old Overholt and bourbons from Kentucky, Illinois (Ten High brand), Indiana (Old Indiana) and Virginia (Virginia Gentleman) were all doing OK, but it was the blended category that was the powerhouse. A brand extension from Seagrams was introduced to the U.S. in 1964 as a premium whiskey packaged in a purple bag, Crown Royal.

At the beginning of the Korean War, distillers ramped up production to crazy levels because they thought the government would tell them they had to make alcohol for the war effort, but they never did, and a GLUT of whiskey followed flooding the market and spelling disaster for the category.

## STANDARDS OF IDENTITY

If you've never visited Liquor.com before, you should. It's an awesome site. My friend Noah Rothbaum was the editor in chief there, and he's also the author of *The Business of Spirits*. He came up with the following rationale for why drinking bourbon is actually an act of patriotism, and I think I must agree with him. In the late 1950s the world become a much smaller place as businesses around the globe started using metal shipping containers that could be loaded onto ships and then attached to tractor trailers. As a result, goods no longer had to be packed in wooden or metal barrels. In order to save the coopers who were in danger of going out of business and to protect the source of barrels for whiskey aging, the 88th Congress of the United States unanimously declared bourbon as a "distinctive product of the United States" and that distillers could only use a new oak barrel. Therefore, it is not only delicious to drink bourbon, it's your patriotic duty!

So this is where the STANDARDS OF IDENTITY of Whiskey, Bourbon, Straight, etc. were set down by the U.S. Government. These are the exact laws as written in the TTB Standards of Identity we know today:

*Subpart C – Standards of Identity for Distilled Spirits*

*5.22 The Standards of Identity*

*Standards of identity for the several classes and types of distilled spirits set forth in this section shall be as follows*

*(2) "Grain spirits" are neutral spirits distilled from a fermented mash of grain and stored in oak containers.*

*(b) Class 2; whisky. "Whisky" is an alcoholic distillate from a fermented mash of grain produced at less than 190 proof in such a manner that the distillate possesses the taste, aroma, and characteristics generally attributed to whisky, stored in oak containers (except corn that corn whisky need not be so stored) and bottled at not less than 80 proof, and also includes mixtures of such distillates for which no specific standards of identity are prescribed.*

*(1)(i) "Bourbon whisky" "rye whisky", "wheat whisky", "malt whisky" or "rye malt whisky" is whisky produced at not exceeding 160 proof from a fermented mash of not less than 51% corn, rye, wheat, malted barley, or malted rye grain, respectively, and stored no more than 125 proof in charred new oak containers; and also includes mixtures of such whiskies of the same type.*

*(ii) "Corn whisky" is whiskey produced at not exceeding 160 proof from a fermented mash of not less than 80 percent corn grain, and if stored in oak containers stored at no more than 125 proof in used or uncharred new oak containers and not subjected in any manner to treatment with charred wood; and also includes mixtures of such whisky.*

*(iii) Whiskies conforming to this standards prescribed in paragraphs (b)(1)(i) and (ii) of this section, which have been stored in the type of oak containers prescribed, for a period of 2 years or more shall be further designated as "straight"; for example, "straight bourbon whisky", "straight corn whisky"*

*Part 5 – Labeling and Advertising of Distilled Spirits*

*5.42 Prohibited Practices*

*(3) The words "bond", "bonded", "bottled in bond", "aged in bond", or phrases containing these or synonymous terms, shall not be used on any label or as part of the brand name of domestic distilled spirits unless the distilled spirits are:*

*(i) Composed of the same kind of spirits produced from the same class of materials;*

*(ii) Produced in the same distilling season by the same distiller at the same distillery*

*(iii) Stored for at least four years in wooden containers wherein the spirits have been in contact with the wood surfaces except for gin and vodka which must be stored for at least* four years in wooden containers coated or lined with paraffin or other substance which will preclude contact of the spirits with the wood surface;

*(iv) Unaltered from their original condition or character by the addition or subtraction of substance other than by filtration, chill proofing, or other physical treatments (which do not involve the addition of any substance which will remain incorporated in the finished product of result in a change in class or type.)*

*(v) Reduced in proof by the addition of pure water only to 100 degrees; and*

*(vi) Bottled at 100 degrees of proof*

*In addition to the requirements of 5.36(a) (1) or (2) the label shall bear the real name of the distillery or the trade name under which the distillery produced and warehoused the spirits, and the plant (or registered distillery) number in which produced; and the plant number in which bottled (example; D.S.P. KY 1). The label may also bear the name of the bottler.*

It goes on and on, and it's quite fascinating, you can read all of it by searching "TTB Standards of Identity" on the internet or by visiting the following:

*http://www.gpo.gov/fdsys/pkg/CFR-2008-title27-vol1/pdf/CFR-2008-title27-vol1-sec5-22.pdf*

## BOURBON MAKES A MISSTEP

The big selling brands of the 1960s and 1970s were Old Crow, Old Grand Dad, Early Times, Ancient Age and Ten High with Jack Daniels coming on strong. Blended whiskies like Canadian Club, Black Velvet, VO, and Seagrams 7 were big sellers too. Newer bourbon brands like Wild Turkey, Evan Williams, Jim Beam and Maker's Mark were finding their way after being introduced but were overshadowed and often outspent by the bigger brands.

Then in 1976 vodka overtook whiskey as the most popular liquor in the United States. Vodka and Tequila weren't even available in bars in the 1940s and much of the 1950s, and then it shot to the top of the heap. Gin, rum, and blended whiskey were also outpacing bourbon, so the big producers of bourbon whiskey tried to match the lightness of vodka, gin and rum by adding more water to their process. They took the Bottled in Bond 100 proof and added water to get it down to 86 proof. Early Times lowered their proof not only by adding water, but they also started aging their whisky in used cooperage. This made Early Times just a "whiskey" rather than a Bottled in Bond or Straight Whiskey. I don't know if it's a coincidence that today when something is to be done away with we say "86 it!" But that's what lowering the proof of bourbon to 86 did for it as well, sales for these brands declined steadily over the next years.

As a side note, years before the attempt to make bourbon "lighter," Pappy Van Winkle was asked if he would ever lower the proof of his coveted Old Fitzgerald from proof. Pappy replied, "I see no sense in shipping water all over the country."

So bourbons lost their way and sales were declining every year. National players like Jack Daniels and Crown Royal grew, but bourbons were having a hard time to say the least. But the next evolution of bourbon was just around the corner.

### SINGLE BARREL AND SMALL BATCH BOURBONS AND CRAFT

In 1984 the Master Distiller of Ancient Age/George T. Stagg Distillery, Elmer T. Lee introduced Blanton's Single Barrel Bourbon. This was a first. There is no definition of Single Barrel, but it is accepted that single barrel means that just one barrel is used and not mingled with any other barrels as is/ was the normal practice. This meant new equipment had to be used, which meant more people and hands to bottle a small amount of bourbon. Lee's bourbon this became the first $25 bottle of bourbon which was unheard of at the time.

Two years later Parker Beam and Heaven Hill Distillery bottled a 12-year-old 94 proof in a limited release. Their cousin Booker Noe over at Jim Beam came out with his own limited release made up of several choice barrels mingled together at barrel strength. He called it Booker's Bourbon and charged a staggering $50 a bottle. Booker also put a name to what he and Parker were doing and called it "small batch." Neither of them made small batches of anything in those big column stills, but they were able to choose specific barrels from certain areas of a rickhouse or whiskies of specific ages and mingle them together for a unique product. Whiskeys taste differently from barrel to barrel. Mingling them together creates consistency of flavor for a brand. The creation of small batch gave the customer new categories to choose from, whether they understood how it was different or not! Just like the consumer had to be educated on what Bottled in Bond meant almost 90 years before, it was going to take years for them to understand what made single barrel small batch different. Bourbon making is all about patience and taking the right amount of time, so the distillers were prepared to take the time needed to create an educated audience.

There is no one definition of small batch. Each distillery has a different definition that works for them and their operations. Parker and Craig Beam define small batch at Heaven Hill as 100 barrels or less. Fred Noe at Jim Beam pulls different small batches from different areas of a rickhouse. For example, Booker's comes from the "Center Cut" (middle two floors), and Baker's comes from the higher floors. At Buffalo Trace Harlen Wheatley has different styles of rickhouses in which he ages his whiskies, including stone, brick and tin. His small batches each come from a distinct rickhouse. No matter how they create a small batch, these distillers are using their choicest barrels to create an extra aged or extra proof expression of their bourbon.

So if you're still confused about the difference between single barrel and small batch, I'll clear it up right here. Let's say its Friday night of Labor Day weekend at 7 p.m. and my air conditioner goes out. Even though it's going to be 100 degrees tomorrow, am I going to call the repair man to come fix it? Goodness no. I happen to have a nice cool basement with a man-cave in it. I have my bar, my TV and just about anything I need right in my basement. I'm not going to go to the main floor much because it will be over 100 degrees up there, and I'm certainly not going in to the attic where it will be like 130 degrees!

So let's say that Parker and Craig Beam send me three barrels of bourbon and told me to put one barrel in the attic, one on the main floor and one in the basement. Then they said don't turn on my air conditioner or heater for 12 full years. After 12 years the bourbon in each of those barrels would taste completely different from each other. So if I bottled up just the barrel of bourbon in the attic that would be a "single barrel bourbon." But if I took all three barrels, mingled them together and bottled them, that would be a "small batch." Now you'll never be confused about the difference in the two again.

Other distillers followed the new trend with Jimmy and Eddie Russell at Wild Turkey creating Kentucky Spirit, Rare Breed and Russell's Reserve. Lincoln Henderson from Brown-Foreman introduced Woodford Reserve. This was also right when the Single Malt Scotch craze was starting to take hold, and these new categories really brought a lot of needed attention to bourbon and American whiskies in general. Rye whiskey started to explode later too, but unlike bourbon, there were only a handful of distilleries that produced it, so even today that market is starved for more. Craig Beam re-introduced American wheat whiskey in 2006 with Bernheim Original Wheat Whiskey, and other forms of American Whiskey like Mellow Corn whiskey and malt whiskey have unknown potential.

Craft distilling followed the introduction of small batch and single barrel bourbons. There are over 400 craft distillers in the U.S. at the time of this printing, with 250 distilling whiskey and 56 putting up bourbon. As craft brewing did for beer, craft distilling is bringing a local/regional attention to whiskey. This does not really compete with the big producers since the craft distilleries cannot produce at their scale, nor have the aged product they do. But craft distillers like Chip Tate are sure making some noise and good whiskey. My favorite is Corsair Distillery in Bowling Green, Kentucky, and Nashville, Tennessee, headed up by Darek Bell and Andrew Webber. They are doing all kinds of creative things with whiskies and other spirits that the big producers cannot or will not do. It's all quite exciting.

No matter how you slice it, we are clearly in the Golden Age of Bourbon right now, and it looks like it only took 30 years to really get here after the introduction of single barrel and small batch, or 200 years after whiskey itself in America.

# My Bourbon Time Line

*"Too much of anything is bad, but too much of good whiskey is barely enough."*—Mark Twain

**1619**  Virginia General Assembly passed laws against public drunkenness, with the first offense dealt with privately by the minister, and second offense dealt with "publiquely" (that being most probably stocks in the town square).

**1600s-1700s**  Along with establishing grains of rye, barley and corn, fruit trees were planted in abundance.  Farmers realized the trees matured in only six or seven years so they could bring in an orchard of abundance. They put up stores of cider and distilled brandy (also referred to as "mobby").

**1716**  According to Robert Beverley in *The History of Virginia, in Four Parts* (1722). "Their strong drink is Madera wine, Cyder, Mobby Punch (hard cider or brandy), made either of Rum from the Caribbee Islands, or brand distll'd from their apples and peaches; besides Brandy, Wine and strong Beer, which they have constantly from England."

**1775**  Daniel Boone is hired by the Transylvania Company to widen the path through the Cumberland Gap to make passage to make settlement in Kentucky and Tennessee easier.

**JULY 4, 1776**  America declares its independence from Kingdom of Great Britain ruled by King George III

**MAY 27, 1778**
George Rogers Clark and his Kentucky Militia settle on an island at the falls of the Ohio River. The native crop grew so well there they called it Corn Island.

**1780**
The Virginia General Assembly approves a town charter to found the city of Louisville named after King Louis XVI of France who aided the Americans in the Revolutionary War. King Louis' family name is Bourbon. Three separate counties are carved out of the Virginia county of Kentucky; Jefferson, Fayette and Lincoln.

**1783**
The Treaty of Paris is signed ending the Revolutionary War. Around that same year Evan Williams sets up a distilling operation in Louisville.

**1784**
The population of Kentucky was approximately 30,000.

**1785**
Basil Hayden Sr. led a group of 25 Catholic families from Maryland into what is now Nelson County, Kentucky and starts distilling a few years after.

**MAY 1, 1786**
Bourbon County is established and shortly after tavern rates were set for apple brandy, peach brandy and whiskey.

**1789**
George Washington is elected as the first President of the United States. In Georgetown, KY, Virginia Baptist preacher Elijah Craig starts distilling whiskey, and Woodford County is created this year.

**1791**
The first National Tax is imposed on liquor to retire the debt from the Revolutionary War

**1792**

Kentucky becomes the 15th State in the Union and actually a Commonwealth. There are three other Commonwealths: Virginia, Massachusetts, Pennsylvania.

**1794**

The Whiskey Rebellion takes place in Washington County Pennsylvania as a protest to the excise tax on whiskey imposed by President Washington to help retire the debt of the Revolutionary War.

**1795**

Jacob Johannes Bohm (Jake Beam) distills his first whiskey off Hardin's Creek. There are 800 licensed distillers in Kentucky at this time.

**1797-1799**

George Washington finishes his second term as President and retires back home to Mount Vernon where he starts a distilling operation run by a Scot named James Anderson. Mount Vernon becomes the nations top distiller selling 11,000 gallons in 1798. Washington dies in 1799.

**1802**

President Thomas Jefferson repealed the excise tax on whiskey imposed by Washington.

**MAY 18, 1808**

Elijah Craig passes away in Georgetown, KY. *The Kentucky Gazette* eulogized, "His preaching was of the most solemn style; his appearance as a man who had just come from the dead; of a delicate habit, a thin visage, large eyes and mouth; the sweet melody of his voice, both in preaching and singing, bore all down before it." Some Baptist sources say he sold out to the world, but "He possessed a mind extremely active and, as his whole property was expended in attempts to carry his plans to execution, he consequently died poor. If virtue consists in being useful to our fellow citizens, perhaps there were few more virtuous men than Mr. Craig."

**1810**

Distilled spirits by state (in gallons)

| | |
|---|---|
| Pennsylvania | 6,552,284 |
| Virginia | 2,367,589 |
| Kentucky | 2,200,773 |
| North Carolina | 1,386,691 |
| Ohio | 1,212,266 |
| Tennessee | 801,245 |

(*Kentucky Bourbon* – Henry Crowgey)

**1812**

Elijah Pepper builds a log cabin distillery in Versailles, KY.

**1812**

A big distilling operation funded by northern businessmen opens in Louisville under the name Hope Distilling Company. They close only a few years later... perhaps they went too big too soon.

**1826**

The American Temperance Society was founded in Boston, MA.

**1820-1835**

By 1830 every male over the age of 15 drank an average of 90 bottles of whiskey each year. The need to ship bourbon causes the implantation of barrels into the whiskey equation. Regardless of how the practice began of charring the inside of the barrel instead of toasting, charring becomes essential in making Kentucky Whiskey or "Old Bourbon" as it will later become known. Old Bourbon is the county named after the French Royal family and the Port of Old Bourbon Kentucky where a lot of whiskey started out on its journey downstream.

**1831**

Aenaes Coffey is awarded a patent on his continuous still in Britain

The Evolution from Unaged Corn Whiskey • 153

**1836**

Joseph Washington Dant starts a distilling operation in Dant Station, KY using an old fashioned log still.

**1838**

Oscar Pepper takes over the distilling operation in Versailles from his father Elijah and then makes the best decision of his career by hiring Dr. James Crow as his distiller. Crowimplements many scientific practices that are still used today (sour mash process, hydrometers, cleanliness practices).

**1840-1855**

George T. Stagg, T.W. Samuels, William Larue Weller and Henry McKenna open distilleries in Kentucky.

**1846**

Carry Nation is born in Garrard County Kentucky. Later she joins the Temperance movement in Kansas where she is arrested over 30 times for smashing up saloons in her "Hatchetations" garnishing attention for their cause. She died in 1911 before Prohibition, the same year my father Herman Joseph Lubbers is born.

**1857**

**BOURBON is established**: Ben Perley Poore is so struck by his business trip to Kentucky he says to his guests after a welcome toast; "Everywhere sir have I been greeted by gentleman with their hearts in their right hand, their right hand in mine", and must I say it, with bottles of unequalled "old bourbon" in their left hands.

**1860**

David Beam's brother John started up the Early Times Distillery.

**1861-1865**

Civil War. Distillation ceases in the South. Kentucky continues distilling, but their major markets are in the South. They can't reach their customers.

| | |
|---|---|
| **1867** | The Chapeze Brothers started up Old Charter Distillery. |
| **1870** | George Garvin Brown buys the best quality whiskey he can get and puts Doctor William Forrester's name on the label. He sells the whisky through doctors and pharmacies. Old Forrester is born. That same year, Col. Edmund H. Taylor opens the OFC Distillery (Old Fashioned Copper) in Frankfort, KY. |
| **1879** | Frederick Stitzel receives a patent on an improvement on the tiered rack system allowing many barrels to be stored on top of each other without damaging the barrels below. |
| **1880** | The beginning of the "new immigration" — 20 million Southern and Eastern European immigrants flow into New York as Asians from Japan and China arrive in San Francisco by 1920. To supply this influx of thirsty folks with enough alcohol, larger rectifiers and blenders of whiskey would use cheap grain spirits and mingle them with younger whiskies and then add colors like iodine and flavoring like cherry and prune juice. |
| **1880's** | By this time the saloon has become the average Joe's gentleman's club. Many got their mail there, paid their bills there, did their job search from there. They also attended fraternal organization meetings or immigrant association functions. The saloon became the center of many folks' universe. |
| **1882** | R.B. Hayden starts up his distillery and uses his grandfather's recipe from the 1700s. He names it Old Grand Dad in his honor. |

The Evolution from Unaged Corn Whiskey • 155

**1887**   At a tremendous cost, Edmund Taylor opens the Old Taylor Distillery which was built to resemble a castle with sunken gardens. He gives tours of the grounds, and many couples hold their weddings on these beautiful grounds.

**1888**   Four Roses distillery opened.

**1893**   Wayne B. Wheeler teamed up with the Rev. Howard Hyde Russell in Russell's newly formed Anti Saloon League (ASL). Wheeler coins the term "pressure group" to turn up the heat for Prohibition.

**1897**   Distiller Edmund H. Taylor and Ezra Brooks from Kentucky along with the U.S. Secretary of State, John Carlisle (also from Kentucky), are the galvanizing forces behind the passing of the first consumer protection legislation in the U.S. in the Bottled In Bond Act.

**1906**   Following the Bottled In Bond Act, the Pure Food & Drug Act is passed requiring the active ingredients be placed on the label of a drugs packaging, and that drugs could not fall below purity levels established. Whiskey was prescribed by doctors as well, so it was also affected by this law and many distillers advertised the fact that a whiskey followed all the regulations of the Pure Food & Drug Act and used this as a selling point.

**1909**

After the legal battles between whiskey rectifiers and blenders and makers of "straight" whiskey, President William Howard Taft drafts the Taft Decision defining "Blended Whiskey" and "Straight Whiskey." Blended whiskey may add colors and flavors, and straight whiskey can only have water added to it, and must be aged for at least two years in brand new charred oak barrels.

**1914-1918**

Whiskey production ceases in order to produce high proof alcohol for smokeless gunpowder and fuels to run war machinery in WWI.

**JANUARY 16, 1919**

The 18th Amendment passes, and Prohibition is set to go into effect in one year. At the time there were 157 operating distilleries in the whole industry.

**JANUARY 15, 1920**

Known as "Thirsty Thursday" since it was the last day you could buy liquor before Prohibition went in to effect.

**JANUARY 16, 1920**

PROHIBITION STARTS — the beer/liquor industry was the fifth largest employer in the United States, and all of those jobs were taken away. The only way to get a legal drink is by a Doctor's prescription or sacramental wine at church.

**1921**

Nassau, Bahamas received 1,000,000 gallons of Scotch Whisky and London Dry Gin from the U.K. as it passed through their docks and then on to rum runners boats like Bill McCoy's into the U.S.

**1929**

Stitzel-Weller and a handful of distilleries in Kentucky were granted permission to run batches of whiskey for medicinal purposes from depleted stocks since the beginning of Prohibition. This eventually helps this select few who held those licenses a good jump start on production when Prohibition is repealed.

**DECEMBER 5, 1933**

Utah became the state that pushed the vote over the majority to repeal the 18th Amendment with the 21st Amendment. Bottoms Up!

**1934**

Shuttered and new distilleries open up to capitalize on the repeal of Prohibition. Col. James B. Beam and his backers buy the old Murphy Barber Distillery in Cleremont, KY. Heaven Hill opens in Bardstown, KY. Sam Bronfman from Seagrams in Canada opens a massive distillery in Lawrenceburg, IN and starts producing blended whiskey there. Schenley Distillers out of New York also open a distillery in Lawrenceburg, IN. Glenmore opens in Owensboro, KY.

**1936**

To help create jobs, F.D.R. makes it a law that a brand new charred barrel must be used in bourbon production.

**1937**

The Great Flood of '37 invades many distilleries along the Ohio River, and Kentucky River.

**1938**

Churchill Downs offers the mint julep as the official drink of the Kentucky Derby and serves it in a commemorative glass that year, and all the years to follow.

**1939** After aging for four years, the pre-prohibition style of Bottled In Bond whiskies are available and Old Heaven Hill Bottled In Bond becomes the #1 selling bourbon in Kentucky. Most all distilleries producing straight whiskies produce one or more Bottled In Bond marques.

**1941** Just when shelves were starting to get replenished with bourbon, rye and other straight whiskies, WWII breaks out and distilleries once again produce high proof alcohol for the war effort.

**1945** The most popular way to travel the county is by train. Just as you fly today, you can't get out of your seat until the place reaches a safe altitude, you had to remain in your seat on a train until it got up to speed and became more stable. There were two lights in every passenger car. When the lower light was lit everyone had to remain seated, but when the upper light was lit or "high ball" then it was OK to get up and go to the bar car for a drink.

**1948-1953** During World War I and World War II, the U.S. government mandated that distillers make high proof alcohol for the war efforts. When it appears that the U.S. is going to be involved in the Korean conflict, distillers ramp up production and make an unprecedented amount of whiskey. However, the government issues no such mandate and there is an absolute whiskey glut. With so much whiskey on hand, prices of straight American whiskey plummet which contributes to the end of the domination of straight whiskey in the United States.

**1950s-
1960s**

Tiki bars and entertaining at home are very popular. People are makingCuba Libras, Hurricanes, Vodka Gimlets, Mojito's, The Aviation, Martinis, Harvey Wallbangers with rum, gin or vodka. Ex GI's from WWII have a taste for London Dry gin and other spirits they discovered there.

**1964**

The 88th Congress of the United States declares bourbon a "distinctive product" of the U.S. Bourbon cannot be produced outside the U.S. The Standards of Identity for Distilled Spirits is written bringing all the laws together. Container ships are created right around this time, thus making the world a smaller place and protecting your countries style and distinctive whisky is important.

**1976**

Vodka overtakes whiskey as the most popular spirit category. Many bourbons and straight whiskies lower their proofs from Bottled In Bond to 86, or 80 proof, or switch to used barrels (Early Times) to match the lightness of vodka and gins.

**1984**

Master Distiller Elmer T. Lee (George T. Stagg Distillery/Ancient Age) releases Blanton's Single Barrel Bourbon, the first single barrel bourbon offered creating a new sub-category of bourbon. This is followed by Parker Beam and Heaven Hill in 1986 with Elijah Craig 12 year old and his cousin Booker Noe at Jim Beam with his Booker's Bourbon in 1987. Booker coined the term "small batch" to describe what he and Parker and Jimmy Russell over at Wild Turkey were doing by mingling choice barrels together instead of using one single barrel where each barrel tastes a little bit different than the next. So Single Barrel and Small Batch were established.

**1991**   *Malt Advocate Magazine* is launched covering whiskies from around the world. The magazine thrives today under their new name, *Whisky Advocate*.

**1992**   The first Bourbon Fest is held in Bardstown, KY where hundreds of people attend to celebrate in the "Bourbon Capital of the World." Today 60,000 people attend from all over the world the third weekend of September.

**1993**   Jim Beam's grandson and Distiller Emeritus Booker Noe hit the road along with spirits writer Paul Pacult and "The Nose" Richard Patterson from Whyte and Mackay Scotch. They traveled the country introducing people to the new Jim Beam Small Batch Bourbon Collection. This collection was the first nationally promoted and offered small batch bourbons and helped awareness and spark enthusiasm for bourbon, especially when Booker and Richard held their "Great Whisk(e)y Debates" on which was the better whisk(e)y, scotch or bourbon.

**1996**   Brown-Foreman and Master Distiller Lincoln
**1984**   Henderson release their small batch bourbon; Woodford Reserve.

**1998**   *Malt Advocate* holds their first Whiskey Fest in New York City. It becomes so popular it expands Whiskey Fest to Chicago and San Francisco and so popular they sell out well in advance.

**2003**   The American Distilling Institute is founded by Bill Owens "To promote and defend the art and enterprise of craft distilling."

The Evolution from Unaged Corn Whiskey • 161

**2007** The United States Senate unanimously passed a resolution declaring September "National Bourbon Heritage Month."

**2013** Heaven Hill releases a Parker's Heritage whiskey called *Promise of Hope,* after it has been announced that Parker Beam is fighting the dreaded ALS disease, sparking a campaign that raises hundreds of thousands of dollars, and sparks a bourbon called UNITY that all distillers combine their efforts on that is auctioned off during Whiskey Fest New York.

**2014** There are 4.3 million residents in Kentucky and 5 million barrels of bourbon aging in rickhouses. So there are more barrels than people and horses combined in Kentucky!

**2014** Bourbon Thru Bluegrass starts the International Bourbon Festival off in Bardstown, KY.

**2015** Bourbon Thru Bluegrass makes an appearance on the Direct TV Documentary, *Bourbontucky* also available on iTunes.

# 6

# Visiting Kentucky and the Distilleries, and You WILL

*"I only drink two fingers of bourbon each day. Of course I use my index and pinky fingers."* – Jimmy Russell,
Master Distiller Emeritus, Wild Turkey

*"May there be no hell..."* –Booker Noe
*"...and if there is, I'll see you there."* –Fred Noe

So you're a member of the bourbon family now and inspired to come visit us down on the Bourbon Trail. Of course you are! I'm telling you, once you visit, you'll be back. They *all* come back. Year after year, the biggest celebrities and political figures come back to Kentucky for the Derby and just to visit. It's a great place, a fun place, and, as a nice bonus, it's not that expensive to visit. Since we are in the heart of the country, a large percentage of the population can just drive here.

We are in the second Golden Age of Bourbon. Why wouldn't you want to feel, smell, hold, and taste history? Not since Ben Parley Moore wrote his employer about that "unequalled old bourbon" has there been such unbridled enthusiasm about bourbons.

Napa Valley has hundreds of thousands of visitors a year. I've been myself, and it's wonderful. San Francisco is where most people stay and then drive up to the wine country. Then they come back and enjoy the food and nightlife of one of the most stunning cities in the world. The Bourbon Trail is very similar and much more accessible to most of the country than San Francisco. I would argue it is also just as stunning (just a different kind of stunning).

On the Bourbon Trail are the distilleries in Kentucky that welcome more than 250,000 visitors each year. Come on by anytime, but I'd avoid mid-July through August, since most distilleries do not distill during the hottest months. If you'd like a recommendation about the best times, I'd first suggest coming the third weekend in September for the Bourbon Festival. Also, Keeneland race track is open every April and October in Lexington, and Churchill Downs is running every May and November. I'd just avoid the last week of April and the first Saturday in May which is Derby, unless you have a bucket of money to get a hotel. Thunder Over Louisville in April is the largest fireworks display in the world and is one of the coolest days/nights ever. It's the opening ceremonies of the Kentucky Derby Festival, and throughout the day there is an air show, while 600,000 people assemble downtown for the world's largest fireworks display over the Ohio River at night. Military cannons roar as fireworks light up downtown for miles. Don't believe me? Find it on YouTube, then go to www.thunderoverlouisville.org and you'll see. Hotels downtown can get pricey, but you can still find some deals, and it's quite something, especially if you have children.

Don't bite off more than you can chew when visiting the distilleries. You can only visit two on a given day. Don't try to do three, you just won't make it. Trust me.

## LOUISVILLE, KY

**Evan Williams Bourbon Experience** – 528 W. Main Street, Louisville, www.evan williams.com/BourbonExperience. The first operating distillery to open in downtown Louisville in decades. Here you'll see how Louisville contributed in the history of bourbon and how Evan Williams made whiskey in this same block over 200 years ago.

**Kentucky Peerless Distilling Company** – 120 N. 10th Street, Louisville, www.kentuckypeerless.com. Craft distillery open for tours and tastings.

**Bulleit Frontier Whiskey Experience** – 3860 Fitzgerald Road, Louisville (Shively), www.bulleitexperience.com. Open at the old Stizel-Weller distillery of Old Fitzgerald and Pappy

Van Winkle fame. Come all things that go into making Bulleit Bourbon.

**Jim Beam Urban Stillhouse** – 404 S. Fourth Street, Louisville, www.jimbeam.com. A new visitors center in the heart of Fourt Street Live in Downtown Louisville, the Stillhouse is just steps away from most hotels.

**Distilled Spirits Epicenter** – Home of Moonshine University, 801 S. 8th Street, Louisville, 502-301-8126, www.ds-epicenter.com.

**Angels Envy** – www.angelsenvy.com. Currently under construction at the 400 block of East Main Street across from the Louisville Slugger Field.

**Old Forester** – www.oldforester.com. Coming in 2017 to Historic Whiskey Row in the 100 block of West Main near Doc Crows.

**Churchill Downs** – (www.churchilldowns.com) Every April until July, and then in October or November after Keeneland closes down, racing moves to Louisville at legendary track under the twin spires at Churchill Downs. Think of Keeneland as the Sistine Chapel and Churchill Downs as St. Peter's Basilica. I hate it when people say Keeneland is much better than Churchill, or vise versa, because they are both *awesome* in their own right. There's no way Keeneland could (or would for that matter) have 160,000 people attending the Derby, and there's no way Churchill can capture some of the charm of Keeneland. We're lucky to have both available to us here in the Bluegrass State. My good buddy Dave Danielson is the executive chef at Churchill...I can't imagine cooking for tens of thousands of my closest friends, but he does. John Asher is also one of my heroes here at the track. He's as passionate about racing and the historic twin spires as we bourbon geeks are about our bourbon.

**Louisville Mega Cavern** – 877.614.MEGA   Everyone has heard of Mamouth Cave, which is only an hour from Louisville and one of the Natural Wonders of the World no less— definitely something you should go see and experience. But you should also go see the Mega Cavern, which spans some 17 miles underneath Louisville! A great and fun way to experience it is to take the two-hour zip line tour, (http://www.louisvillemegacavern.com/tour-info-zip-tours.html),a zip line adventure totally underground!

**Louisville Slugger Museum** – 800 Main Street, Louisville, www.sluggermuseum.com. See the world's largest bat and watch them make the bats for the major league hitters today. Learn about the bats made for the legends of America's pastime.

**Frazier Arms Museum** – 829 W. Main Street, Louisville, www.fraziermuseum.com. Weapons from the British Royal Armouries along with other historical artifacts and live daily performances. Soon to be a starting point for the Bourbon Tour experiences.

## WESTERN SHELF DISTILLERIES AND ATTRACTIONS

Split them in to two days to visit distilleries and the cooperage:

*Day 1*

### MAKER'S MARK DISTILLERY

3350 Burk Spring Road, Loretto, KY 40037

Phone:270.865.2881

www.makersmark.com

Master distiller is Greg Davis; president and family member ambassador is Bill Samuels, Jr.

The Maker's Mark visitor's experience gives you a look at how Bill Samuels, Sr. and his wife Marjorie (who is responsible for the bottle, name, font and wax) started up the family business again in 1959. A re-creation of their kitchen is here, and you get an inside look at how this family created and built this now-iconic brand. Take your camera, there are photo ops a plenty. You top off your tour by being able to purchase a bottle of Maker's Mark and dip it in that famous red wax your own damn self.

*Maker's Mark distillery house (Maker's Mark is a registered trademark of Maker's Mark Distillery, Inc. and is used with permission.)*

**Directions from Louisville:** Take I-65 South from Louisville to Exit #112, (Clermont/Bardstown). At the ramp turn left onto Hwy. 245 South to Bardstown.

Take Hwy. 245 to the intersection of Hwy. 62, turn right and continue on Hwy. 62 East for approximately two miles. Hwy. 62 runs into Hwy. 150, where you will turn left and continue approximately two miles, past My Old Kentucky Home State Park. At the intersection of Hwys. 150 and 49, turn right onto Hwy. 49 South and follow the brown historical landmark signs to Holy Cross, which will direct you to go straight on Hwy. 527 South. Follow Hwy. 527 to St. Francis (5 miles), where you will turn left onto Hwy. 52 East into Loretto. Continue on through Loretto for approximately three miles,

1) Maker's Mark Distillery, 3350 Burk Spring Road, Loretto, KY 40037

2) Independent Stave Cooperage, 712 E. Main Street, Lebanon, KY 40033

3) Heaven Hill Distilleries Bourbon Heritage Center, 1311 Gilky Run Road, Bardstown, KY 40004

4) Jim Beam American Outpost, 526 Happy Hollow Road, Clermont, KY 40110

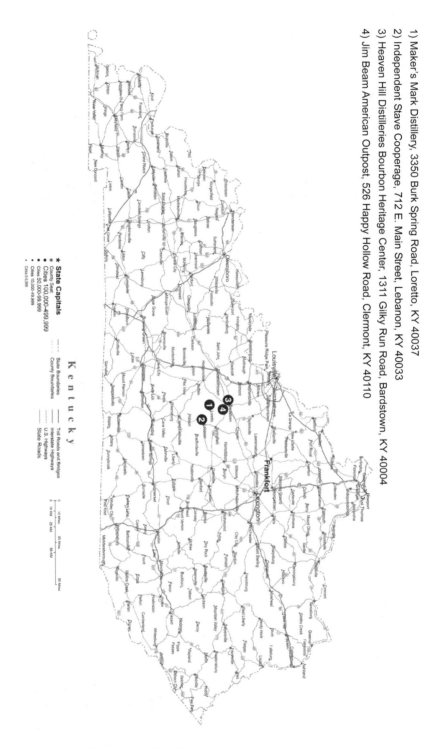

and at the end of Burks Spring Road you will see the sign, "You have just found the home of Maker's Mark." Approximately one-and-a-half hours driving time.

**Directions from Lexington:** Take U.S. 60 West six miles to Martha Layne Collins Blue Grass Parkway. Merge onto the parkway toward Elizabethtown and drive 30 miles to Exit 42 (Springfield/Lebanon). Take the exit and turn left toward Springfield/Lebanon on KY 555 S. After 14.8 miles, KY 555 S becomes KY 55 but continue straight for 8.9 miles to the traffic signal (Gen. Thomas Statue). Turn right onto KY 55 Bypass and drive to the next light (Circle K). Turn right onto KY 49/52 and continue 6.3 miles. Turn right onto KY 52 continuation and continue 2.2 miles. Turn right onto Burk's Spring Road and historic Maker's Mark Distillery is straight ahead. Approximately one hour, 15 minutes driving time.

### INDEPENDENT STAVE COOPERAGE (BARREL MAKERS)

712 E. Main Street, Lebanon, KY, 40033

Phone: 270.692.4674

www.independentstavecompany.com

This is something you've really got to see. The way they make barrels is just amazing! No nails, screws or glue here. Bending wood and using metal hoops along with hundreds of years of experience is what you'll see here at this facility. By law, bourbon must be aged in brand new charred-oak containers, so almost all the barrels you see being made are for the bourbon industry. The coolest thing is that this is a family-owned business run by the Boswells.

**Directions from Louisville:** Take I-65 South toward Nashville for approximately 20 miles to Exit 112 (Clermont/Bardstown). Turn left onto Hwy. 245 toward Bardstown and drive 19 miles. Turn left onto Hwy. 150 E and drive 15 miles. Turn right onto KY 55 (Hardees® on the corner). Centre Square in Lebanon is nine miles straight ahead. From Centre Square drive one block south on KY 55/Spalding Ave. to the light at

Main Street. Turn left onto U.S. 68/Main St. and continue for about one mile. Independent Stave Cooperage is on the right. Driving time is about one hour, 15 minutes (63 miles).

**Directions from Lexington:** Take U.S. 60 West six miles to Martha Layne Collins Blue Grass Parkway. Merge onto the parkway toward Elizabethtown and drive 30 miles to the Springfield exit (Exit 42). Take the exit and turn left toward Springfield/Lebanon on KY 555 S. After 14.8 miles, 555 S becomes 55 but continue straight for 9 miles to Centre Square. From Centre Square drive one block south on KY 55/Spalding Avenue to the light at Main Street. Turn left onto U.S. 68/ Main St. and continue for about one mile. Independent Stave Cooperage is on the right. Driving time is around one hour, 10 minutes (59.8 miles).

*Bourbon Heritage Center (Photo courtesy of the Louisville Convention and Visitors Bureau)*

## Day 2

### HEAVEN HILL DISTILLERIES BOURBON HERITAGE CENTER
1311 Gilky Run Road, Bardstown, KY 40004
Phone: 502.337.1000
www.bourbonheritagecenter.com.

Master distillers are Parker Beam and his son Craig Beam, and their ambassador is Bernie Lubbers.

Heaven Hill's Heritage Center really raised the bar for everyone else when they built their multimillion-dollar facility. They received *Whisky Magazine*'s Global Icons of Whisky

Award for Visitor Attraction of the Year in 2009. A fire destroyed a total of six rack houses and their distillery in 1996, so the distillery is no longer here at this facility. But they more than make up for this; trust me, you will be treated to one of the best experiences on the Kentucky Bourbon Trail.

*Parker and Earl Beam at Heaven Hill (Circa 1970) Courtesy of Heaven Hill Distillery*

**Directions from Louisville:** Take I-65 South to Exit 112 (Clermont/Bardstown). Turn left onto Hwy. 245 South. Take Hwy. 245 South to the end, then make a right onto 150 West. Turn left at the first light onto 49 South (by the McDonald's®). Follow 49 South one mile to Heaven Hill Distilleries Bourbon Heritage Center. It'll take you about 50 minutes to get there from Louisville.

**Directions from Lexington:** Take Bluegrass Parkway West to Exit 25 (U.S. 150), turn right onto U.S. 150 West. Turn left at the first light (by the McDonald's ) onto 49 South for one mile to the Bourbon Heritage Center. It will take you about an hour to get here from Lexington.

## Jim Beam American Outpost

526 Happy Hollow Road

Clermont, KY 40110

Phone: 502.543.9877

www.jimbeam.com.

The Master distiller/family member and bourbon ambassador is Fred Noe.

Jim Beam is the #1 selling bourbon in the world, so although the grounds are breathtaking, the distillery is large and industrial. But don't think that they're cutting any corners,

*Booker Noe statue on Beam Hill (Jim Beam is a registered trademark of Jim Beam Brands Co. and is used with permission.)*

goodness, no! Beam takes as much care as any of the smaller, quainter distilleries, just more of it. Colonel Beam built big after Prohibition, and that's one of the reasons we're still around. He just had no idea any of you all would be coming around to visit, so the distillery was set up to make *a lot* of whiskey. But they've done a great job renovating and showing off everything that goes on at the world's largest bourbon distillery, as well as giving you an inside look at the process.

**Directions from Louisville:** Take I-65 South toward Nashville to Exit 112 (Clermont/Bardstown). Go left off the exit, and 2.5 miles on the left is the Beam Distillery. You'll see signs for the Jim Beam American Outpost off Happy Hollow Road. Driving time is around 25 minutes.

**Directions from Lexington:** Take Bluegrass Parkway west to Exit 25 (U.S. 150). Drive toward Bardstown and turn right onto KY 245. Drive 13.5 miles, then turn right onto Happy Hollow Road.

## FOUR ROSES WAREHOUSE AND BOTTLING FACILITY AT COX'S CREEK

624 Lotus Road

Cox's Creek, KY

www.fourrosesbourbon.com.

The Visitor Center features antique bottles, advertising and other memorabilia from the Four Roses archives. Tours highlights operations at the facility, including warehousing, barreling and bottling. The Visitor Center also includes a premium bourbon tasting bar that allows guests the opportunity to sample Four Roses products following a tour.

**Oscar Getz Museum of Whiskey History** – 114 N. 5th Street, Bardstown, KY. www.whiskeymuseum.com. Chronicles the history of American whiskey from Colonial days to the 1960s. Lots of cool old pictures of distillieries and vintage bottles of whiskey.

**Willet Distillery** – 1869 Loretto Road, Bardstown, KY. Located across from Heaven Hill Bourbon Heritage Center. Master distiller is Drew Kulsveen. Come tour the facility and see how they craft their bourbon and rye whiskey. You can also visit one of their rickhouses.

**Limestone Branch Distillery** – 1280 Veterans Memorial Hwy., Lebanon, KY. www.limestonebranch.com. Master distiller is Steve Beam (yes, another Beam) and my buddy Steve Fonte is their ambassador. They make some tasty sugar shine moonshine-esque whiskey and the historic Yellowstone bourbon here. You'll sometimes see Tim from the TV series "Moonshiners" here making some of his whiskey.

**Barton 1792 Distillery** – 300 Barton Road, Bardstown, KY. www.1792bourbon.com. Right in the heart of Bardstown, this distillery is run by my buddy Ken Pierce as Master Distiller, and they make some of the best high rye recipes around.

OTHER WESTERN SHELF ATTRACTIONS:

**Knob Creek Gun Range** – (www.knobcreekrange.com) Located in West Point, KY, just about 30 minutes south of Louisville, on the way to Jim Beam actually. Open 9:00 a.m. to 6:00 p.m. every day *but* Tuesday, so *don't go Tuesdays*. It's an old quarry and now a gun range and you can buy/sell weapons there, too. But every mid-April and mid-October is the Machine Gun Shoot, when at night they fire off live tracer rounds and just about every other type of weapon imaginable, and I think a few arrows and sling shots, too! It's just something to see and hear, and it's located right off Knob Creek! (This is no affiliation with Knob Creek Bourbon...but both are located in same area.)

**Mammoth Cave** (www.nps.gov/maca) is just an hour away... If I have to tell you anything about Mammoth, retake geography class.

## EASTERN SHELF DISTILLERIES AND ATTRACTIONS

For your visit to the Eastern Shelf, I'd do it this way:

*Day 1*

### BUFFALO TRACE DISTILLERY

113 Great Buffalo Trace

Frankfort, KY 40601

Phone: 502.696.5926

www.buffalotrace.com

*Filling bottles at Buffalo Trace (photo courtesy of the Louisville Convention and Visitors Bureau)*

Master distiller is Harlen Wheatley and distiller emeritus is Elmer T. Lee.

I love the grounds at this distillery. I love the O.F.C. (remember the Old Fire Copper from Colonel Edmund Taylor?) above some of the brick rack houses here. They have different types of brick, block and traditional rack houses. The log buildings on the property are really cool, too, and you can even rent the lodge for gatherings and meetings.

**Directions from Louisville**: Take I-64 East to Exit 53B (U.S. 127 North). Continue straight about five miles, cross the Kentucky River, and you'll see the Holiday Inn. Turn left, continuing on 127 North which is also Wilkinson Blvd. The distillery is one mile down on the left.

**Directions from Lexington**: Take I-64 West to Exit 58. Go north on U.S. 60 until it becomes 127/421. Go straight and follow signs to Civic Center/Downtown, about 5.5 miles. Do not make any turns until you see the distillery on your right.

1) Buffalo Trace Distillery, 113 Great Buffalo Trace, Frankfort, KY 40601

2) Woodford Reserve Distillery, 7855 McCracken Pike, Versailles, KY 40303

3) Wild Turkey Distillery, 1525 Tyrone Road, Lawrenceburg, KY 40342

4) Four Roses Distillery, 1224 Bonds Mill Road, Lawrenceburg, KY 40342

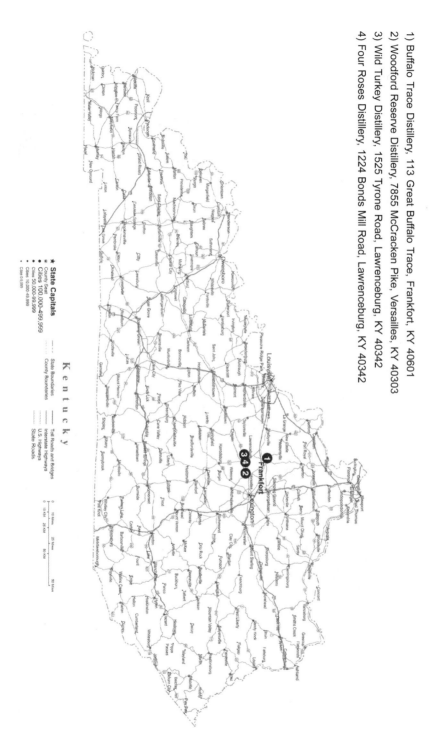

Kentucky

**State Capitals**
★ County Seat
● Cities 100,000-499,999
● Cities 50,000-99,999
● Cities 10,000-49,999
  Cities 0-9,999

State Boundaries
County Boundaries

Toll Roads and Bridges
Interstate Highways
U.S. Highways
State Roads

Visiting Kentucky and the Distilleries • 175

## WOODFORD RESERVE DISTILLERY

7855 McCracken Pike

Versailles, KY 40303

phone: 859.879.1812

www.woodfordreserve.com

Master distiller is Chris Morris. Woodford is the gorgeously renovated former Labrot & Graham Distillery. Brown-Foreman spent millions of dollars rebuilding this distillery, and it shows. The brick rack houses are really

*Woodford Reserve Barrel Head (photo courtesy of the Louisville Convention and Visitors Bureau)*

cool, and the triple pot stills are something to see, since this company is the only one in the bourbon business to use them. They have many events at this distillery, including some really nice bourbon dinners, so call ahead and see what they'll have going on when you visit.

**Directions from Louisville:** Take I-64 East to the U.S. 60 exit (Frankfort Versailles). Turn right toward Versailles. Go 2.5 miles and turn right on Route 3360 (Grassy Springs Road) until it ends. Turn right on McCracken Pike to the distillery.

**Directions from Lexington:** Take U.S. 60 (Versailles Road) out of Lexington toward Frankfort. Just after you pass State Road 1685, turn left onto Route 3360 (Grassy Springs Road) until it ends. Turn right on McCracken Pike to the distillery.

## Day 2

### WILD TURKEY DISTILLERY

1525 Tyrone Road
Lawrenceburg, KY 40342
phone: 502.839.4544
www.wildturkeybourbon.com

*Wild Turkey Distillery (photo courtesy of the Louisville Convention and Visitors Bureau)*

Master distiller is Eddie Russell, and distiller emeritus is his dad, Jimmy Russell. This distillery sits way up overlooking the Kentucky River, and that alone is one of the coolest sights you'll see there. They've just renovated the distillery, so go take a look and enjoy it all. If you're lucky enough, maybe Jimmy Russell will be there to have a chat and pose for a picture or two.

**Directions from Louisville:** Take I-64 East to 151 South. Take U.S. 62 East to the distillery. Driving time is around 50 minutes.

**Directions from Lexington:** Take U.S. 60 West to Versailles, then take U.S. 62 West to the distillery. Driving time is around 30 minutes.

## FOUR ROSES DISTILLERY

1224 Bonds Mill Road

Lawrenceburg, KY40342

phone: 502.839.3436

www.fourroses.us.

*Four Roses Distillery (photo courtesy of the Louisville Convention and Visitors Bureau)*

Master distiller is Jimmy Rutledge. This distillery is built in the Spanish Mission style, and it's really picturesque. The rack houses you see across the way don't belong to Four Roses; those are the property of Wild Turkey, whose distillery is a few miles away. Four Roses is a small distillery, but Jimmy Rutledge does some of the coolest distilling there with their two recipes and five strains of yeast which can give them many options for a final product. Their Brand Ambassador is my buddy Al Young, and he wrote a great book on the history of Four Roses called, *Four Roses – The Return of a Whiskey Legend*. Al was inducted into the Kentucky Distiller's Hall of Fame in 2011, too!

**Directions from Louisville**: Take I-64 East to Exit 53 (U.S. 127 South). Go 14 miles to Highway 513 West (There's no sign there for the distillery, so pay attention). Go right on Highway 513. It's just one mile to the distillery on the right.

**Directions from Lexington**: Take U.S. 60 East to Bluegrass Parkway West. Take Exit 59B off Bluegrass Parkway and drive a 10th of a mile to Highway 513 West (there's no sign to the distillery, so pay attention here). The distillery is just down a mile on the right.

**Town Branch** – 401 Cross Street, Lexington, KY. www.kentuckyale.com. Town Branch makes some really great whiskey under the eye of Dr. Pierce Lyons through his Master Distiller Mark Coffman. Tours and tastings daily.

**Barrel House Distilling Company** – 1200 Manchester Street, Lexington, KY. www.barrelhousedistillery.com. This is a small batch distillery in a historic distilling and brewing area of Lexington. Along with whiskey and moonshine, they distill rum and vodka.

OTHER EASTERN SHELF ATTRACTIONS:

**Keeneland Race Track** – (www.keeneland.com). Keeneland sits right across from Bluegrass Field Airport on Versailles Road, and has live racing in April and October (short card, so check their website for dates) and Keeneland Thoroughbred sales during different parts of the year if you want to see horses sell for millions and millions of dollars. It's one of *the* coolest places on earth, and you can just taste the history there. Don't come in your blue jeans, though; dress up and join in the Old Southern charm of Keeneland.

**Kentucky Gentlemen Cigars** – 1056 Ninevah Road – Lawrenceburg, KY – 502.839.9226 (www.kentucky-gentlemencigars.com) – Take Exit 53 Frankfort/Lawrenceburg (same exit as Buffalo Trace). Cigars are made right here and filled with flavorings from Kentucky heritage including bourbon, moonshine or mint julep, so you can experience cigars available nowhere else or customize your own blend from varieties from all over the world.

## OTHER DISTILLERIES IN THE AREA:

**Huber's Orchard Winery and Vineyards** – 19816 Huber Rd., Borden, IN. www.huberwinery.com. Over 600,000 visitors a year can't be wrong, and they've been making wine on site for decades. Now they are distilling brandy and whiskey. This is great fun for the whole family, with lots of things to do, including pumpkin picking and other crops.

**Corsair Distillery** – www.carsairdistillery.com. They have locations in both Bowling Green, KY and Nashville, TN. Both give tours, so check their website for details. Darek Bell and Andrew Webber make some of the most tasty innovative craft spirits in the industry. This is my favorite craft distillery open today!

**Prichards Distillery** – www.prichardsdistillery.com. Phil Prichard is one of my all-time favorite guys in the industry. What a character... and he makes some of the best rum you'll ever taste. He makes some whiskey too, but his passion is rum. They have two locations to visit, one in Kelso, TN and the other in Fontanel, TN. Check the website for details on each.

## WELCOME TO KENTUCKY

Since I'm the whiskey professor, I'll help guide you on your first visit here. Our airport in Louisville is a great little airport–one terminal. We have Southwest, U.S. Air, United, Continental, American, Delta, Frontier and a few others that fly here. We're only a five-hour drive from St. Louis and Chicago and seven hours from Atlanta. You can fly in to Bluegrass Airport (LEX) in Lexington, but I would venture to guess that Standiford Field (SDF) in Louisville is going to have more and cheaper options. Louisville is right in the middle of bourbon country and is a 25-minute drive from Jim Beam, and 45 minutes from Bardstown. On the other side, Lexington is only 72 miles from Louisville. It's not going to cost you much to get here, but you will need to rent a car or hire transportation to take you around to the distilleries if you'd like to do it that way, or come with a group. Mint Julep Tours (mintjuleptours.com) is a great company to tour with if you don't want to get a car or if you have a group of people you want to bring along with you. There are many hotels right downtown that start around $100 a night, and some on the outskirts of town (in Brooks or Shepherdsville) that are half that.

Taking tours is fun and interesting. Every distillery gives a different tour, and each has its own unique history and qualities. At some you'll see the distillation firsthand. At others you'll go into a rack house and see the barrels aging and smell the evaporation of the "angels' share" (what the angels drink ... the bourbon evaporating from the barrels). Louisville and Lexington are the cities you'd stay in as your home base, and then you'd journey out from there to the distilleries. You could also stay in Bardstown if you wanted to get that real small-town feel, being right there in the heart of the Bourbon Capital of the World. But there isn't as much nightlife or restaurants there compared to Louisville or Lexington. Once you've driven out through the rolling fields of horse country, met the passionate and friendly folks at the distilleries, and enjoyed the restaurants and nightlife here, you'll be back. Lexington is a fun college town, home to the University of Kentucky Wildcats and Transylvania University, with great restaurants and night life. And unlike most of the country, the bars in Louisville are open until 4:00 a.m. every night of the week, so bring your "A" game.

*Louisville*

Louisville has created someting really cool. The city is actually involved as an active partner to promote bourbon tourism and the responsible enjoyment of our native spirit.

**URBANBOURBONTRAIL**

A few years ago they formed the Urban Bourbon Trail, and it is a shining example of how a city and it's thriving food and drink scene can work together to create something special. More than 750,000 people come to visit each year and that number just keeps growing and growing.

To be on the Urban Bourbon Trail list, you must carry a minimum of 50 bourbons in the back bar. Most of the places on the trail carry many more, but 50 is a good start. There's around 30 accounts that are officially on the list but those change, close or re-open under other names from time to time. For a current list, visit www.bourboncountry.com. You can obtain a passport at any of the accounts, and after you visit part of the trail (or all of the trail!), you get a cool t-shirt or other items to boast of your accomplishment.

There are five bars and restaurants that have been proud members of the Urban Bourbon Trail since its inception in 2008. They include the following:

**The Bar at Blu** – 280 W. Jefferson St. 502-894-4285. www.blugrille.com. For a modern Louisville experience, step into a fresh new space of contemporary design at BLU. Sample 60+ bourbons from the "Wall of Bourbon" or try one or more of the bourbon flights.

**Bourbon's Bistro** – 2255 Frankfort Ave. 502-894-8838. www.bourbonbistro.com. Marty Rose from the *Courier-Journal* says "Even in the land of bourbon, where massive catalogs of whiskey are the pride of many bars, Bourbon Bistro stands out as one of the key destinations on Louisville's Urban Bourbon Trail." Brown Hotel Lobby Bar – 335 W. Broadway. 502-583-1234. www.brownhotel.com. It's easy to let your imagination take you back to another era as you sip an Old Fashioned in the lavish lobby bar of the Brown Hotel, which *Southern Living* described as "straight from a 1930s movie set."

**The Old Seelbach Bar** – 500 4th Street. 502-585-3200. www.seelbachhilton.com. Opened in 1905, the Seelbach Hotel has hosted gangsters, politicians and celebrities for generations. Listed on the National Register of Historic Places, the Seelbach's gilded-era luxury served as F. Scott Fitzgerald's inspiration for *The Great Gatsby*, and the hotel's Oakroom restaurant was a favorite hangout of Al Capone.

**Proof on Main** – 702 W. Main Street. 502-217-6360. www.proofonmain.com. Located in downtown's 21c Museum Hotel, Proof on Main features a diverse selection of Kentucky's finest bourbons. Named one of three American "New Whiskey Temples" by *GQ*. Proof offers a library of small batch and single barrel bourbon as well as proprietary bourbon selections.

## HOTELS

### THE SEELBACH HOTEL

500 S. Fourth Street

Louisville, KY 40202

phone: 502.585.3200

www.seelbachhilton.com

The Seelbach is a historic property built in 1905 which recently went through a 12 million dollar renovation. F. Scott Fitzgerald and Al Capone were just a couple of the visitors to this hotel. The Al Capone Poker Room is off the famous Oak Room Restaurant, complete with slanted mirrors (to peek at his

*Old Seelbach Bar (photo courtesy of the Louisville Convention and Visitors Bureau)*

opponents' hands) and secret panels and passages to escape the Feds during Prohibition. F. Scott Fitzgerald was so inspired from his stay that he used the Seelbach as the backdrop for Tom and Daisy Buchanan's wedding in *The Great Gatsby*. The Old Seelbach bar oozes history and is famous in cocktail books for the Seelbach Cocktail made with bourbon, champagne, bitters and triple sec.

## THE BROWN HOTEL

335 W. Broadway

Louisville, KY 40202

phone: 502.583.1234

www.brownhotel.com

*The Brown Hotel (photo courtesy of the Louisville Convention and Visitors Bureau)*

The Brown was built for four million dollars back in 1923 and has been a magnet for celebrities and prominent guests for the Derby or visitors to the Bourbon Trail ever since. Extensive renovations in the 1980s restored it to its full elegance in English Renaissance design, and it remains one of the most treasured landmarks in the South. In the lobby bar, you'll be able to sip and enjoy a wide variety of bourbons and classic cocktails. The English Grill is a great restaurant, and I suggest you treat yourself and request the chef's table. There is a minimum number of people required for this table, but if you tell them the bourbons you want to pair and taste with dinner, they will accommodate. It's one of the most awesome dinner experiences I've ever had. Just across the street on Broadway is Freddie's Bar, and you'll swear you've walked back in time to the 1950s. It is one of the coolest, oldest bars in the city. Not a huge bourbon selection, but a place you've almost gotta experience.

## THE MARRIOTT HOTEL

280 W. Jefferson Street
Louisville, KY 40202
phone: 502.627.5045
www.marriott.com/hotels/travel/sdflm-louisville-marriott-downtown

The Marriott is right in the heart of downtown Louisville with 616 rooms. Built just a few years ago, this hotel is contemporary and comfortable. The Blu Lobby bar is cozy but open to the gorgeous lobby. Blu is where all the bourbons are showcased on the back bar, and it is also where my buddies Hickory, Jim and Chris play bluegrass every Thursday night from 9 p.m. until midnight. Hickory loves Basil Hayden's bourbon, Jim likes Baker's, and Chris likes Knob Creek, so your

---

### IF YOU STAY AT THE MARRIOTT

*Since Hickory and Clare are both Basil Hayden's fans, I'll tell ya this story that I share during my bourbontations around the country.*

**Bahsil or Basil?** *I always refer to Basil Hayden's bourbon as "Baaaahsil" Hayden's bourbon, not "Baysil" Hayden's bourbon. People invariably ask me if it is pronounced Basil, or Basil Hayden's. I answer with this story:*

*I have a neighbor (this is true) who lives six doors down from me, and not only is he a great guy, but he has one of the coolest names I know: Basil Doerhorfer. (I think he's Irish.) He's in his 70s and is about 6'5" tall with a full head of wavy white hair, and he's a real skinny fellow. Every day he walks his little Chihuahua-mix dog in front of my condos, and it just looks funny with him being a slender 6'5" and with that little dog on a leash. One day I saw him and said, "Hey, Basil, how are you doing?" He replied, "Well, young man, basil is an herb, Baaahsil is the name." To which I replied, "Well, in that case I'll just call you Dick then." We both had a chuckle, but since then I've always called him and the bourbon Baaahsil.*

---

song request might just move to the top of the list if you buy them a bourbon. One of my favorite bartenders, Clare (also a Basil Hayden's girl), joins the band and sings a couple songs with the boys, too. It's a fun night and a great place to stay while visiting Louisville. If I'm in town on Thursday nights, you'll

*Hickory, Chris, Clare and Jim at the Blu Bar (photo by Bernie Lubbers)*

find me there, and most times Hickory invites me up to sing and play with them, too. It's a great fun night for all, so by all means, come on by.

### 21c Museum Hotel
700 W. Main Street
Louisville, KY 40202
phone: 502.217.6300
www.21chotel.com/hotel

What is a museum hotel? Well, everything in the hotel/restaurant is a museum exhibit! It's something to see, and it's not just me who says that.

*The Bar at Proof on Main (photo courtesy of the Louisville Convention and Visitors Bureau)*

*Conde Nast Traveller* rated it the #1 hotel in the United States and the #6 hotel in the *world*! A boutique hotel that's not snooty. It has a great sense of humor, as you'll find by the exhibits and the large red penguins that move around the hotel and restaurant called Proof (the cheese grits are to die for). You'll see some of the master distillers and us bourbon ambassadors at Proof from time to time, and when you come in, you'll know why. Even the bathrooms are intriguing. Luxury accommodations with good ole Kentucky hospitality, and it's the only museum in America dedicated solely to art created in the 21st century (get it? 21c?). Whether you visit Proof or stay at 21c, you will not think you are in Kentucky. London maybe, or New York or San Francisco, but thank God it is Kentucky!

## THE GALT HOUSE HOTEL
140 S. Fourth Street
Louisville, KY 40202
phone: 502.589.5200
www.galthouse.com

The Galt House is located right on the Ohio River and is a large hotel with two towers. The rooms have recently been renovated and most of them are huge. A.J.'s lobby bar overlooks the river and

*Jockey Silks at the Galt House (photo courtesy of the Louisville Convention and Visitors Bureau)*

Fourth Street Live, and the Jockey's Silks Bar boasts over 100 bourbons, some that aren't even available anymore! Rivue Restaurant sits at the top of the West Tower and overlooks Louisville and the Ohio River for great views of the Bluegrass. Jeff Ruby's Steakhouse is in the front of the Galt House and is one of the hottest spots to sip a bourbon, listen to great music, and enjoy great steaks and seafood. My good buddy and singing partner Robbie Bartlett and her band play almost every weekend there. She drinks Jim Beam Black Label and ginger ale with about five cherries in it, if you want to send one up to her. Jeff Ruby's also has a signature Maker's Mark dessert.

## HILTON GARDEN INN
350 W. Chestnut Street, Louisville, KY

This is a newer hotel located on Fourth Street in the Theater District and also has the only roof top bar located on the 8th floor overlooking downtown Louisville. The 8 UP Elevated Drinkery and Kitchen is a place to see and be seen, and they have a great cocktail program and good bourbon selection.

Visiting Kentucky and the Distilleries • 187

EMBASSY SUITES

505 S. Fourth Street, Louisville, KY

Another fairly new hotel across the street from the historic Seelbach Hotel on Fourth Street, the Embassy Suites is located in a historic building where every room is unique. Also home to a great seafood and steak place called Brendon's Catch 23.

## RESTAURANTS

**8 UP Elevated Drinkery and Kitchen** –350 W. Chestnut –Louisville, KY. Located in the Hilton Garden Inn. The only (so far) roof top bar in the city.

**Asiatique** –1767 Bardstown Road–Louisville, KY 40205– 502.451.2749 (asiatiquerestaurant.com). On the edge of the Highlands just about three miles from downtown, its food, decor and multilevel dining rooms are all fascinating. They boast Pacific Rim cuisine in a relaxed elegant atmosphere and deliver just that.

**Bistro 1860 Wine Bar and Spirits** – 1765 Mellwood Avenue – Louisville, KY. (www.Bistro1860.com). Chef Michael Crouch formally of Bourbon's Bistro came down with the owners Ron Kayrouz and Terry Fereday, and I have to tell you, this is one of my all-time favorite places to have a nice dinner and treat myself to some fine food and spirits.

**Bourbon's Bistro**–2255 Frankfort Ave.–Louisville, KY 40206– 502.894.8838 (www.bourbonsbistro.com). Voted the best whiskey bar/restaurant in 2006 in the Icons of Whisky Awards in *Whisky Magazine*, this is a wonderful place owned by John and Jason, two bourbon fans and all-around good guys whom you'll see almost every night sipping on some good Kentucky straight bourbon whiskey. Located just two miles from downtown, the restaurant is also easy to get to. On Mondays they often have master distillers and ambassadors like myself host bourbon dinners. Call ahead and see if one is going on; they're always fun and educational with delicious food. My favorite meal in the world is there, and if you see the pork chop on the menu, tell them you want it the way Bernie gets it, complete with the glass of Old Grand Dad.

**Bristol Bar & Grille** (Downtown)–614 West Main Street–Louisville, KY 40202–502.582.1995 (www.bristolbarand grille.com). This has been a popular eatery in Louisville for as long as I can remember, and they have several locations around town. The one on Main is officially on the Urban Bourbon Trail now since it's right on Whiskey Row.

**Buck's**–425 W. Ormsby (in the Mayflower)–Louisville, KY 40202–502.637.5284 (www.bucksrestaurantandbar.com). This is a lil' hidden gem in the city, located in Old Louisville just off Fourth in Ormsby in the historic Mayflower building. Buck always liked "moon gardens," which are all-white flower gardens, so the place is just covered in white flowers. Dinner is served on all kinds of fine china that doesn't match, which is pretty cool, and Rick Bartlett (my singing partner Robbie's brother) plays piano and sings there almost every night.

**Derby Café at the Kentucky Derby Museum**–704 Central Avenue–Louisville, KY 40202–502.634.0858 (derbycafe.com). So many people come to this museum at historic Churchill Downs, and with all the special events that take place here, it just made sense. Come see and drink history here at the Café.

**Dish on Market**–434 W. Market Street–Louisville, KY 40202–502.315.0669 (www.dishonmarket.com). My buddy Anderson opened this place, and it's got a brisk breakfast and lunch business Monday through Friday, and they serve up damn good grub. In addition to breakfast and lunch, they have happy hour until 7:00 pm. The restaurant has a nice little bourbon selection, and Anderson has been to several of the distilleries and has a genuine passion for bourbon.

**Doc Crow's Southern Smokehouse and Raw Bar**–127 W. Main Street–Louisville, KY 40202–502.587.1626 (www.doccrows.com). Located in historic Whiskey Row, this restaurant celebrates seafood from the coast and diverse BBQ styles from the interior. Located right next to the Yum Center and the Second Street Bridge.

**Ramsi's Cafe on the World**–1293 Bardstown Road–Louisville, KY 40204 (www.ramsiscafe.com) Ramsi, the son of the only female liquor-store owner in Jerusalem, moved to Kentucky and married a local girl, and they've raised their family above this popular eatery in the heart of the Highlands. It truly does feature more than 100 dishes from all over the globe, including the Cubean Burrito (favorite of Rob, my buddy from Heaven Hill), hummus and (my favorite) the Jamaican Jerk chicken sandwich. Ramsi's features a great Sunday brunch, and as they are part of the Urban Bourbon Trail, you can taste bourbons from any distillery you visit while there.

**Village Anchor**–11507 Park Road–Louisville, KY 40202–502.708.1850 (www.villageanchor.com). Located in an old train station in the fashionable Anchorage neighborhood, the Village Anchor is a cool old building with great comfort food. Downstairs is the Sea Hag bar, and Kyle is the resident bourbon guru. Kevin owns the place and has already won a few awards for this, his first-ever restaurant.

So there you have it, the Urban Bourbon Trail (that's just fun to say, isn't it?). Just remember that several of the accounts on the Urban Bourbon Trail are busier for happy hour or dinner. Blu Café (Marriott), Proof and Bourbon's Bistro have the better later-in-the-evening scene, especially Thursday at Blu with Hickory and the boys playing bluegrass 'til midnight.

There are also several locally owned bars and restaurants you should check out. I'm always one to support the little guy, and the local guy, too. If you want to go to where the locals drink and hang out to get a real taste of Louisville, I'd suggest taking a two-mile car ride to the Highlands to one of these accounts. It's also quite a bit more affordable to hang out and have many of the same bourbons at these places, and they all have excellent bourbon selections.

OUT OF DOWNTOWN:

**The Back Door**–1250 Bardstown Road–Louisville, KY 40204 (in the back of Mid City Mall). John Dant owns the place, and it is a favorite hangout for locals. Six pool tables, darts and Golden Tee golf all contribute to make this a great place to hang out with friends. They boast a really nice bourbon selection, and Chris, Dave, Hunter, Flash, Queenie, Carrie, Mary, Steve and the whole staff will give you suggestions on drinks and bourbons. They have Old Grand Dad and just about everything there, as well as some of the best pub grub in town. Helpful hint: Don't order a double, you're getting one anyway. Prices are low there. They are only closed one night a year: New Years Eve. Can you believe it? I asked John why, and he said it was because he got tired of babysitting amateurs. There should be a sign on the front door saying "Welcome to the Back Door, open 364 days a year, closed New Year's Eve. PROFESSIONALS ONLY."

**Diamonds (No 2)** – 630 Barrett Ave.-Louisville, KY 40204 between Broadway and Baxter Ave. Facebook page under Diamond Pub and Billiards. Eighteen Diamond Pool tables; that's 18, folks. If you're serious about playing pool, this is the place for you, and it's a great place to watch sports. Live music just like the Diamonds No. 1 in St. Matthews, and yes, my singing partner Robbie and I just might be singing there sometime, and Hickory plays there, too, so keep an eye out. Jared runs the joint, and Griff usually has his UK shirt on somewhere around the place.

*Me and Robbie Bartlett – Come see us at Diamonds!*

**Highlands Tap Room**–1279 Bardstown Road–Louisville, KY 40204 (across from Mid City Mall and Skyline Chili). Tommy owns the place, and Kevin, Sheila and Will are my buddies there who bartend. The Tap Room is known for the most fun karaoke in town. They have a decent bourbon selection as well and a great outdoor area for conversation and watching folks on Bardstown Road...good people watching.

**Left Field Lounge** – 2282 Bardstown Road–Louisville, KY 40204-facebook page under **Left Field Lounge**. Awesome little hole-in-the-wall bar where I watch the UK ball games. Bartenders Bill, Lee and Chelsea are always attentive and colorful,to say the least, as are us regulars there. Eddie from Shenanigan's owns the joint, and so you know they got Old Grand Dad and some awesome bourbons, since I go in there.

**Molly Malone's Irish Pub**–933 Baxter Avenue–Louisville, KY 40204. This is an authentic Irish bar with authentic Irish folk working there. Donnell owns the place, and they've done so well they've opened a second Louisville location in St. Matthews, and another in Covington, Kentucky. They have a trivia night early in the week and great live music on the weekends.

**Nachbar**–969 Charles Street–Louisville, KY 40204 (at Krieger St.). They have an absolutely brilliant beer selection and a nice bourbon list. Retro is big there, so Old Fitzgerald, Old Forester and Old Grand Dad are popular. Chill hipster scene. One of my favorite places to take visitors just to have a nice beer and a shot, and to hang out with friends. It's where all the cool kids hang out.

**O'Shea's**–956 Baxter Avenue–Louisville, KY 40204. Another great Irish pub. Tommy O'Shea owns this place, as well as Flanagan's down one block and Patrick O'Shea's downtown at Second and Main. If the weather is nice, they have one of the best outside areas in the whole state!

**Outlook Inn**–916 Baxter Avenue–Louisville, KY 40204 (at Christy)–Look for the Falls City Beer sign outside (my dad and grandfather's brewery). There are a couple pool tables in the back, but this is just a great little corner bar. They also have Falls City Beer on tap there, so have an old one (old Grand Dad) and a cold one (Falls City).

**Shenanigan's Pub**–1611 Norris Place (at Deerwood Ave.). Good food, drink and 16 flat screens to watch all the sports and live music most weekends. Eddie owns the joint, and Rick keeps it rollin'.

### St. Matthews Area – Lots of locally owned pubs and eateries, only 5 miles from downtown

**Diamond Pub and Billiards**–3814 Frankfort Avenue-Louisville, KY 40207-(Facebook page is Diamond Pub and Billards). Great pool hall and music hall with about a dozen Diamond Pool tables (thus the name), including two regulation big boy tables. They have a great bourbon selection and live music almost every night. Lloyd bartends there during the day shift, and at night Kevin sings — ask him to sing "Sara Smile", he crushes it! DZ will probably be bartending on the patio bar, Wes out front, with MC and Blake weaving in and out keeping things straight, and Jason walking the floor as the enforcer. Melissa will probably be drinking some Pucker Vodka listening to the music too along with the owner, Griff, and Jared will be busy running the joint. Griff loves Knob Creek Single Barrel Reserve, so take his lead, buy him and you one, and enjoy yourselves there.

**Frankfort Avenue Beer Depot**–3204 Frankfort Avenue–Louisville, KY 40206 (directly next door and shares a parking lot with Patrick's). It just serves beer (thus the Beer Depot) and has some of the best BBQ in town. Known for "Beerhalla" miniature golf out back, since the "Valhalla" golf course is here in Louisville, too. Relive your own Ryder Cup at FABD, as the locals call it.

**Gerstle's Pub**–3801 Frankfort Avenue–Louisville, KY 40207. With great live music and a great bar, this is one of the most recognized neighborhood bars in Louisville. My cousin's band, Dallas Alice, performs there from time to time, as do other great acts. It's the home of the Minnesota Vikings, so if you're a fan of the Vik's, get your ass to Gerstle's to watch the game. You can go down and taunt the Packers fans at

Dutch's at half-time. The Pranksters perform there, and they are one of the best bands on the entire planet, no joke. They are easily the best band playing on a Sunday night anywhere in the United States. They play every Wednesday and Sunday, but I really love Sundays. They also have Falls City Beer on tap there. The Pranksters play originals and cool covers. They've been together for like 100 years, so they nail everything they perform. They cover "The Walrus." I mean come on, if the Beatles were all here alive today, they couldn't play "The Walrus."

**Molly Malone's**–3900 Shelbyville Road–Louisville, KY 40207. This is Molly's St. Matthews location. If you follow soccer or rugby, this is going to be your spot. Molly's has a great beer selection and nice bourbons to choose from, too. Brendan runs this place, not from across the street but from across the pond in Ireland, and he's a great guy. The whole staff is terrific, and Molly's is always poppin' with fun people. The food is pretty damn good, too.

**Patrick's**–3202 Frankfort Avenue–Louisville, KY 40206. This is a little neighborhood pub just down the street from Gerstle's. It has pool tables and a nice little patio out back, and has one of the coolest beer coolers I've ever seen. It's an antique in the shape of a beer bottle, but it still keeps the beer nice and frosty cold.

**R Place Pub**–9603 Whipps Mill Road–Louisville, KY 40242. Known for its outdoor sand volleyball leagues, this bar is owned by Cres and Scott and is a great neighborhood hangout. Jim Beam's R&D folk have a volleyball team every year playing on Thursday nights, and the Pittsburgh Steelers fans pack in here for football season.

## PLACES TO EAT

Here are some suggestions of places to eat breakfast, lunch and dinner. Louisville is home to some of the best locally owned restaurants in the country. Per capita we have more restaurants and eat out more often than most cities in the nation.

## BREAKFAST PLACES:

**Ghyslain On Market**–721 East Market-Louisville (Behind Creation Gardens) 502.690.8645 (www.ghyslain.com/restaurants/ghyslain-market). Full service bistro with homemade gelato and an assortment of Ghyslain's gourmet chocolates. Monday-Sunday 7:00 a.m. to 9:00 p.m.

**North End Café**-1722 Frankfort Avenue-Louisville, KY 40206 (northendcafe.com). Located just a couple miles from downtown is a great neighborhood place with great food all day, but I really enjoy breakfast here. They also have a great bourbon selection. Don't be bashful about ordering a Bloody Mary and substituting bourbon for the vodka. It's one of my favorite cocktails. And they just opened a new location in the Highlands, 216 Bardstown Road.

**Toast on Market**-620 East Market-Louisville, KY 40202 (toastonmarket.com). Toast has great breakfast and is always popular any day of the week. Toast is just what a breakfast place should be. You may have to wait a little bit to get a table, but once you get one, it's not a drawn-out thing. It's where Goldilocks would enjoy breakfast; it's just right.

**Wagner's Pharmacy**–3113 South 4th Street (4th Street and Central)-Louisville, KY 40214. Since 1922, Churchill Downs is Wagner's and Wagner's is Churchill Downs, and yes, it's inside a pharmacy. It's the city's most famous breakfast joint, especially during Derby Week. Racing history drips from the walls and the ceiling. D. Wayne Lucas, Nick Zito, and other horse trainers and celebrities all pack in to this hole-in-the-wall joint across from the track to sop up gravy with biscuits and have some of the best sausage, eggs, and bacon, southern style.

## LUNCH/DINNER PLACES:

**610 Magnolia**–610 Magnolia Avenue-Louisville, KY 40208– 502.636.0783. (www.610magnolia.com). Chef/owner Edward Lee gives a contemporary approach to Southern cooking and it's farm to table. Six course prix-fixe, seasonal menu changes weekly. Don't just come in jeans—it is "smart casual," so be creative.

**August Moon**–2269 Lexington Road Louisville–KY 40206 (augustmoonbistro.com). A fusion of Chinese and Malaysian cuisine, renowned chef Peng S. Looi has been invited as a guest chef at the James Beard Foundation on numerous occasions. You can get an awesome dinner here, too, as you can imagine, with a very cool atmosphere. They have an *awesome* homemade chili pepper oil that is hot and spicy and just wonderful drizzled on anything.

**Bambi Bar**–2701 Bardstown Road–Louisville, KY 40205–This bar is famous for the Bambi Beer Walk and the Bambi Burger. It has one of the best dang burgers in town. The #1 has fries, the #2 has cheese, and the #3 comes with onion rings. It doesn't get any simpler than that. It's a dive bar, folks, so don't wear a tie or a dress, just put on your jeans and go on in.

**Bearno's by the Bridge**–131 W. Main Street (at the Second Street Bridge)–Louisville, KY 40206–502.584.7437. Bearno's serves pizza and Italian food, and sometimes acoustic acts there, too. It's a nice little bar to hang out or watch a ballgame.

**Bistro 301**–301 W. Market (Third and Market)–Louisville, KY 40206–502.584.8337–A great place with good food, Bistro is close to the Marriott and other downtown hotels and right across from the downtown convention center. Matt's the owner, and he's a good guy who likes his bourbon. I did his first bourbon dinner there, and it was a really fun, delicious experience. Look for more in the future.

**Bistro Le Relais**–2817 Taylorsville Road–Louisville, KY 40205–502.451.9020 (lerelaisrestaurant.com). Located in historic Bowman Field, Louisville's original airport, the Bistro is fine dining with exquisite French cuisine. Anthony Dike is the owner. The bistro has first-class service and an intimate, 1940s art-deco interior reminiscent of the café from the movie *Casablanca*.

**Eiderdown** –983 Goss Avenue (at Goss and Krieger), Louisville – 502.290.2390 (www.eiderdowngermantown.com). Owned by the folks who also own Nachbar one block up,

Eiderdown is in the Schnitzelburg neighborhood, and German beers are big here (of course!). The food is awesome. If you want a bourbon, they don't have it here, but they do at Nachbar, an easy walk for an Old Grand Dad or Old Fitz.

**El Camino** –1314 Bardstown Road, Louisville. (www.elfreakingcamino.com). This is the second location for the Silver Dollar folks, and they hit it just right with the Tequila/Mezcal heavy bar with a nice bourbon selection. Think California beach tacos and all that great surfing culture and food and put that in the middle of the Highlands, add great cocktails by Suzie and Larry and you get El Camino.

**Garage**–700 E. Market Street, Louisville, KY–502.749.7100 (www.garageonmarket.com). Located in an old service station, you'll see a 1970 Camaro wrecked into an old Trans Am out front. This bar and eatery features wood-fired pizzas with a Southern perspective. It is owned by the same folks at 21c and Proof, so you know they did it up right.

**Gary's on Spring** –204 S. Spring St. Louisville, KY 40206–502.584.5533 (www.garysonspring.com). Contemporary American cuisine with casual fine dining and a damn nice appetizer menu and upstairs bar/lounge that I personally love with a nice selection of bourbons.

**Hammer Heads** –921 Swan St., Louisville, KY 40206 (Germantown, Swan Street near Breckinridge) (www.louisvillehammerheads.com). No reservations and limited seating, but worth the wait if you have one. Chefs and owners Chase Mucerino and Adam Burress prepare awesome food in an old dive bar that has reopened in Germantown. Cozy, fun atmosphere and great food. No bourbon here yet, but a great beer selection.

**Harvest**–624 E. Market Street, Louisville, KY–502.384.9090 (www.harvestlouisville.com). Decent bourbon selection, but the food is excellent and FRESH. They only use food harvested within a 100-mile radius of the restaurant, and they have a map and pictures up around the place of all the farmers they partner with. The menu changes often because of what is available, obviously. Pretty cool concept, and yes the food is excellent.

**Haymarket Whiskey Bar**–331 Market Street-Louisville, KY 40202-502.442.0523.A cool little live music joint that sells craft beer and great bourbons and whiskey. Beer garden, concert venue, bar. Matthew Landan owns the place and is very passionate about his craft beers; he's even gonna start making some there. He likes his old bourbons, too, so get an Old Grand Dad or J.T.S. Brown there anytime.

**Impellizzeri's Pizza**–1381 Bardstown Road, Louisville, KY 40204–502.454.2711 (impellizzeris.com). Famous in Louisville, and right in the Highlands. Impellizzeris Pizza uses only the finest and freshest ingredients, which is why it's no wonder they've been voted "Best of Louisville Magazine" a whopping SIX TIMES! They offer this award-winning pizza alongside a full menu of Italian-style dishes from appetizers to salads to hoagie sandwiches and mouth-watering pasta dishes. They've opened a new location on Main Street just down from the new Yum Center Arena, too.

**Jack Fry's**–1007 Bardstown Road–Louisville, KY 40204–502.452.9244 (jackfrys.com, at Baxter Avenue and Highland Avenue at the foot of the Highlands). Many locals will tell you that Jack Fry's is the best restaurant in Louisville, period. Great live jazz during the week, wonderful food, and the décor takes you back to the 1960s. It doesn't get much better than this.

**Jeff Ruby's**–325 W. Main Street–Louisville, KY 40202–502.584.0102 (jeffruby.com). Eat where O.J. can't. Jeff Ruby asked O.J. Simpson to leave his place a couple Derbys ago. He serves up some of the best steak and seafood around. My buddy Robbie Bartlett's band plays there almost every weekend. It's not cheap, but it's worth every penny.

**Kern's Korner**–2600 Bardstown Road–Louisville, KY 40205–was founded by Mr. Kern, who used to work with my dad at the Falls City Brewing Company. Kern's has great chili, soups and burgers and is a great place to hang out with the locals and have a casual lunch.

**Lilly's**–1147 Bardstown Road–Louisville, KY 40204 – 502.451.0447 (lillyslapeche.com). Lilly's bills itself as a Kentucky bistro, and its menu is shaped by the produce and meats available from community farms and its own organic garden. Lilly's is located right in the heart of the Highlands, just a couple miles from downtown hotels.

**Meta** – 425 W. Chestnut Street – Meta was opened by Jeremy Johnson here in town and it's in a cool spot that was previously a strip joint. They've made it a very legit cocktail bar in the same block as 8 UP. It's cool to hit both when you're in the block. No food here, but they serve awesome cocktails.

**Molly Malone's**–933 Baxter Avenue–Louisville, KY 40204– 502.473.1222 (mollymalonesirishpub.com). This is an authentic Irish pub with authentic Irish people. They have a pub quiz early in the week, and dining inside and out.

**O'Shea's Irish Pub**–(www.osheaslouisville.net).Wherever you find yourself either downtown, the Highlands or St. Matthews, you'll find one of these great fun pubs.

**Patrick O'Shea's**–123 West Main Street–Louisville, KY 40202– 502.708.2488 (www.osheaslouisville.net). At the foot of the Second Street Bridge, this gorgeous building is a great place for lunch or dinner. It's a great place to hang out downtown, as well.

**The Post** – 1045 Goss Avenue - Louisville (Germantown) - www.the postlouisville.com. My old poker buddy Nash and his wife opened this place, and it quickly became one of the places to go for great pizza. It has a good bar too with comfortable seating. This is just an all-around cool casual place to grab a whole pie or a slice of the day along with a good bourbon or beer.

**Seviche**–1538 Bardstown Road, Louisville, KY 40205 – 502.473.8560 (www.sevicherestaurant.com). Award-winning chef/owner Anthony Lamas shows off his Latin culture with his modern flare. Seviche is a Louisville local favorite, so better make a reservation, although the bar is a great experience, too. I saw Anthony and his crew down at Epcot Food & Wine Festival this past year.

**Silver Dollar**–1761 Frankfort Avenue, Louisville, KY 40206– 502.259.9540. Facebook page is under "The Silver Dollar." My buddy Larry Rice and his partners Shawn Cantley opened this awesome place in an awesome spot. Located in the renovated old Albert Stoll Fire House, Silver Dollar has a 42-foot-long bar made from reclaimed wood from old tobacco barns and distillery rackhouses. Awesome old bourbon choices like Old Grand Dad, Very Old Barton and Old Fitzgerald. The staff there are some of the best around, and the place is jamming every night. I love that the music is very Western and rockabilly and played on vinyl on a real turntable. The food is awesome too and matches the music with a chef-driven menu filled with the vivid flavors from the Southwest, dubbed "gastro-honky tonk" by our local food critic, who gave a glowing 3.5 star review (out of 4).

**Rye On Market** –900 E. Market Street, Louisville, KY 40206– 502.749.6200 (www.ryeonmarket.com). Right in the heart of the thriving area called NuLu, head chef William Tyler Morris came in from the Breslin Hotel in New York. Proprietor Michael Trager-Kusman is the driving force who never settles for second best.

**Wick's Pizza**–975 Baxter Avenue, Louisville, KY 40204– 502.458.1828 (wickspizza.com). Home of the "Big Wick," this is a Louisville favorite when it comes to pizza. It has good entertainment on the weekends, too.

## LEXINGTON, KENTUCKY

Lexington is a smaller city than Louisville, but it's just as much fun. I went to college there at the University of Kentucky. *The Bourbon Review* is published there, and it's the perfect place to stay when you visit the distilleries on the Eastern Shelf: Buffalo Trace, Woodford Reserve, Wild Turkey and Four Roses.

I'd suggest visiting Wild Turkey and Four Roses one day, and then Woodford Reserve and Buffalo Trace the next. Lexington doesn't have the equivalent of the Urban Bourbon Trail (yet), but there are a few places, including hotels, that carry a nice selection of bourbon.

## Downtown Lexington Hotels

**Crowne Plaza**–1375 S. Broadway, Lexington, KY 40504–859.255.4281. Just a mile or so down the road from the Hyatt, the Crowne Plaza Campbell House was renovated in 2005. Bogart's is the bar there, and it has a variety of bourbons.

**Gratz Park Inn  Lexington**–120 West Second Street, Lexington, KY 40507 (www.gratzparkinn.com). Gorgeous locally owned hotel, right downtown where ya need to be. It's the only historic boutique hotel in Lexington, and it's just a couple blocks off Main Street on land first settled in 1781.

**Hyatt Regency**–401 W. High Street, Lexington, KY 40507–859.253.1234. The Hyatt is right across the street from the Hilton and ideally located near downtown watering holes. The Hyatt is actually connected to Rupp Arena where the University of Kentucky plays basketball, so if you want to see Wildcat basketball madness up close, go for it! They've got a very nice lobby bar in the atrium with a nice bourbon selection, so it's a great place to start or end your evening on your Lexington visit.

**Lexington Hilton**–369 W. Vine Street, Lexington, KY 40507–859.231.9000. This hotel is right in the heart of Lexington and within walking distance to many fine restaurants and watering holes. It has the Bigg Blue Martini Bar off the lobby–a great name for being in the home of the Big Blue Kentucky Wildcats. The bar also has a nice bourbon selection and live music often on the weekends.

**Marriott Griffin Gate**–1800 Newtown Pike, Lexington, KY 40511. Located a few miles out of town and right off I-64, this hotel boasts a great golf course that was host to a couple Senior PGA Tour events. Large hotel, nice bar, too.

## Where to go for a cocktail/after-dinner drinks:

**Al's Bar**–601 N. Limestone, Lexington, KY 40508. Josh is one of the owners and he prides himself on specializing in local "everything," from ingredients in food to over 30 bourbons. He also hosts a great variety of local music talent nearly every night of the week. Their house specialty cocktail is called the "Kentucky Cocktail," which is your favorite bourbon mixed with a local ginger ale called Ale 8. Can I suggest an Old Grand Dad with that, anyone?

**Austin City**–2350 Woodhill Drive–Lexington, KY 40509 (austincitysaloon.com). Just a couple miles from downtown Lexington, this is a shit-kicking country bar with great bands. My buddy Puddin' Howell plays there regularly. This is where Troy Gentry of Montgomery Gentry won a contest sponsored by Jim Beam, and to this day, Jim Beam and Montgomery Gentry have a mutual partnership spreading good music and good bourbon wherever they travel.

**Belle's Cocktail House** – 152 Market Street, Lexington. Larry Redmond from Bluegrass Tavern and the boys from *Bourbon Review* magazine have a bourbon-heavy hand in this awesome weekend destination. Come on in and enjoy the music, drinks and diverse crowd.

**Bluegrass Tavern**–115 Cheapside Street, Lexington, KY 40507. Also owned by Larry Redmond, this bar offers more bourbon and American whiskey than any other bar, period. That would be 187; Larry's counted them. Led by head mixologist, Chris, all the bartenders wear a white shirt, black trousers and black tie, and they are eager to help you select a bourbon and/or a cocktail if you need such a suggestion. I've helped train the staff there, too, since I've done a couple bourbon tastings there. It's located right on the pavilion downtown on Cheapside, so in nice weather it's a huge outdoor patio party on the whole block.

**Cheapside Tavern**–131 Cheapside Street, Lexington, KY 40507–859.254.0046 (www.cheapsidebarandgrill.com). Good food and live music, too. It's located on the opposite end of the block from Redmond's. My Louisville buddy and singing partner, Robbie Bartlett, performs there from time to time. Cheapside Street has been turned into a pavilion and is one rockin' outside area when the weather permits, which is often!

**Jakes Cigar Bar**–263 East Brannon Road–Nicholasville, KY 40356 (www.jakescigarbar.com). Located just 10 minutes south of downtown Lexington on Nicholasville Road (US 27) in the Brannon Crossing Shopping Centre. Jack Glancy owns the joint and it's only been open since April 2010, but it's the only place you can go in Lexington (or Louisville, for that matter) to enjoy fine cigar brands from all over the world, along with a choice of 50 bourbons. They don't have food, so it's a perfect after-dinner stop. Take the short drive out to Brannon Crossing and have a great smoke, great bourbon and stellar conversation.

**Parlay Social**–257 W. Short Street (right next to Dudley's), Lexington, KY 40507–859.244.1932 (www.parlay-social.com). Cool cocktail bar with live music. I did the first bourbon tasting there and met the owners Bob Estes and Joy Breeding, and it's a very cool place to enjoy bourbon.

**The Grapevine**–4101 Tates Creek Centre Drive–Lexington, KY 40517. The Grapevine is a comfortable neighborhood bar with good pub grub. They also have TVs to watch all the Wildcats games and a stage with live music, where the owner of the joint gets up and plays, too. FUN!

## BREAKFAST

**Tally Ho's**–395 S. Limestone, Lexington, KY 40508. The only place for authentic college grub! This is a little greasy spoon, where extra grease is no extra charge. It takes me back to my college days every time. It's one of the few places in the world where I order a chocolate milkshake with breakfast! Yummie!

## BREAKFAST/LUNCH

**Ramsey's**–496 E. High Street, Lexington, KY 40507–859.259.2708. There are three other Ramsey's in town, so check out their website for them (www.ramseysdiners.com). Ramsey's offers great breakfast and just good food all the way around. Sunday mornings are particularly fun with their brunch menu. Plan on waiting awhile though, but even waiting for breakfast there is kind of cool.

## DINNER

**Baker's 360**–201 East Main Street, Lexington, KY 40507–859.523.7797 (www.bakers360.us). Great steakhouse and seafood. A buddy of mine from San Diego recently went there and said it was the best sushi he's ever had, and he's from California! After dinner it turns into a nightclub and bar. Really cool new spot in Lexington.

**Dudley's**–259 W. Short Street, Lexington, KY 40502–859.252.1010 (www.dudleysrestaurant.com). Dudley's Restaurant has been a mainstay on the Lexington gathering and dining scene for the last 28 years. Great food and atmosphere. I like it!

**Malone's/Harry's**–3347 Tates Creek Drive, Lexington, KY 40502–859.335.6500 (www.malonesrestaurant.com, in the Landsdowne Shopping Center). Always makes the top 10 great steak houses in the United States by all the inflight magazines I see when I'm traveling around the country. Awesome seafood, too. Malone's is the more formal (although dress is casual), and Harry's is the hangout bar area with a great menu as well. Malone's ownership is proud to claim that they carry prime beef that's considered to be the top 1.5-2% of the beef served in the whole world! Now that's a statement. They have the Big Lex cocktail, which is Maker's Mark bourbon with Kentucky Proud blackberries and strawberries infused into a simple syrup with a splash of 7UP and a squeeze of lemon and lime.

**Merrick Inn**–1074 Merrick Drive, Lexington, KY 40502–859.269.5417. Merrick Inn is without a doubt the oldest and most traditional dining experience in Lexington. The bar area and patio are an experience all on their own.

**Portofino**–249 E. Main Street, Lexington, KY 40507–859.253.9300. Portofino is in a nicely renovated building downtown and serves northern Italian food. If you're looking for some good wine on your visit to bourbon country, know that Portofino earned the *Wine Spectator* Award eight years in a row, from 2003 through 2010, for their varied selection.

Sal's–3373 Tates Creek Road, Lexington, KY 40502 (www.bluegrasshospitality.com). Actually in the same shopping center as Malone's and Drake's. That's how good these places are: They compete directly with themselves! It's just a great experience, and once you go, it won't be for the last time. The outdoor patio at Sal's is always hopping from Keeneland's spring meet through the summer, of course, and until the fall meet ends before it gets too cold. Trust me, this is where all the pretty people are.

## SOME GOOD PACKAGE LIQUOR STORES FOR WHEN YOU VISIT THE BOURBON TRAIL...AND YOU WILL VISIT!

So you're in Kentucky visiting distilleries, and you'd like to purchase some bourbon to take back with you? Where do you go? Also, you're in Kentucky, so certainly there are some bourbons you can buy only in this state, and not where you're from. Knob Creek and Old Grand Dad are my two favorites, but you can certainly buy those in almost every part of the country.

## THE BOURBON CAPITAL OF THE WORLD

You'll drive right through Bardstown when you go to visit Heaven Hill, Thomas Moore, Independent Stave Cooperage, Maker's Mark or Jim Beam, so you might as well stop and buy some great bourbons that you can only find here in the Bourbon Capital of the World. And don't forget to visit Bardstown during Bourbon Festival, which is always the third weekend in September.

## STORES IN BARDSTOWN

Toddy's–100 S. 4th Street-Bardstown, KY 40004 – 502.348.1444. This was Toddy Beam's store (does the name sound familiar?), and it's a small 'lil store in downtown Bardstown that is just chocked FULL of bourbon...as well it should, being in the Bourbon Capital of the World.

Liquor World–93 N. Salem Drive (just off Hwy 245)-Bardstown, KY 40004- 502.349.7560. This store is a little larger and  has more of what Toddy's carries.

**Kroger's**-102 W. John Rowan Boulevard (Hwy 245 at N. 3$^{rd}$ St.)-Bardstown, KY 40004- 502.348.2977. This is located smack dab on Hwy 245, which you'll most likely take to get to Heaven Hill and Maker's Mark.

### STORES IN LOUISVILLE

If you're staying in Louisville, you'll probably choose a hotel downtown and then venture out to grab a bite to eat in the Highlands or out East, so here are stores that will be close by. Stores in Louisville tend to be bigger; you'll get a kick out of just how BIG the bourbon spreads are in the stores. Some even have sections for each category of bourbon. You'll be in bourbon heaven.

### *DOWNTOWN*

**Theater Square Marketplace**–651 S. 4$^{th}$ Street, just behind the Brown Hotel. It's a small store, but there's a cool market, bagel shop and damn-nice restaurant there. George and Eric own the place. It's a great store, and one of the few that's located right in the heart of downtown.

### *HIGHLANDS*

**Karem Deeb/Morris' Deli**–2228 Taylorsville Road (Bear to the left off Bardstown and Trevillian at the McDonald's) 502.458.1668. Karem Deeb is the favorite store of my good friends Paul and Amber Halloran. It's in the Lake Side area of town, just a couple miles down Bardstown Road, just over the Highlands. Morris' Deli has some of the best country ham sandwiches, so make a lunch date of it. It's a small store, too, but it has a decent bourbon selection, and it's close to downtown hotels.

**Old Town Liquors**–1529 Bardstown Road–502.451.8591. It's just about 2.5 miles from downtown in the heart of the Highlands, which is where you'll probably be going to eat, anyway. Gordo owns the place, and although he's known for his wine selection, he carries a nice bourbon selection, too. Bring your dog—he's always got a water dish out and treats for your pooch.

These next stores are larger stores with bigger bourbon spreads.

*EAST END*

**Liquor Barn St. Matthews**–4301 Shelbyville Road 40207-502.897.7773. Baker runs this store and he's a bourbon nut. He has selected several barrels of Knob Creek, Four Roses and others for his own personal single-barrel selections. You can also get growlers of Falls City Beer (the beer company where my dad worked for 45 years, and which my grandfather and 12 other saloon keepers founded in 1905).

**Party Mart**–4808 Brownsboro Road-40207-502.895.4446.Jerry Rogers owns the place, and he's a wine guy from way back, but he loves his bourbon, too. He's got a terrific bourbon spread, and you'll find some great ones that you can only get here in Kentucky. Party Mart is about a 15-minute drive from downtown, but it's worth the ride.

**Westport Whiskey & Wine**–1115 Herr Lane-40222-502.708.1313. My buddy Chris Zaborowski is the owner/operator, and he's really into education. He hosts regular spirits/wine education "classes" there, and I and other ambassadors and master distillers have all done several tastings there. Chris and his staff are very educated and helpful and can set you up with some great bourbons that you can only get here in Kentucky.

**Liquor Barns Louisville**–Voted the best package store for whisk[e]y in the U.S. for 2012 *Whisky Magazine*'s Icons of Whisky Awards. These are large box stores with awesome selections, great cheeses, and all kinds of specialty foods. Your jaw will drop when you see the bourbon selection; the stores have many kinds of Knob Creek and other great single-barrel selections that Brad has picked out himself. There are three locations:

**Fern Valley**-3420 Fern Valley Road (on the way to and from Bardstown and distilleries off I-65 Fern Valley exit) 40213-502.968.1666.

**Hurstbourne**-1850 S. Hurstbourne Parkway- 40220-502.491.0753.

**Springhurst**–4301 Towne Center Drive (Westport Rd at I-265) 40241–502.491.0753.

**Evergreen Liquors**–12017 Shelbyville Road-40243-502.244.1957. If you go out to the Village Anchor on the Urban Bourbon Trail, you'll be right near this store. I like it because they only put bourbons in their bourbon section—not Jack, Crown or SoCo—just bourbons, and they also have a dedicated bonded bourbon section.

STORES IN LEXINGTON

**Liquor Barns**–Three locations. Icons of Whisky 2012 award winner (Best in the U.S.).

**Hamburg Pavillion**–1837 Plaudit Place (at Man O' War Blvd) 40509- 859.294.5700.

**Harrodsburg Road**-921 Beaumont Centre Parkway (at New Circle Rd) 40513-859.223.1400.

**Richmond Road**–3040 Richmond Road-40509-859.269.4170.

**Thoroughbred Shop**–2005 Versailles Road (We pronounce that "Ver-sayles" here) 40504- 859.254.038. Thoroughbred Shop is an Icons of Whisky 2012 award winner (Highly Commended U.S.A.). They always have a great selection of bourbons, with some that are not stocked at other stores. Handy location for when you are visiting Buffalo Trace Distillery and Woodford Reserve.

**Red Dot Liquors**–1139 U.S. 127-Frankfort, KY 40601-502.223.5054. My buddy Michael at Silver Dollar says stopping here is never a disappointment when it comes to bourbons that are either hard to come by or are new and different.

# 7

# How to Host a Bourbon Tasting at Your Home

*"They say that some of my stars drink whiskey. I have found that the ones that drink milk shakes don't win many ballgames."*
– Casey Stengel

Now that you know about the history and heritage of our native spirit, and you know how to read a label and find your favorite bourbons, you're going to want to show off your knowledge and host a bourbon tasting for your friends and family. The first thing you'll want to do is figure out a fun tasting of four or five bourbons/whiskies. That might sound like a lot of alcohol, but if you only pour a quarter-ounce of bourbon in each tasting cup, it's equivalent to just one drink. You'll want to start with the lowest-proof bourbon and go up to the highest proof. If you start with the higher-proof bourbons and go lower, their more intense flavors will overpower those of the lower-proof bourbons. Always drink smart and be aware of your guests; if they need a lift home, of course provide one.

Not all of your guests will be bourbon drinkers, so you'll want to have drinks for them as well. You might want to have a featured cocktail for them to try. A delicious cocktail would be Ms. Annis' Bourbon Sour since you can batch them and pour them out as your guests arrive. It's a very refreshing cocktail that even vodka and gin drinkers will enjoy.

Appetizers are a must since you will be sampling spirits. Various sliced meats, cheeses and crackers are always good, and then whatever your favorite apps are for any party.

Map out the bourbons you'd like to sample. It's best to start with a younger bourbon, either 80 or 86 proof, and then move up in age and/or proof. Remember that some bourbons are high rye bourbons (Old Grand Dad, Basil Hayden's, Four Roses), and some use wheat instead of rye (Maker's Mark, W.L. Weller, Van Winkle). And then you have the single-barrel and small-batch bourbons (Blanton's, Knob Creek, Evan Williams Vintage, etc.).

Here are some tastings I've done in the past just as an example for you:

### SAMPLE ONE — STAY BONDED: TASTING OF BOTTLED IN BOND WHISKIES

Mellow Corn Bottled in Bond Corn Whiskey

Evan Williams Bottled in Bond Bourbon

Rittenhouse Rye Bottled in Bond

Henry McKenna – 10-year Bottled in Bond


### SAMPLE TWO — THE EVOLUTION OF BOURBON

Georgia Moon unaged Corn Whiskey

Mellow Corn Bottled in Bond Corn Whiskey

Bernheim Wheat Whiskey

Evan Williams Bottled in Bond Bourbon

Elijah Craig Bourbon


Whatever you choose, it will be fun putting bourbons and whiskies together to taste. Pick one or two that you've never tasted before, so you can experience it along with your friends during the tasting.

The Stay Bonded Tasting is a great one because you can see and taste the difference in Corn Whiskey, Bourbon Whiskey and Rye Whiskey. It also shows how a used barrel affects a whiskey (Mellow Corn) compared to a brand new, charred barrel (the other three). Then you can taste the difference between the three recipes with them all at four years old and 100 proof. Finally, you can see what six additional years of aging does with a bourbon whiskey for difference in Evan Williams Bottled in Bond and Henry McKenna Bottled in Bond.

For the Evolution of Bourbon Tasting, it follows the story of how bourbon went from uaged corn whiskey to bourbon as told in this book in Chapter 5.

Now look at your guest list and see how many people are coming and multiply that number by five or six or however many bourbons/whiskies you will be tasting. If you have five whiskies to taste and you have two or three people over, you'll need five glasses for each plus yourself; so you'll need 20 glasses/cups. If you have 15 or 20 people coming, you will need 100 glasses/cups for the tasting. Not many people have 100 shot glasses or wine glasses, so in that case I'd go to the liquor/party store and buy hard plastic or two-ounce or two-and-a-half-ounce shot glasses. They usually come in packages of 50 and cost three or four dollars each.

Next you will need to craft a "tasting mat" for the glasses/cups to sit on. You can make one yourself by using a blank sheet of paper and, with a Sharpie pen, tracing around one of the plastic glasses to make a circle (see my sample on the next page). If there are five bourbons in your tasting, trace five glass-sized circles on the mat with a Sharpie, and then put the name of the bourbon down in the order left to right, using one or two columns. You can print the name of each bourbon/whiskey under the circle. You also might want to note the age and proof and whether it's a bourbon, scotch, rye, Irish, etc.

Put a cup on each circle and pour out the bourbon for your guests right before you all sit down. You don't want to pour more than 30 minutes before you sit down, as that little amount of whiskey in the glass will be exposed to the air and can turn it cloudy. You're only pouring a quarter-ounce or so in each glass. You can use a jigger to pour them out accurately if you prefer, or just use a speed pourer. You will also want to have small bottles of water for your guests so they can add water to the bourbon if they like or just sip between tastes. Crackers on the table would be good, too, so guests can cleanse between tastes if they wish.

Then lead your guests in a tasting. Here's how I'd lead them for each brand, with a little bit about what flavors they will be discovering in each expression.

Start out by telling them that bourbon and rye whiskey are truly American creations. Canadian Whiskey has different grains distilled separately and then blended together. Scotch and Irish whiskies use only barley. Bourbon uses predominantly corn, rye and barley, all ground and cooked, fermented, and distilled *together*. Rye uses those same grains cooked, fermented, and distilled together, but the predominant grain in the recipe is rye.

Corn is the native crop of North America, and because of that and its rich history and heritage in helping to form this country, Congress declared bourbon the native spirit of the United States. President Lyndon Baines Johnson signed it into law in 1964. So not only is it delicious to drink bourbon, it's your patriotic damn duty to drink bourbon! Also share with them some of your stories of bourbon: the proof story, George Washington and Jacob Beam, how the barrel first became charred, and how bourbon got its name.

There are certain flavors you get from the grains. You get the sweetness and the full body from the corn. Rye brings a really nice spice flavor. Think of eating some corn bread, and then some rye bread. This will help you imagine the different flavors of corn and rye. We use just a little bit of barley, and we use it mostly for the starches to help convert the sugars into alcohol by the yeast, so we are getting little or no flavor from the barley. If the distiller uses wheat instead of rye, more of the sweetness of the corn will come through, so wheated bourbons are typically softer and sweeter than rye bourbons.

Aging the bourbon in the charred barrels is responsible for 75% of the flavor of the finished product. All of the red/amber color of bourbon and rye comes from the barrel. The liquor goes in the barrel clear like vodka, and years later the natural sugars in the wood impart the color and flavors to the whiskey. Wood notes you want to look for in these whiskies are vanilla, maple, caramel, ginger, various toasted nuts and oak. Some people with astute noses and taste buds will taste different flavors like leather, tobacco, peppermint, and on and on, but they all come from the interaction of the grains with the barrel. The length of time it spends in the barrel will dictate how many wood notes are in the whiskey. It takes six years to start getting big vanilla notes in a bourbon. So if you taste really pronounced vanilla notes, then that bourbon is probably six or more years old. If you taste more citrus notes in a bourbon, that bourbon is more than likely four or five years old in the barrel.

So let's taste these and see what notes we get. Booker Noe used to tell folks to use these four steps in tasting bourbons.

**Step One:**  Look at the color and compare it to the others on the mat. The darker the color, the longer the bourbon has been aged and the higher proof it will be compared to the lighter ones on the mat.

**Step Two:**  Nose the bourbon/whiskey. Put your nose into the glass, but part your lips so you are not taking all that high-proof alcohol up your nose. This isn't wine, its high-proof alcohol with many layers of aromas and flavors, so don't take it all in your nose at once.

**Step Three:**  Place your tongue on the side of the glass and put enough whiskey in your mouth to get to the middle of your tongue and then "chew" it. This will achieve the same result as "swishing," but since it is high proof, the chewing will distribute the spirit to your entire palate. Fred Noe, Booker's son, calls this the "Kentucky Chew," and it's something his dad taught him. It works really well in tasting bourbon.

**Step Four:**  Assess the finish. Is it short? Medium? Long? Is it empty, does it fade away cleanly or linger? Short finishes usually dictate lighter proof and/or younger aging. For some people a short finish is preferred to a long finish. You just don't want an empty finish or one that is metallic or unpleasant.

**Finish off the tasting with the "Bourbon Pledge."** This is something I wrote a couple years ago, and it really helps to emphasize to people that bourbon is the native spirit of the United States. It also ends the tasting on a really nice note.

You can copy the pledge from the book here, put four on a page, and print it at Kinko's, too.

---

**THE BOURBON PLEDGE**

I pledge to open my heart and my taste buds

to the native spirit of the United States: bourbon!

I acknowledge the history

and heritage of this unique spirit.

I understand that all bourbon is whiskey,

but not all whiskey is bourbon.

I pledge to always have

bourbon whiskey available:

For those who arrive as strangers

yet leave as friends,

And for those who arrive as friends

and leave as family.

This I pledge from this taste forward.

So raise your favorite bourbon to salute our

country's native spirit...BOURBON...Cheer's, ya'll!

---

Now that you've educated your friends about the great joys of our native spirit, you're ready for the next stage of bourbon party planning.

## HOW TO HOST A KENTUCKY DERBY PARTY IN YOUR HOME

Do you want to have a Kentucky Derby party? Of course you do! Big hats and bourbon: a winning combination. It's a great party theme, and you get to watch the event live on TV. Over the years I've noticed the best Derby parties I've thrown and attended include betting, cocktails and, of course, a little food. So here are some suggestions for your Derby party.

## BETTING

Betting makes everything more fun. Why do you think Jai Lai has lasted so long? Thanks to technology you can bet on the big race as well as all the other races at Churchill Downs all day long. Remember there's a race following the Derby too. You can make live bets, get track odds and even see a program of all the races by setting up an account at www.twinspires.com.

I suggest setting up your account a day or two prior to first Saturday in May just to make sure it's all set to go. Encourage your guests to set up their own accounts too, so they're not all mooching off you. Or, if you are daring, you can play "bookie" and make a little money by taking a percentage of their winnings. It's easy, and there's no charge... well, unless you pick the wrong horses! Just tell your guests to bring their ipads or tablets to the party, and they can bet on the races on their own. It's so funny when the person who seems to think they know the most about the ponies loses, and the ones that bet on names and colors win!

## COCKTAILS

What's a party without cocktails? With the Derby it's all about bourbon cocktails too. So here are a few suggestions.

If you're expecting a fairly large crowd, it's nice to have a batched cocktail that you can prepare ahead of time. I get a two gallon container with a pour spout, but you can use a pitcher also. The Bourbon Sour Cocktail is great to batch up, and it's simple.

### Bourbon Sour

Get a can of frozen concentrated lemonade, and put that in the container. Then fill that same can with water, and add it to the container. Then fill that same can with pulp free orange juice and add that to the mix. Finally, fill the lemonade can with bourbon. Repeat all the steps as needed to fill up the container (or pitcher), and then all that's left to do is fill glasses with ice, pour and serve.

During Derby week thousands of people attend breakfast at the track, prepared by my buddy, Executive Chef David Danielson. Can you imagine a job where your first week back to work you have to feed around 400,000 people? But he does it every year with a smile on his face because he works at one of the most iconic venues on the planet (and the *Most Exciting Two Minutes In Sports*). While enjoying breakfast that week, folks get to watch the early morning workouts of the majestic thoroughbreds that will be competing in the Kentucky Oaks and Kentucky Derby. The following two cocktails compliment breakfast and brunch if you want to start your party early.

**Bourbon Lettuce and Tomato Cocktail**

This drink is quite simple since you've probably already made it hundreds of times. It's just a Bloody Mary using bourbon instead of vodka. You see vodka only adds alcohol to a Bloody Mary, but bourbon brings alcohol AND flavor to this classic drink. I use Evan Williams Black Label 86 proof bourbon in mine. It's a great everyday whiskey, and the five years of aging and 86 proof bring some good barrel notes to compliment and enhance the Bloody Mary's ingredients. If you want to get cute, garnish it with a baked slice of thick bacon!

**Dawn at The Downs Cocktail**

This is your elegant morning option. In a champagne flute pour one ounce of bourbon (I like Elijah Craig 12 for a little more spice or Evan Williams Single Barrel for a little more vanilla flavor), and then fill the rest of the glass with Martinelli's Sparkling Apple Cider. You can garnish with an apple slice to give it a little extra "oomph."

**And now for the main attraction: The Mint Julep**

Of course the Mint Julep is the official drink of the Kentucky Derby and has been since Larwin won the race in 1938 with Eddie Arcaro up in the stirrups. In 1938 that bourbon would more than likely have been "Bottled in Bond" since prohibition ended four years before, and it takes four years for a bourbon to meet this standard. "Bottled in Bond" is my favorite category in whiskey, so here's how I'd build my Mint Julep as taught by Suzie Hoyt over at the Silver Dollar in Louisville:

- Tear five or six mint leaves off the stalk and place them all in your palm.

- Clap them with the fingers of your opposite hand... this "wakes up" the mint.

- With a bar spoon, take those leaves and run them around the inside of your glass (or sterling silver mint julep cup) then discard the leaves.

- Add 0.5 ounces simple syrup.

- Add two ounces of Evan Williams White Label Bottled in Bond Bourbon.

- Fill the glass half way with crushed ice and give it a little stir, then continue adding ice to the brim and lightly pack it. Finally, add more crushed ice and crown the ice with your hand (a la snow cone style).

- Insert a full sprig of mint in the ice.

- Insert a short straw. (There's no other way to drink it because of all the crushed ice, plus the straw makes you put your nose close to the mint. Folklore says that the Mint Julep was the original reason for the invention of the straw).

### Another oldie but goodie: The Old Fashioned Cocktail

As bourbon history has it, around 1880 the Old Fashioned Cocktail was first made at the Pendennis Club in Louisville, KY (also the home of Henry Baines Sauce) when the distiller Colonel James Pepper ordered a drink from the bar. He asked for a bourbon cocktail made in the "old fashioned" way, meaning it was to be made with muddling fruit and using sugar and bitters. You'll need:

- Two ounces of whiskey (I like Evan Williams Single Barrel Bourbon or Bernheim Original Wheat Whiskey)

- Two dashes of Angostura® bitters

- A splash of water

- One teaspoon of sugar

- One maraschino cherry

- One orange wedge

   Mix the sugar, water and bitters in an old-fashioned glass. Drop in a cherry and an orange wedge. Muddle into a paste using a muddler or the back end of a spoon. Pour in the bourbon, fill with ice cubes and stir.

### A LITTLE FOOD

   You might want to give the food you serve at your party a little Louisville as well. One of our local treats is a spread called Benedictine. A Louisville restaurateur and cookbook author named Jennie Carter Benedict came up with this cucumber and crème cheese spread around 1900. You can use it for finger sandwiches or as a dip.

### Benedictine Spread

   You'll need:

- One large cucumber

- Eight ounces cream cheese, softened

- Two tablespoons grated onion

- 1/4 teaspoon salt

- One tablespoon mayonnaise

- A dash of green food coloring (optional)

   Pare, grate and drain the cucumber before combining with remaining ingredients in food processor. Refrigerate until needed.

### Pimiento Cheese Spread

   This is also good as either a dip or for finger sandwiches and is just as easy to make. You'll need:

- One cup shredded sharp Cheddar cheese

- 1/4 cup diced pimiento

- 1/4 cup mayonnaise

- Two teaspoons lemon juice

- Salt and black or red pepper, to taste

In a bowl, combine the cheese, pimiento, mayonnaise and lemon juice. Then add salt and pepper as desired. Beat with an electric mixer until well blended. This makes about 1 cup.

## Derby Pie

Derby Pie is a Kentucky Derby tradition, and it's passionately trademarked by Kern's Kitchen in Louisville, KY. So why not have the real deal for your party? You can order the authentic derby pie online their website.

 www.derbypie.com

## Bourbon Ice Cream

I like to make this special treat for my guests. It's very good and so damn easy. Put a couple scoops of ice cream in a wine glass and then pour a shot of bourbon over the top. That's it! Your guests will enjoy this awesome Kentucky dessert. I use vanilla ice cream which compliments the bourbon well. I have also used mint chocolate chip ice cream, which makes it a Mint Julep dessert. Garnish it with a sprig of mint or half of a Thin Mint cookie if you want to get fancy!

At the track it's not just the social event of the season, but also the fashion event of the season. It's all about the hats and attire. I like to have a more casual gathering, but I insist everyone (that's men included) wear a great Derby hat.

Celebrities are a big part of the race too, so why not put a red carpet out for your guests to arrive on? You could go so far as to have your kids and/or the neighbor kids ham it up and dress in fedoras and trench coats to pelt your guests on the way in with TMZ-style questions, "Mister Clooney...Is it true you're dating Lady Gaga?" They will all LOVE it including the kids!

Another great tip to remember is that the race is known as the *Run for the Roses*, so have roses everywhere for ambience.

The Kentucky Derby is like the Super Bowl and Mardi Gras all rolled into one event at Churchill Downs. You and your guests will have a blast, and you all just might win some money along the way. Finally, when your guests sing "My Old Kentucky Home" along with the 160,000 attendees of the even they are watching on TV, bourbon cocktails at the ready, don't be surprised if you spot a tear or two in your guests' eyes.

# 8

# My Favorite Bourbon Recipes

*"My grandmother is over 80 and still doesn't need glasses. She drinks right out of the bottle."* –Henny Youngman

There are several classic bourbon cocktails: julep, sour, old fashioned, Manhattan and highball. Each has a great history behind them. The oldest bourbon cocktail is probably the Julep.

## THE MINT JULEP

It's a Kentucky thing . . . or is it? The mint julep has certainly been associated with bourbon and Kentucky for a long time. Its origins are somewhat sketchy, but I'll throw in my two-cents worth on why it's so strongly connected to bourbon and the great Commonwealth of Kentucky .

A drink with the staying power and legendary status of the mint julep usually needs a few passionate bar keeps to either feature it on the menu and/or link it to an event. A couple good examples of this are the Pimm's Cup at the Napoleon House in the French Quarter and the Irish Coffee at Buena Vista in San Francisco. At both of these places, they make hundreds of their house specialties every single day! Who knows how it started, but when you visit either one, you've got to—no you MUST—have one of those drinks.

When you come to Kentucky, odds are you'll order an Old Fashioned (created at the Pendennis Club in Louisville), a Manhattan or, of course, a mint julep. One thing you'll find out is that we locals do not drink mint juleps on occasions other than Oaks Day and Derby Day. But with the popularity of the Bourbon Trail Distillery Tours and the Urban Bourbon Trail (21 bars that carry at least 50 bourbons on their bars), visitors have been wanting to sample this refreshing Southern delight.

The mint julep can be traced back to the Middle East from a drink called the julab made from water and rose petals. This practice probably started in order to make the water more palatable. Back then, water was the liquid of last resort. Unless you had a fresh stream on your property, you'd better be careful of the water you drank. That's one reason people drank beer/wine/spirits, added things like bitters, or brewed it and added leaves to it.

The julab certainly found its way to the New World, and the julep was born. The julep was a Southern drink, perhaps since its cousin, the mojito, was popular down in the Caribbean Islands. The mojito is similar to a mint julep; it's basically a mint julep with muddled limes added to the mint and rum used as the base spirit. I'm sure rum was used in some early versions of the mint julep. The bourbon-based mint julep evolved and became popular probably because of passionate people who loved it, such as the most notable and very well-liked politician from the great Commonwealth of Kentucky, Henry Clay. Mr. Clay served as United States senator on three separate occasions from 1807-1811, 1831-1842, and finally from 1849 until his death in 1852. He also served a term as secretary of state from 1825-1829. Senator Clay made the mint julep famous at the world-renowned Willard Hotel's Round Robin Bar in Washington DC. He famously dismissed a British naval officer's claim that rum or brandy would work as well as bourbon. Clay said of the mint julep, "The mint leaves fresh and tender, should be pressed against the goblet with the back of a silver spoon."

His fellow congressmen no doubt took that drink and shared it along with his passion to constituents in their districts, and I can imagine them saying something like, "This is what the good folks in Kentucky drink to cool off during those humid summers there in the Bluegrass State."

After the Civil War, Temperance Movement, WWI and Prohibition all but killed bourbon, Churchill Downs made the mint julep the "official drink" of the Kentucky Derby in 1938. The Kentucky Derby was and still is THE social event of the season, and is the epitome of fashion and style for all classes of folks. From factory workers to celebrities to royalty in front of all the media, the Derby leads the fashion and style for the upcoming year.

It just so happened that the year before, in 1937, the management of the track noticed that the well-dressed people were *stealing* the cool mint julep glasses from the bar! So ever since, they have sold the glass with the mint julep at Churchill Downs on Oaks and Derby Day. Today they sell 150,000 mint juleps in those two days alone, but it all started that first Saturday in May in 1938 when Lawrin won the garland of roses with Eddie Arcaro up in the stirrups.

Growing up, my parents would always go to the track on Derby Day to entertain guests of the brewery, so my dad's sisters would babysit us for the day. Aunt Bern taught me how to make mint juleps, and since I made them every year for us, I think I make a pretty damn good one. But like most Louisvillians, I only drink them on Oaks and Derby Day.

Sterling silver mint julep cups are also something that highlights this drink. I mean, what could be more aristocratic then sipping out of sterling silver? I have my parents' set of silver Mint Julep cups, and I always take one with me as I travel the country and the world. In the 1960s and 70s, my parents liked to throw parties, and when they did, they served all the drinks in those cups. They weren't mint juleps since it wasn't Derby, but highballs and the like. If they had more guests than cups, they'd borrow the neighbors, and since we all had our own monograms on them, we always knew whose was whose.

Nearly 160,000 people attend the Derby every year, and most of them are from out of town (we locals like to throw our own parties that day and watch the spectacle on T.V.). That's a lot of folks returning to their hometowns after being swept up in the magic of the Derby and our passion for bourbon. I'd like to think that they go back home saying, "This is what the folks in Kentucky drink." So just like Henry Clay started back in the first Golden Age of Bourbon, the Kentucky Derby and now the Bourbon Trail and the Urban Bourbon Trail all have secured the mint julep as truly one of the most iconic drinks not only in the bourbon world, but in the spirits world, as well.

My Favorite Bourbon Recipes • 223

### DERBY DAY, 1966—I MADE MY FIRST MINT JULEP

My real first experience with bourbon was tied to the Derby, as it is for many Kentuckians. Since the brewery where my dad worked owned box seats at Churchill Downs for executives and customers, my parents had to go to the Kentucky Derby every year. Darn! They'd leave early that first Saturday of May, and they wouldn't get back home 'til seven or later that night. Four of my dad's sisters would come over and watch us and enjoy the festivities of Derby Day. Aunts Regina, Bernadine, Michelle and Margaret–or as we called them, Jean, Bern, Mike and Maggie–were more like our grandparents than aunts. So it made Derby even more special in our house when they visited.

Now, in Louisville on Derby Day, the local TV stations broadcast the entire day of races and festivities before the featured race, the Kentucky Derby, the most exciting two minutes in all of sport. So it's like the Macy's parade, only all day long. When I was seven years old, my aunt Bern decided to start a new Derby tradition and put *me* in charge of making the family mint juleps. The result is that I make a *killer* mint julep. Aunt Bern had the best recipe; it's *so* easy and works in any-sized container.

To start, you take a silver mint julep cup–or a gallon pitcher, it doesn't really matter–and pour a quarter-inch of sugar on the bottom. Then you pile in about an inch (loosely stacked) of mint leaves fresh off the stalks. Muddle those loose leaves into the sugar with a wooden spoon. Pack crushed ice on top of it and then put the container in the fridge all day (or overnight).

When you're ready to serve, add the bourbon and more crushed ice along with several sprigs of mint sticking out of the top so you can bury your nose in it as you sip and savor and enjoy! The melted ice and sugar make the simple syrup for the julep. Just so you don't think too poorly of my Aunt Bern, she's the one who always added the bourbon when I was seven. I wasn't in charge of alcohol until I was at least nine.

Right before the big race, when "My Old Kentucky Home" played, we would all sing along and pass the silver mint julep cup around to everyone in the family, young and old. And then when the bell rang and the gates opened up and the track announcer said, "And they're off..." we would again pass around this tasty refreshing piece of history as we watched the race unfold on TV. I swear it was one of the most thrilling times to be alive! I get goose bumps and a little misty just writing about it here. (Let me go grab a drink–ahhhh OK. ) So who won the Derby that year in 1966 when I made my first mint julep? Kauai King with Don Brumfield up.

In my comedy act, I explain the Derby to folks who have never been there. I say that the Kentucky Derby is like Mardi Gras, except everyone's facing the same way.

When you see me at different events, more than likely I will have one of those cups from my family's sterling silver mint julep sets. Since my parents and my aunts are all drinking with the angels now, it's a way to pay tribute to the important place bourbon has had in my history.

As a side note, the mint julep is based on an Arabic drink called a "julab" made with water and rose petals. Hmmmm ... a drink made from water and leaves. Is it just me, or does that remind anyone else of tea? It morphed into the mint julep here in the United States with either rum or bourbon and mint leaves. The bourbon version has been the most popular, as it has been the official drink of Churchill Downs and the Kentucky Derby since 1938. Who won the Kentucky Derby that year? Lawrin with Eddie Arcaro aboard.

### AUNT BERNADINE'S MINT JULEP

**Ingredients:**

Sugar

Basil Hayden's eight-year-old 80-proof bourbon–you want a lighter bourbon that doesn't overpower the mint, so pick your bourbon accordingly.

Fresh mint

Ice/water

In the bottom of any container (works with a glass, a pitcher, or an infusion jar) put about a quarter-inch of sugar. Add a small amount of water, pull 10 or more mint leaves off the stems, and then muddle them in the bottom of the container with the sugar.  Fill the container with ice and place in the fridge for several hours.  Pull from fridge and fill the container with Basil Hayden bourbon. Top it off with water, if needed. If larger than a glass, put in 1.5 ounces per every 12 ounces of the container. For example, if it's a 24-ounce container, put in three ounces of bourbon.  If it's a 36-ounce container, put in 4½ ounces, and so on.

## SOUR

The whiskey sour is a classic and was written about in the very first cocktail book in 1862 by Jerry Thomas.  Jerry is the father of American mixology.  His creativity and showmanship established the image of the bartender as a creative professional. His book in 1862 was titled, *The Bar-Tender's Guide* (alternately titled *How to Mix Drinks* or *The Bon-Vivant's Companion*).

The sour recipe I will share with you is my absolute favorite and a favorite at every bourbon festival.  I first had it at the Bourbon Gala about six years ago.  It's the Noe family's recipe, and it's so simple and so delicious!

### MS. ANNIS' BOURBON SOUR

Fred Noe's mom (Booker's widow) made this recipe.  It's a refreshing twist on a classic.

**Ingredients:**
Take equal parts of:
Jim Beam Black
Orange juice
Frozen concentrated lemonade
1 can of water
Ice cubes

You can pre-batch them for a party.  Just take the equal parts of Beam Black, frozen lemonade and orange juice and water, mix and then pour over the ice in a glass.  You can just use the lemonade container as your measuring cup.  If you want to make them frozen in the summertime like Fred Noe does, put the mixture in a blender.  We serve these every year at the Bourbon Festival in Bardstown, and they are a hit with everyone. People don't believe us, but Fred and his wife, Sandy, son Freddie, and friends all work together and pre-batch them for the Bourbon Gala. We save a jug for our table because they're just that delicious!

## Old Fashioned

The old fashioned is the first drink we know of that used bourbon as the base spirit. The drink was invented by a bartender at the prestigious Louisville gentleman's club, the Pendennis Club, around 1870. A member and distiller, Colonel James E. Pepper, asked him to make a bourbon drink in the "old-fashioned way." The bartender took that to mean as a "smash" with muddled fruit. Colonel Pepper liked it so much he ordered it wherever he traveled and brought it to the Waldorf Astoria in New York City, where it became a standard.

The drink was so popular that the lowball glass it was served in began to be known as the old-fashioned glass.

**Ingredients:**

Slice of orange cut in a half moon

Cherry

2-3 dashes of bitters

Sugar - small lump or a cube

Soda water

Knob Creek bourbon

In a lowball glass, add a cherry, half-moon orange slice, a sugar cube and a splash of water. Muddle the contents and then add a shot of Knob Creek bourbon and ice, and top off with soda water.

### STOCKING YOUR BAR WITH BOURBON

*So now you know what bourbon is, how it's made, even how to read a label. Now it's time to go out and stock your bar with some great bourbons so you can share with your friends and family. You can't really go wrong with any bourbons, so don't be afraid. When asked my advice on what bourbons to stock at home, I always say go for the classic old-school bourbons with the iconic names and history. Follow the history, and you'll find yourself with some great stuff. If you've been paying attention in this book, you should have a pretty good idea of what bourbons I'm talking about. Then go out and have some small-batch and single-barrel bourbons at a bar or restaurant and find the ones you like and add them. Like when you build a house you need a good foundation before you can add the amenities, it's the same deal here. Get a nice foundation of all types of bourbons and ryes, and then you can add to them with the small-batch and single-barrel bourbons. So if you're asking me, here's what I'd put on my bar for my foundation:*

Old Grand Dad–*86, 100 bonded and 114. Get one or all three, you can't go wrong.*

Heaven Hill–*bottled in bond 100 proof–a good bonded bourbon you just gotta have*

Evan Williams–*86 proof–It doesn't get much more classic than that.*

Old Crow Reserve–*86 proof – old school and a great four-year-old bourbon for the price*

Old Forester–*86 proof, 100 proof–the flagship for Brown-Foreman and just a great bourbon*

Wild Turkey–*101 proof–the Kickin' Chicken*

Old Overholt Straight Rye–*80 proof–classic Monongahela-style rye*

Rittenhouse Rye–*bottled in bond 100 proof–classic Monongahela-style bottled in bond rye*

Jim Beam–*four-year-old 80 proof, and Black Label eight-year-old 86 proof–It is the #1 selling bourbon in the world, for goodness sakes, find out why for yourself.*

J.T.S. Brown – *It's what Fast Eddie Felson (Paul Newman) drank in the movie* The Hustler

Old Charter–*eight-year-old and 10–year-old–high corn recipe and good value for the years aged*

Ancient Ancient Age–*10-year-old 86 proof–10-year-old bourbon, nuff said!*

Old Fitzgerald–*86 proof–This is what Pappy Van Winkle made famous, and it's a wheat bourbon, so it's a nice way to top your bar off.*

*Right here you're not even at $200.00. Isn't that crazy?*

*From here you can then start adding your Knob Creek, Basil Hayden's, Maker's Mark, Elijah Craig, Blanton's, etc. Find out if you like a high rye bourbon or a wheated bourbon and then play around with all of those that share similarities in recipes, ages and proof. Find out your common denominators.*

*My bar at my house – pretty strong on bourbon, wouldn't you say?*

## THE MANHATTAN

The Manhattan was created in 1870 for Winston Churchill's mom, Lady Randolph Churchill (Jennie Jerome), at the Manhattan Club in New York City during a fundraiser she hosted for presidential candidate Samuel Tilden. The success of that party made that drink fashionable, and people started ordering it by referring to the name of the club where it had originated. It was made with American whiskey, sweet vermouth and Angostura Bitters. It can be made with rye whiskey, a bourbon, or even a Canadian whiskey, but the classic Manhattan is now made with bourbon or rye whiskey.

**Ingredients:**

Knob Creek bourbon

Sweet vermouth

Bitters

Mix three parts Knob Creek, one part sweet vermouth and add bitters to your taste. Put ingredients in a Boston shaker glass first without ice, then add ice ¾ to the top of the glass. Using a bartender spoon, stir the Manhattan, do not shake. Stirring adds just enough water to the Manhattan, shaking would add too much. When the cocktail comes up to the same level as the ice, you've stirred it enough. Strain the drink into a martini glass, garnish with a cherry (classic) or a lemon peel, and serve.

*Here's Steven at one of my staff trainings at EO (Employees Only, Hudson and Christopher). EO is one of my all-time favorite places to get a cocktail in the Village. It's also near Daddy O's and PDT. Always fun to hang out with the gang, too: Igor, Jason, Dushan, Bill and Henry. They also have a place call Maca, near the Brandy Library and Ward III in Tribeca.*

## HIGHBALLS

A highball is simply a shot of bourbon (or any spirit) topped off with a carbonated mixer (ginger ale, 7UP, cola, soda, etc.). Back in the day, trains were the fashionable way to travel. On the train there were two lights in each compartment, one on top of the other. When the train left the station and got up to speed, the train's engineer lit the light on the top position, and it came to be called the "highball." When the highball was lit, people knew it was OK to walk to the club car. They knew it was time to go get a cocktail.

### WHISKEY PROFESSOR–A.K.A BBG (ORIGINALLY CALLED A HORSES NECK)

**Ingredients:**

Old Grand Dad 86 or the Bonded (or if you're up for it, the 114)

Ginger ale

Aromatic bitters

Lemon peel

Sprig of mint

Ice

In a highball glass, pour a shot of bourbon, then two to three dashes of aromatic bitters, and top off with ginger ale. Garnish with a spiral of lemon. (The spiral of lemon is reminiscent of a horse coming out of the stall, and for us in Kentucky, that's something we know about.) I've changed the name of this drink to the whiskey professor, because I can, and because it's my favorite bourbon cocktail and I'm spreading it all over the world, so there! We also call it the BBG for my buddy and master mixologist Bobby "G" Gleason, who first turned me on to these. (BBG–get it?) BBG also stands for the ingredients: bourbon, bitters and ginger ale. The first time you tell a bartender what BBG stands for, you'll never have to tell him again, he'll know. So order a whiskey professor and enjoy!

## Presbyterian – a.k.a. Press

**Ingredients:**

Old Grand Dad 86

Ginger ale

Soda water

Peel of lemon

Fill a highball glass with ice and add one shot of Old Grand Dad 86-proof bourbon. Fill the rest of the glass with equal measures of ginger ale and soda water. Take a slice of lemon peel and zest it on top of the drink.

It's said that when people had parties at their homes back in the '50s and '60s, bourbon and ginger ale looked pretty dark, and folks knew they were drinking a cocktail. But if you added soda water, it looked like your Presbyterian neighbor was just drinking ginger ale, since the soda lightened it up. Truth or fiction? I don't know, but it's a damn good story.

Here follows some bourbon twists on other classics

## BLT – Bourbon, Lettuce and Tomato – (it's a Bloody Mary with bourbon and a couple other unique touches)

**Ingredients:**

Jim Beam Black eight-year-old bourbon or the equivalent

Bloody Mary mix (preferably homemade, but your favorite mix will do)

Hickory bacon salt

Two slices of thick-sliced crisp bacon

Celery (the "L" of the BLT here)

Rim a tall glass with hickory bacon salt. Make a Bloody Mary as you usually would in your favorite way, but use Jim Beam Black Bourbon instead of vodka. Take two slices of thick-sliced flavorful gorgeous crisp bacon and make an "X" over the glass. Take a bite of the bacon and sip and you have a BLT. Let,s face it, vodka adds no flavor whatsoever to the Bloody Mary, but the eight-year-old bourbon adds those great barrel notes after aging, that compliment the Bloody Mary. The bacon, well, if I have to explain that, you shouldn't be drinking it!

I attend the annual New Orleans convention celebrating the art of the cocktail–Tales of the Cocktail. Whatever you do, *go* next year. Go to the website and find seminars to attend and make plans to attend the different dinners and events.

## OLD TUB BOTTLED IN BOND TOAST

*Fred Noe is the seventh generation of Beams to run the Jim Beam distillery...which just happens to make them one of the most illustrious distilling families in the world. Yet Fred takes the time to text or call me and wish me a happy birthday. He takes the time to talk to anyone who is interested in bourbon. He is more than a mentor, he is a friend.*

*The Bourbon Fest 2007 previewed the first bottles of Jim Beam with Fred Noe's image added to the family pictures on the label. They had a big media event for that special day, of course. There was an empty rocking chair to represent each of the six previous generations, and Fred's dad, Booker's, chair had his fishin' hat and can on his. Fred and Booker used to travel around doing the Great Whiskey Debate. The Great Whiskey Debate was something that was created by their PR partner and friend, Jim Kokoris, at which Booker or Fred would debate that bourbon was the better whiskey of the world, and Richard Patterson of The Dalmore Scotch would debate that scotch was the better whiskey of the world. It is a great event to witness. One of the "props" they used was a full bottle of Old Tub Bottled in Bond Bourbon (a brand that was first made by third-generation David Beam and continued until the 1970s). Jim and Fred always said they'd open that bottle some day. So later that week when we were all at the Bourbon Q BBQ celebration, Jim brought that bottle of Old Tub to the party to give it to Fred.*

*Fred took that bottle of Old Tub Bottled in Bond Bourbon, and everyone took turns getting pictures with it. Now you can't get Old Tub anymore, but Fred insisted we not just open the bottle but finish it off. I mean, how many times do you get your picture on the side of one of the biggest icons of American history? But still, a lot of people I know would have saved that bottle and never opened it. Not Fred. We all took a taste and toasted Fred's milestone on the porch of Colonel Jim Beam's house with all that history around us...It's a moment I'm sure I could never describe as vividly as it happened, but I know I will never forget it as long as I live.*

*My cousin Bobby up front, me, Hickory, Fred, David, Virgil and Bourbon Festival enthusiast.*

*Left, Old Tub Bottled in Bond. Right, Mine and Hickory's buddy (and bass player) Chris Douglas taking in the magic and greatness of the Old Tub.*

My Favorite Bourbon Recipes • 235

I've found that New Orleans as a city makes the best Bloody Marys by far. My guess is they are more familiar with hungover people than most cities. Right behind the host hotel, the Monteleone, is a little corner bar called the Chart Room. I call it the "Back Door of the French Quarter," so you know I love it. During Tales of the Cocktail, you can find master distillers, ambassadors and the top mixologists in the world there at any given time. I walked by one morning and saw my buddy Phil who owns the famous whiskey bar in New York, Daddy O's, my buddy and teammate, Matt, and a few others sitting at the bar at the crack of 11:00.

When you see a collection of professionals like this, you know it's going to be a long day and night, so you definitely need your vitamins. I then introduced them and the bartender Julie to the BLT. They didn't have bacon, but Julie made up the best damn Bloody Mary with Old Grand Dad *bonded* in it...and let me tell you, it was delish. I will not rest until Old Grand Dad is the Pabst Blue Ribbon of bourbon, and I won't rest until all the Bloody Marys made around Bourbon Street are made with bourbon in them. Help me spread the word.

BOURBON MIMOSA

**Ingredients:**

Knob Creek bourbon, or your favorite that works with this

Chilled sparkling apple cider

Cinnamon

In a champagne flute add a shot of Knob Creek bourbon and then top off with chilled sparkling apple cider. Sprinkle some cinnamon on the top. If you want to get real fancy, garnish with a thin slice of apple and slide it on the rim.

This drink is an absolute hit when I attend Kentucky Derby morning parties before we go to the race track. For any occasion you would be drinking a regular mimosa, think of this as an alternative. It's a great way to enjoy bourbon, especially for vodka and rum drinkers.

## Cook Like a Whiskey Professor

I don't cook much, but when I do, I like to cook with bourbon. (Surprise!) Here are a few of my favorites for you.

**Bernie's Spicy Bourbon Chicken**

Boneless skinless chicken breasts

Your various favorite spices

½ cup brown rice

Broccoli, or any combination medley of your favorite vegetables

Chicken broth

Old Grand Dad Bonded 100-proof bourbon whiskey

Preheat oven to 450 degrees. Slice chicken breasts in half. On a piece of aluminum foil, place each boneless chicken breast in its own piece of aluminum foil on the shiny side. Make sure the foil is long enough to be able to hold chicken inside and fold at both ends.

Sprinkle your favorite seasonings and spices on the chicken. I like ground cayenne, cumin, freshly ground black pepper, poultry seasoning and a little ground paprika for really nice color. Don't be bashful with any of these spices. After seasoning both sides, you may add broccoli or any other veggies, too. Then join the long end of the foil at the top and fold shut. That leaves the two ends of the foil. Fold one end shut and then add up to a tablespoon of chicken broth and the same amount of bourbon. Seal the final end. You'll figure out which amount of broth and Old Grand Dad you like after you make this recipe a couple times.

Place the chicken in the foil on a baking sheet on the center rack for 20 minutes. Prepare a half-cup of brown rice while the chicken cooks.

The chicken will be perfectly done after 20 minutes. Be careful opening the end of the foil (the steam escaping is very hot since you just pressure-cooked it in the sealed foil). Pour the bourbon/broth "gravy" in a bowl, and then the chicken. Slice the chicken in the broth with the veggies, and add rice.

The best thing about this is you can make several of these aluminum packs of chicken and put them in the fridge. It just takes the time to preheat and 20 minutes of cooking. Perfect for dinner for one or two, but it can also be perfect for a dinner party. It looks like you've slaved and prepped all day. They'll never know how easy it is.

**Bernie's Bourbon Cream**

Wine glass

Mint chocolate chip ice cream

Baker's seven-year-old, 107-proof bourbon

This is the easiest dessert to serve at home or take to someone's house. It's *always* a hit. All you do is take a wine glass and add a couple scoops of mint chocolate chip ice cream into them. Then pour over it a shot of Baker's seven-year old, 107 proof bourbon. Garnish with some fresh mint and, if you want to get really fancy, add some fruit, but that's it. When your guests spoon out the ice cream and the bourbon, it's just like a mint julep dessert! So simple, and you'll be the star every single time, especially with the after-dinner drinks you make with the leftover bourbon!

# 9
# Bourbon: Our Native Spirit

*As a nation, "… we have improved man's lot and enriched his civilization with rye, bourbon, and the martini cocktail. In all history has any other nation done so much? Not by two-thirds."*
–Bernard DeVoto, THE HOUR: A Cocktail Manifesto

In 1964, Congress declared bourbon the native spirit of the United States. Why would the U.S. government take the time to bother with bourbon? It's because bourbon whiskey developed in tandem with United States history. Let's face it, folks, if there was no bourbon, there'd be no NASCAR! And what would America be without that?

*Bobby G., Fred Noe and me (photo courtesy of the author)*

## BOTTLING BOURBON

*Bourbon was first bottled and labeled in 1870 by a pharmaceutical salesman named George Garvin Brown. One of his friends was a doctor who was a Civil War hero with a sterling reputation, and the doctor would often complain that the bulk whiskey he prescribed (barrel whiskey) wasn't consistent. He would say he just couldn't rely on it. Being an enterprising man, George Brown bought several barrels of bourbon, used a hydrometer to measure the proof, bottled it, and sold it as superior medicinal bourbon. For credibility, he put the name of that noted physician and Civil War hero, Dr. William Forrester, on the label, and Old Forrester was born. After Dr. Forrester passed away, the distillery dropped one "r" and the Old Forester brand is still around today. As a matter of fact, it is the only bourbon that was available before, during and after Prohibition. I quite like the Signature 100 proof.*

*Other distilleries adopted this practice of bottling and labeling their bourbons, but mostly after 1897 with the Bottled in Bond Act. George Garvin Brown and his brother J.T.S. Brown went on to found Brown-Forman in Louisville, Kentucky. J.T.S. Brown was the preferred bourbon of Fast Eddie Felson, played by Paul Newman, in the movie* The Hustler. *J.T.S. Brown bourbon is still around today, too. What does the J.T.S. stand for? John Thompson Street Brown—I love that name.*

President Lyndon B. Johnson signed it into law. Then the United States Senate in 2007 unanimously passed the resolution declaring September as National Bourbon Heritage Month. Like I said, it had to be a unanimous decision by the Senate. Bourbon is the one and only alcohol that is designated as our native spirit. So it is not only delicious to drink bourbon, it's also your patriotic duty!

Just think about all the rich history and heritage surrounding bourbon: how the United States has used bourbon and whiskey as money and paid our troops with bourbon whiskey; the way bourbon has become its own style of whiskey, unique from Irish, scotch, Canadian, and Tennessee whiskey; the corn that gave it sweetness and the charred barrels that gave it magic, color and characteristics. Just think about all of the family names that are still in the bourbon business: Elijah Craig, Evan Williams, Dr. James Crow, Edmund Taylor, the Medleys, the Ripys, Albert Blanton, George Washington, Colonel Oscar Pepper, the Beams, Pappy Van Winkle, the Samuels, the Browns, the Wathens, the Willets, and on and on. It's great to see people embracing bourbon in the manner they have in the past 10 years. I believe that with the increased interest people have in visiting the Bourbon Trail and all the distilleries on it here in Kentucky, the industry might easily double and triple in size. But don't worry about the quality. Remember, we *can't* cut corners.

I think that what Ben Perley Poore witnessed in Kentucky in 1857 is still true today. When you meet my fellow whiskey professors, distillers, ambassadors and me, you will surely be greeted by gentlemen with our hearts in our right hand, and our right hand in yours, and surely in our left a bottle of unequalled old bourbon.

DISTILLER'S ROW BY – BERNIE LUBBERS  (23 BOURBONS MENTIONED IN THE SONG)

My **OLD GRAND DAD (1)** He passed away, but he lived 94 years to the day

He's laid to rest, right up on **HEAVEN HILL (2)**,  with a spray of **FOUR ROSES (3)** on his grave

He'd drink a quart, each and every day; of some good store bought **JIM BEAM (4)**

Dr. **FORESTER (5 – OLD FORESTER)** said, "Hey **PAPPY (6 – PAPPY VAN WINKLE)**; you better cut it down" but then the good doc passed away so who's to say

**CHORUS**

So raise a red eye  to OLD GRAND DAD (only counts once) He lived to be an **ANCIENT AGE (7)**

That **OLD CROW (8)** sure left his **MAKER'S MARK (9)** & now he's drinking with the **ANGELS (10 – ANGELS ENVY)** far away.

When the weekends rolled around, oh the stories they would flow

Like **BRANCH** water **(11 - TOWN BRANCH)** pouring down **KNOB CREEK (12)**

**EVAN WILLIAMS (13)** start to sing, brother **ELIJAH's (14 ELIJAH CRAIG)** voice would ring,

**JIMMY'd (15 – RUSSELS RESERVE)** passed the jug to CRAIG & **PARKER BEAM (16 – PARKER'S HERITAGE)**

**CHORUS**

*Here I am, singing my heart out about the joys of Bourbon. You can tell my fellow musician loves this song.*

**WILD TURKEY'S (17)** they all were, and like **EAGLES THEY WERE RARE (18 – EAGLE RARE)**

They bottled and bonded all the day.

And all in to the night at **BASIL HAYDEN'S (19)** shear delight, they'd tell stories by the **CABIN STILL - 20)** they raised.


**CHORUS**


He'd throw **OLD FITZ (21)** if he didn't get his **V.O.B. (22 – VERY OLD BARTON)** and now he's drinking there with **BOOKERS (23)** far away!

*On the set at my home bar during the shooting the bourbon documentaries* Bourbontucky *and* Straight Up: Kentucky Bourbon *with my favorite Heaven Hill whiskey, Henry McKenna Single Barrel which is Bottled in Bond, of course!*

# Appendix I:
## Frequently Asked Questions

You can imagine that as a whiskey professor, I get asked a lot of questions about our native spirit when I tour the country. A lot of them get repeated, so I figured that putting down some of the most frequently asked questions here might help. Also, after reading this book, you just might know the answers yourself. Cover up the answer and see how well you do:

**When distilling the distillers beer or mash into white dog, are different cuts of the distillate used to make different labels of bourbon (e.g. more middle run for higher quality labels vs. more first cut or tails for lesser quality)?**

When you use a column still, you don't make "cuts" as you do with a pot still for single-malt scotch. With pot stills you trim off the heads and tails on each batch. Column stills are very efficient. You only have to trim off heads when you start the still up, and then it brings the spirit off the still at a constant proof 24 hours a day, as long as you run the still, which is usually five or six days. Then you only trim off the tails on the last day. We do that with all our bourbons, not just small batch. There's no such thing as "good cuts," "bad cuts," or "best cuts. They are all the best cuts. What separates the bourbons therefore is age and proof. A greater age on a bourbon and higher proof can make the bourbon more expensive. But they are all made with the same exacting, high standards by the laws that define bourbon from other whiskies. (i.e. 51% corn, distilled to no more than 160 proof, aged in a brand new charred- oak barrel at no more than 125 proof, bottled at no less than 80 proof, with nothing added to the bourbon other than water to get it to barreling or bottling strength).

Even when using pot stills and separating heads and tails on each batch, they would never use the heads and tails, only the heart. There would be too many fusel oils and congeners in the heads and tails.

### Are there any bourbons distilled outside Kentucky? If so, what are they?

Ninety-seven percent of the bourbon in the world is distilled in Kentucky. But there are more and more bourbons made outside Kentucky as the popularity of bourbon continues to climb. The biggest brand made outside Kentucky is *Virginia Gentleman.* Hudson Baby Bourbon is being produced up in New York. There are bourbons being distilled in Austin, Texas, Colorado and Florida, too. But these are tiny little craft distillers and probably will be available only in their local markets, kind of like a local brew pub. So bourbon can be distilled anywhere in the United States, but since the overwhelming majority is distilled in Kentucky, a lot of people think that it has to be made in Kentucky. That is one of the myths of bourbon.

### What type of glass is best for drinking bourbon neat?

I like to use a snifter or a nice rocks glass, sans the "rocks." I like a glass that I can get my nose into a bit. But that's a personal preference. There are some who like a tulip-shaped glass, and those are nice, but I can't get my schnoz into them, so I like a snifter. Try some out and see what works best for you; there are no rules. When you visit, you'll find out that we bourbon drinkers are not as pretentious as the scotch drinkers.

I have put together a whiskey cellar with roughly twelve different bourbons right now. Most of these are sealed with a cork. How should store them? On their sides? Upright? How long will they keep before they go "off"?

Keep your bourbons standing straight up, and if the corks are a good seal, they should never go "off". Unlike wines, bourbons are distilled at a higher proof, so they won't get "corked" or go bad. Bourbon will not age in the bottle, either. Just keep them out of direct sunlight, and you'll enjoy them for years. But don't wait years to enjoy them; we've got lots of barrels resting in our rack houses for you, so enjoy all you want ... you keep drinking it, and we'll keep making it.

**When my uncle introduced me to good bourbon, he had a bottle of "branch water" on his bar. I tried to find "branch" on the Internet but it does not seem to exist anymore. Does anyone sell it or has bottled water replaced it?**

"Branch water" is a term that refers to the water from the head of a stream before it "branches" off. Not many of us are lucky enough anymore to live on acreage that has such magical properties, so I'd suggest we use a good nonmineral bottled water, or water from a purifier.

**When did distillers start storing whiskey barrels in rack houses, rather than stacking on the floor of other buildings? I'm wondering if it was between the 1860s (still on floors) and about 1880.**

I've been doing research on this one for a while now, and it's been pretty fun. I'm glad you've asked the question. I know that one of my heroes in bourbon history, Colonel Edmund Taylor, was very influential in bourbon-making and aging. In 1869 Colonel Taylor purchased a small distillery on the banks of the Kentucky River at Leestown, Kentucky. Colonel Taylor was the first person to employ the "rick" system in warehouses on a consistent basis. The ricks lifted the barrels off the floor and into the ricks we still use to this day. They are stacked three barrels high per floor in the "one high," the "two high," and the "three high," and rolled down the ricks which are two 4x4's designed to hold 11+ barrels deep in a rack house.

Colone Taylor was also a supporter who helped pass the Bottled in Bond Act of 1897, the first consumer protection legislation in the United States. The B.I.B. Act states that a bourbon must be at least four years old, exactly 100 proof, from one distillery (with the actual maker listed on the bottle) and barreled in one season. So raise a glass of Bottled in Bond Old Grand Dad to Colonel Taylor! We employ today a lot of what he pioneered long ago.

**I'm used to drinking Jack & Coke, but a friend turned me on to the Knob Creek bourbon. Since I like to mix my drink is it OK to mix the Knob Creek with Coke or something else, or do you prefer not to?**

I'm glad your friend turned you on to bourbon and especially one of my favorites. The only rule I have about it is one I picked up from my buddy and master mixologist, Bobby "G." Drink what you like, like what you're drinking, but know what you're drinking. If you like it mixed with Coke, by all means mix it with Coke.

Jack Daniels tends to be younger, meaning it hasn't been aged as long as Knob Creek (nine years in the barrel) or Elijah Craig (12 years in the barrel), for example. Even the white label Jim Beam (four years old) drinkers tend to like Coke, 7UP, or ginger ale mixed in with their bourbon. The longer the bourbon has rested in those barrels, the more of those vanilla, maple, caramel, and ginger flavors are there, and the less you might want to add to it so you can taste them. This is why a lot of folks just use a cube or 2 of ice, or just a splash of water or ginger ale.

If you like it with cola, by all means drink it that way, but know that cola tends to mask the flavors that we have been aging for. It also contains a lot of sugars and flavors on top of that to boot. Ginger ale actually brings out some natural vanillas and other flavors from the barrel. So try it with ginger ale sometime, or half ginger ale, and half soda. This is also called a Presbyterian. It's a classic drink and very refreshing.

But if you like bourbon with Coke, you drink it with Coke. Booker Noe was asked by a woman one time if it was a sin to mix Booker's Bourbon and Coke. She really liked the taste of it. Booker looked at her and said, "Ma'am, if you take the best bourbon in the world and mix it with Coke, you'll have the best damned bourbon and Coke in the world."

**How do you measure alcohol content? How do you regulate it during production? How much variability is there from batch to batch?**

That's a great question. And we have to thank technology for helping us make it a little easier and a lot more consistent now. In the 1980s, computers were being used more in the actual cooking and distilling. Before that, people had to turn valves and control temperatures, etc. Now it's all done by computers, so it's controlled a lot more tightly. Once the computer has the steam under the still, it can keep the bourbon pouring off the still at a desired proof. But we still use the old-fashioned way and use a hydrometer to check the proof level every hour, just like Dr. James Crow did back in the 1800s. So there is hardly any variability on a run (batch). Keep in mind that a "batch" is five or six days long. That's the advantage of using column stills instead of pot stills. The proof stays constant. Two people in the control room overseeing the computer system can do the job of 15 people turning valves and adjusting dials by hand. The operators can override the computer system and open valves, but still by using the computer system. If that totally fails, they can go down into the distillery and turn the valves by hand. With as much technology as we have today, we still have to have guys like Fred Noe, Craig Beam, Tommy Crume and other distillers who know how to go in and do it by hand if needed.

## Can a whiskey still be considered a bourbon if it contains more than 80% corn, or does that automatically make it "corn whiskey"?

This is a question that is debated over and over, and I don't know why. The laws are really clear here. The law on bourbon whiskey states that it must contain at least 51% corn. It mentions no upper limit for percentage of corn or other grains specifically, so yes, as long as it follows all the laws of bourbon, the whiskey can be 80% or more corn and still be considered bourbon. Period. Corn whiskey is defined as "whiskey produced at not exceeding 160 proof from a fermented mash of not less than 80% corn grain, and if stored in oak containers stored at not more than 125 proof in used or uncharred new oak containers."

If you're more inspired now than ever about the native spirit of the United States and want to attend some of the events and meet folks like myself, Fred Noe and all the whiskey men and women who are ambassadors, please come and enjoy. Some whiskey events across the country include: Bourbon Festival in Bardstown, KY, Whiskey Guild/Whisky Life and Spirits Cruises, WhiskeyFest, Whisky Live, Tales of the Cocktail, Aspen Food and Wine, Epcot Food and Wine, Beer Bourbon and Bar-B-Q, and the Philadelphia and Pittsburgh Whiskey Festivals. Just Google these and they'll pop right up.

You can also follow me on Facebook and Twitter.

You can see a video of me on YouTube singing a song I wrote and performed with Hickory and the boys titled, "The Bourbon Trail." I mention 18 bourbons in the song:

## A FINAL NOTE

*As I finish this book, I'm on holiday in Munich, Prague and Berlin. Most people hate airports. I love them. True, they can be a pain, but what the hell, you're going somewhere! I also love train travel. Since I took the train between cities in Europe, I knew it would be the perfect opportunity to finish this incredible project. I'd like to thank my employer, Heaven Hill, for the opportunity to serve as whiskey professor on behalf of their great brands. Also, I can't thank Fred Noe enough for his never-ending passion and the knowledge and experience he shares so graciously with us all. When I asked him if he would write the foreword for this book, he didn't hesitate and added that it would be his honor to do it. What a class act! Fred makes you feel like you're a part of the Beam family, and when you meet him, you'll feel like you've known him all your life. This is also true of all the other master distillers: Jimmy and Eddie Russell (Wild Turkey), Greg Davis (Maker's Mark), Harlen Wheatley and Elmer T. Lee (Buffalo Trace), Parker and Craig Beam (Heaven Hill), Fred Noe and Kevin Smith (Jim Beam), Jimmy Rutledge (Four Roses) and Chris Morris (Woodford Reserve). I've learned a lot from all of them, and they're all inspiring to be around.*

*I also want to thank my buddy Tom Mabe (comic, musician, jingle writer, TV show host) for introducing me to my publisher. I heard stories of getting rejection letter after rejection letter with publishers, and I must tell you, I'm one for one. I approached one publisher and he said, "I want to do it." Thanks, Tom Doherty and everyone at Blue River Press! And a big thanks to my editor, Holly Kondras!*

*I encourage you to sign up and become members on the websites of your favorite brands: heavenhill.com, jimbeam.com, knobcreek.com and makersmark.com. When you sign up, you'll be invited to cool tastings and gatherings. Most brands have websites, so Google your favorite brands and sign up for all the ones you enjoy.*

*Me with our distillers in front of Bonded Warehouse Y: Charlie Downs, Craig Beam, Parker Beam, Denny Potter .*

# Appendix II:
# Where to Go for Bottled in Bond Bourbon

*"Bottled in Bonds are the Eagle Scout of Whiskies"*
*– Bernie Lubbers*

For those of you with ambition, I am listing here for your benefit all the restaurants and/or bars that carry "Bottled in Bond" bourbons. Consider it your new set of travel destinations for the coming months (or years).

## BOTTLED IN BOND ACCOUNTS IN USA

### Louisville, KY

**Bistro 301** — 301 Market St, bistro301.com

**Blu Bar at the Downtown Marriott** — 280 W. Jefferson St., blugrille.com

**Bourbons Bistro** — 2255 Frankfort Ave, bourbonsbistro.com

**Charr'd** — 1903 Embassy Square Blvd in the Marriott East, no website available

**Dish on Market** — 434 W. Market, dishonmarket.com

**Down One** Bourbon Bar — 321 W. Main St., downonebourbonbar.com **(order the Lubbers Flight)

**Feast BBQ** — 909 East Market St., feastbbq.com

**Haymarket Whiskey** — 331 East Market St., www.haymarketwhiskeybar.com

**Jockey's Silks** — at the Galt House Hotel, 140 N. 4th Street, galthouse.com

**Joe's Older Than Dirt** — 8131 New LaGrange Rd, joesotdirt.com

**Meta** — 425 West Chestnut St., metalouisville.com

**Monkey Wrench** — 1025 Barret Ave, monkeywrench.com

**Proof/21c** — 702 W. Main St., proofonmain.com

**Roux** — 1325 Bardstown Rd, rouxlouisville.com (upstairs bar)

**Seelbach Hotel** — 500 4th St., www.seelbachhilton.com

**Side Bar** — 129 S. 2nd St., sidebarwhiskeyrow.com

**Silver Dollar** — 1761 Frankfort Ave.

**The Back Door** — 1250 Bardstown Rd., thebackdoorlouisville.com

**The Brown Hotel** — 335 W. Broadway, brownhotel.com

**Village Anchor** — 11507 Park Road in Anchorage, villageanchor.com

Louisville Restaurants with Bars

**Bristol Bar & Grille** — 1321 Bardstown Rd (Highlands) and 614 W. Main (Downtown) bristolbarandgrille.com

**Doc Crows** — 127 W. Main St., doccrows.com

**Harvest** — 624 E. Market St., harvestlouisville.com

**Joy Luck** — 1285 Bardstown Rd, thejoyluck.com

**Lilly's** — 1147 Bardstown Rd, lillyslapeche.com

Jeffersonville/New Albany, IN (just across the bridge)

**Match** — 207 Spring St. in Jeffersonville, matchcigarbar.com

**The Exchange** — 118 Main St. in New Albany, exchangeforfood.com

**Feast BBQ** — 116 W. Main Street in New Albany, feastbbq.com

LEXINGTON, KY

**Belle's** — 156 Market Street, no website available

**Bluegrass Tavern** — 115 Cheapside St., thebluegrasstavern.com

**OBC Kitchen** (Old Bourbon County) — 3373 Tates Creek Rd (at Sals), obckitchen.com

CINCINNATI, OH/ NKY

**OKBB** (Old Kentucky Bourbon Bar) — 629 Main St., Covington, KY, facebook page 1OKBB

**Goodfellas/Wiseguys** — 603 Main St., Covington, KY, goodfellaspizzeria.com

**Japps Since 1879** — 1136 Main St., Cincinnati, OH, japps1879.com

**Bakersfield** — 1213 Vine St., Cincinnati, OH, Bakersfieldotr.com

**Goodfellas/Wiseguys** — 1211 Main St., Cincinnati, OH, goodfellaspizzeria.com

DAYTON, OH

**Century** — 10 S. Jefferson St., centurybourbon.com

INDIANAPOLIS, IN

**Bakersfield** — 334 Massachusetts Ave., bakersfieldtacos.com

**Bru Burger** — 410 Massachusetts Ave., bruburgerbar.com

**Old Point Tavern** — 401 Massachusetts Ave., facebook page

**Thunderbird** — 1127 Shelby St., thunderbirdindy.com

# MIDWEST

## Chicago, IL

**Sable** — 505 North State St. (at the Palomar Hotel), sablechicago.com

**Big Star** — 1531 North Damen Ave. (Cash Only), bigstarchicago.com

**Twisted Spoke** — 501 Ogden Ave, twistedspoke.com

**The Barrelhouse Flat** — 2624 North Lincoln Ave., barrelhouseflat.com

**Delilah's** — 2771 North Lincoln Ave., delilahschicago.com

**Longman & Eagle** — 2657 North Kedzie, longmanandeagle.com

**Sportsman's Club** — 948 North Western Ave., drinkingandgathering.com

**California Clipper** — 1002 North California Ave., californiaclipper.com

**Franklin Room** — 675 North Franklin Street, franklinroom.com

**Untitled** — 111 West Kinzie, untitledchicago.com

## Kansas

**4 Olives** — 121 South 4th St., Manhattan KS, 4olives.biz

**Bourbon & Baker** — 312 Pointz Ave., Manhattan KS, bbmanhattan.com

**Rye** — 10551 Mission Rd., Leawood KS, ryekc.com

## St. Louis

**Sanctuaria** — 4198 Manchester Ave., santuariastl.com

**Hendrick's BBQ** — 1200 S. Main St. in St. Charles, hendricksbbq.com

## SOUTHEAST

### ATLANTA, GA

**Holeman + Finch Public House** — 2277 Peachtree Rd. N.W., Atlanta, holeman-finch.com

**Bourbon Bar** at Intercontinental Hotel — 3315 Peachtree St., in Buckhead, southernart.com

**Local Three Kitchen and Bar** — 3290 Northside Parkway, Atlanta, localthree.com

**Kimball House** — 303 East Howard Ave., Decatur, GA, kimball-house.com

**Mac McGees** — 111 Sycamore St., Decatur, GA , macmcgeeirishpub.com

**Mac McGees** — 936 Canton St., Roswell, GA, macmcgeesirishpub.com

### CHARLESTON, SC

**Proof** — 437 King St., no website available

**The Cocktail Club** — 479 King St., thecocktailclubcharleston.com

**Husk** — 76 Queen St., huskrestaurant.com

**Boone's Bar** — 425 King St., boonesbar.com

### NEW ORLEANS

**The Avenue Pub** — 1732 St. Charles Ave., theavenuepub.com

**Bar Tonique** — 820 N Rampart St., bartonique.com

**Barrel Proof** — 1201 Magazine St., barrelproofnola.com

**Cure** — 4905 Freret St., curenola.com

**Oxalis** — 3162 Dauphine St., oxalisbywater.com

### DISTRICT OF COLUMBIA

**Bourbon** — 2321 18th St. N.W., bourbondc.com

**Jack Rose Dining Saloon** — 2007 18th St. N.W., jackrosediningsaloon.com

**Rebellion** — 1836 18th St. N.W., rebelliondc.com

**Smoke & Barrel** — 2471 18th St. N.W., smokeandbarreldc.com

NASHVILLE, **TN**

**Patterson House** — 1711 Division St., thepattersonnashville.com

**Whiskey Kitchen** — 118 12 Ave. S., mstreetnashville.com

# NORTHEAST

## MASSACHUSETTS

**JM Curley** — 21 Temple Place, Boston, MA, jmcurleyboston.com

**Citizen Public House & Oyster Bar** — 1310 Boylston St., Boston, MA, citizenpub.com

**The Saloon in Davis Square** — 255 Elm St. in Somerville, MA, saloondavis.com

**Red Bones in Davis Square** — 55 Chester St. Somerville, MA, redbones.com

**The Bancroft in Burlington** — 15 Third Ave. in Burlington, MA, the-bancroft.com

## NEW YORK CITY

**American Whiskey** — 247 W. 30th St., americanwhiskeynyc.com

**Copper & Oak** — 157 Allen St., brandylibrary.com

**Fools Gold** — 145 East Houston, foolsgoldnyc.com

**Brandy Library** — 25 North Moore St. in Tribica, brandylibrary.com

**Daddy O's** — 44 Bedford St. in the West Village, daddyonyc.com

**Maysville** — 17 W 26th St., maysvillenyc.com

**Umami Burger** — 432 Avenue of The Americas and North 4th Street in Brooklyn, umami.com

**Noorman's Kil** — 609 Grand St., Brooklyn, noormanskil.com

**The Shanty** — in Brooklyn at the Brooklyn Distilling Co., 79 Richardson St. (between Leonard and Lorimer), nydistilling.com/the-shanty

## WEST

### Austin/Dallas/Ft. Worth, TX

**Anvil** — 1424 Westheimer, Houston, TX, anvilhouston.com

**Cpt Foxheart's Bad News Bar** — 308 ½ Main St., Houston, TX

**Coltivare Pizza & Garden** — 3320 White Oak Dr., Houston, TX, Coltivarehouston.com

**East Side Showroom** — 1100 E 6th St., Austin, TX, eastsideshowroom.com

**The Blackheart** — 86 Rainey St., Austin, TX, blackheartbar.com

**HG Sply Co** — 2008 Greenville Ave., Dallas, TX, hgsplyco.com

**The Ranch** — 857 W John Carpenter, Irving, TX, theranchlc.com

### Nebraska

**Grane** — 120 S. 21$^{st}$ Ave., Omaha, granewhiskey.com

**Le Bouillon** — 1017 Howard St., Omaha, bouillionomaha.com

**V Mertz** — 1022 Howard St., Omaha, vmertz.com

**Nite Owl** — 3902 Farnam, Omaha, niteowlomaha.com

**Wine 121** — 12100 West Center Rd., Omaha, wine121.com

**Brix** — 225 North 170$^{th}$ St. Omaha, brixomaha.com

**Tavern Square** — 814 P St., Lincoln

**City Spirits** — 2620 Stockwell, Lincoln

### Denver, CO

**Ace** — 17$^{th}$ and Pennsylvania, aceeatserve.com

**Whiskey Bar** — 2201 Larimer St., whiskeybardenver.com

**Williams & Graham** — 3160 Tejon St., williamsandgraham.com

## Los Angeles Area

**Ace Hotel** — 929 South Broadway, Downtown LA, acehotel.com/losangeles

**Seven Grand** — 515 West 7th St., Downtown LA, sevengrandbars.com

**City Tavern** Downtown LA — 735 South Figueroa St., #133, Downtown LA, citytaverndtla.com

**Cole's Red Car Bar** — 118 East 6th St., Downtown LA, 213nightlife.com/colesfrenchdip

**The Varnish** — 118 East 6th St., Downtown LA, 213nightlife.com/thevarnish

**Faith & Flower** — 705 West 9th St., Downtown LA, faithandflowerla.com

**Umami Burger** — 852 South Broadway and 738 East 3rd St., umami.com

**Lock & Key** — 239 South Vermont, Koreatown, lockandkey.la

**Butchers & Barbers** — 6531 Hollywood Blvd., Los Angeles, butchersandbarbers.com

**Harvard & Stone** — 5221 Hollywood Blvd., harvardandstone.com

**No Vacancy** — 1727 North Hudson Ave., novacancyla.com

**Black Market Liquor Bar** — 11915 Ventura Blvd. in Studio City, CA, blackmarketliquorbar.com

**Firefly** — 11720 Ventura Blvd. in Studio City, fireflystudiocity.com

**1886 Raymond Restaurant** — 1250 South Fair Oaks Avenue, Pasedena, CA, theraymond.com

**Areal** — 2820 Main St. in Santa Monica, arealrestaurant.com

**The Chestnut Club** — 1348 14th St. in Santa Monica, thechestnutclubsm.com

**Oldfields Liquor Room** — 10899 Venice Blvd., oldfieldsliquorroom.com

**Scopa Italian Roots** — 2905 West Washington Blvd., Ventura, scopaitalianroots.com

**Sonny's Hideaway** — 5137 York Blvd., sonnyshideaway.com

SAN DIEGO, CA

**Seven Grand** — 3054 University Ave., sevengrandbars.com

**Polite Provisions** — 4696 30th St., politeprovisions.com

**Neighborhood/Noble Experiment** — 777 G St., nobleexperimentsd.com

**Bourbon Street Bar & Grill** — 110 E. Commonwealth Ave., Fullerton CA, bourbonstreetfullerton.com

**Playground 220** — 220 E. 4th St., Santa Ana CA, playgrounddtsa.com

SAN FRANCISCO, CA

**Bourbon & Branch** — 501 Jones St., bourbonandbranch.com

**Brass Tacks** — 488 Hayes St., brasstackssf.com

**Elixir** — 3200 16th St., www.elixirsf.com

**Hard Water** — Pier 3 Embarcadero, hardwaterbar.com

**Local Edition** — 691 Market St., localeditionsf.com

**Rickhouse** — 246 Kearny St., rickhousebar.com

**Smokestack** — 2505 3rd St., magnoliasmokestack.com

**Trick Dog** — 3010 20th St., trickdogbar.com

**Tradition** — 441 Jones St., tradbar.com

PORTLAND, OR

**River Pig Saloon** — 539 Northwest 13th Ave., riverpigsaloon.com

**Old Gold** — 2105 North Killingsworth St., theoldgoldpdx.com

**Richmond Bar** — 3203 Southwest Division St., therichmondbar.com

**Southland Whiskey Kitchen** — 1422 Northwest 23$^{rd}$ Ave., southlandportland.com

**Paddy's** — 65 Southwest Yamhill St., paddys.com

**Pope House Bourbon Lounge** — 2075 Northwest Glisan St., popehouselounge.com

**Clyde Common** — 1014 Southwest Stark St., clydecommon.com

**Multnomah Whiskey Library** — 1124 Southwest Alder St., mwlpdx.com

SEATTLE

**Canon Whiskey & Bitters** — 928 12$^{th}$ Ave., canonseattle.com

**Liberty** — 517 15$^{th}$ Ave. E., libertybars.com

**Ma'Ono Fried Chicken and Whiskey** — 4437 California Ave.

**Rob Roy** — 1433 4$^{th}$ Ave., robroyseattle.com

**Rocco's** — 2228 2$^{nd}$ Ave., roccosseattle.com

**Smith** — 332 15$^{th}$ Ave. E., smithseattle.com

**Tavern Law** — 1406 12$^{th}$ Ave.

**Zig Zag Café** — 1501 Western Ave., zigzagseattle.com